D0549339

1/10/94
55856
GEOG
910
LB94/1020
GJ2
£7.50
6

Access to Geography 4

Richard Kemp • Paul Carvin • Zoë Carvin

Oxford University Press 1994

Acknowledgements

The publishers and authors would like to thank the following people for their permission to use copyright material:

Aerofilms pp.1, 47 (top left), 64 (left), 114; A.G.E. FotoStock pp.49, 50, 51, 70, 72 (bottom left), 81; J Allan Cash Ltd pp.71 (bottom), 72 (bottom right), 72 (top and bottom right); Bryan and Cherry Alexander pp.46 (right), 47 (bottom left), 55; Mandy Reynolds/Bath City Council p.26 (bottom right); John Cleare Mountain Camera p.34; Cleveland Public Library p.120; Colorific pp.107 (bottom left, top right), 122, Steve Bendow/Colorific p.107 (top left); Commission of the European Community pp.6, 84 (top); H Girardet/The Environmental Picture Library p.47 (middle), Chris Westwood/The Environmental Picture Library p.30 (top left), The Environmental Picture Library p.46 (left); John and Penny Hubley pp.92, 95; By courtesy of the Italian State Tourist Office (E.N.I.T.) London p.26 (top right); Guido Alberto Rossi/The Image Bank p.56, Juergen Schmitt/The Image Bank p.82, The Image Bank p.124; Frank Lane Picture Agency p.30 (top right); Life File Photo Library/Mike Evans p.71 (top), Emma Lee pp.71 (middle), 74, Miguel Arana p.76 (bottom); Thomas Hoepker/Magmun Photos p.20; Meadowhall Centre Ltd pp.110, 111; Metrolink p.119; NATO p.84 (bottom); OECD p.84 (upper middle); Panos Pictures/James Morris p.98 (bottom), Bruce Paton p.91, 94, 96 (top and bottom), 104, David Reed p.90; Peter Scoones/Planet Earth Pictures p.56 (bottom), Planet Earth Pictures p.46 (top); Popperfoto p.24; John Sanford/Science Photo Library p.47 (bottom right); Sheffield City Council Library and Information Services p.109; J L Grande/Spanish National Tourist Office p.48, Ramon G Lopez Alongso/Spanish National Tourist Office p.75; Spectrum Colour Library pp.18 (bottom), 26 (middle, bottom left), 112, 118, G R Richardson/Spectrum Colour Library p.29; Daher/Frank Spooner Pictures p.9; Swift Picture Library p.64 (right); Telegraph Colour Library pp.76 (top), 107 (bottom right); Topham Picture Source pp.18 (top), 21, 23, 41, 42 (top and bottom); Anna Tully pp.86, 98 (top); United Nations p.84 (lower middle); John Walmsley pp.117 (top and bottom); Mike Williams pp.58, 60, 62, 63; Brian J Woodruffe p.10.

The cover photograph is reproduced by permission of Picturepoint Ltd.

The Ordnance Survey map extracts on pp.44, 58, and 115 are reproduced with the permission of the Controller of Her Majesty's Stationary Office © Crown Copyright.

The diagrams are by Stefan Chabluk and the maps are by Line and Line. Other illustrations are by Oxford Illustrators pp.29, 32 and Nigel Paige pp.31, 105, 112, 119.

Every effort has been made to trace and contact copyright-holders, but this has not always been possible. We apologise for any infringement of copyright.

Oxford University Press, Walton Street, Oxford OX2 6DP

Oxford New York Toronto
Delhi Bombay Calcutta Madras Karachi
Kuala Lumpur Singapore Hong Kong Tokyo
Nairobi Dar es Salaam Cape Town
Melbourne Auckland Madrid

and associated companies in
Berlin Ibadan

Oxford is a trade mark of Oxford University Press

ISBN 0 19 833474 5

Printed in Hong Kong

Introduction

Access to Geography has been carefully planned and written to meet the needs of the National Curriculum. Books 1-3 cover Key Stage 3, and Books 4-5 cover Key Stage 4. The themes, topics, and case studies used are drawn from the National Curriculum programmes of study and are designed to cover all the appropriate statements of attainment.

The whole course has been designed as a practical response to the National Curriculum. The books have been organised to match as much as possible the good practice geography teachers have developed in recent years. Each book is divided into half a dozen units, each based around a familiar unifying theme. Within each unit the material is organised in double-page spreads, the most practical format for classroom use.

The course is designed for students across a broad range of ability. The lively page design, the high quality visuals, the carefully written text, and the range of student activities mean that the material is very accessible.

Matching your scheme of work

Books 4 and 5 have been designed to provide a coherent and progressive Key Stage 4 course. Used in the planned order, the units make for a varied mix of themes for study. It is also possible to use the units from Books 4 and 5 in a more flexible way; the authors know from experience that at Key Stage 4, for a range of reasons, teachers often want to have more flexibility in the way that they plan or execute their scheme of work for GCSE.

Differentiation

The material in Books 4 and 5 reflects the general levels within Key Stage 4. The activities allow students to work to their own particular level.

Geographical enquiry

Each book contains a variety of 'assignments', which are designed to encourage students in the development of their enquiry skills. Each unit also has one or more 'Resource Bank' spreads, each of which contains a selection of background and extension material relevant to the theme being studied; this material can be used either for extension studies or to support enquiry work.

Regional case studies

Integrated within the course are regional case studies. These exemplify and extend the material developing human, physical, and environmental themes and issues.

Access to Geography is a practical and straightforward response to the needs of the National Curriculum at Key Stages 3 and 4.

Contents

EC ISSUES

TOURISM IN THE EC

FRAGILE ENVIRONMENTS

SPAIN

NIGERIA

URBAN ISSUES

What is the European Community?

Resource Bank

TREATY OF ROME CREATES COMMON MARKET

Six nations - France, West Germany, Italy, Belgium, The Netherlands, and Luxembourg - have signed the Treaty of Rome creating the European Common Market. This largely economic grouping of the countries with a total population of 160 million people will develop over the next fifteen years. It aims at free movement of people, goods, and money between the member states.

British Prime Minister Harold MacMillan said that he hopes to establish a wider continental trading structure which could include the Common Market, Britain, and other countries. Many people believe that the Market's development will be a threat to Britain, leading to new friction rather than greater European unity. Britain is pushing for a European Free Trade Area (EFTA) to include the whole of Western Europe, but with less surrender of sovereignty than joining the EEC.

The signing ceremony of the Treaty of Rome, 25th March 1957. 'The Six' create a common market for Europe

Figure 1

Figure 2 The history of the European Community

- **18th April 1951** Formation of European Coal and Steel Community (ECSC)
- **20th November 1959** EFTA set up by the UK, Austria, Denmark, Norway, Sweden, Portugal, and Switzerland
- **8th November 1961** The UK formally applies for membership of the EEC
- **14th January 1963** President De Gaulle of France claims that the UK neither thinks nor acts like a continental nation and should not yet join the EEC
- **29th July 1968** Six member states agree to free movement of workers within the EEC
- **1st January 1973** The UK, Denmark, and the Irish Republic become full members of the EEC (EUR 9). Norway had applied but withdrew application

Figure 3 The aims of the European Community

- A common trade policy.
  Tariffs to be removed to create a larger home market and a cheaper and wider range of goods.
- Freedom to work.
  Citizens from any member states should be free to work in any Community country, without work permits and with the same rights as nationals of that country.
- The stability and harmonisation of currencies.
  Through the European Monetary System, set up in 1979. Member states use a special currency - the European Currency Unit (ECU). It also regulates the value of individual currencies through the Exchange Rate Mechanism (ERM).
- To develop and improve agriculture.
  Through the Common Agricultural Policy (CAP), the most important of the Community's common policies. It absorbs 65 per cent of the total Community budget.
- To help regions and groups with economic difficulties.
  Through the creation of the European Regional Development Fund (ERDF) in 1975.
- To have common policies throughout the Community.
  There are common policies for fisheries, industrial intervention, economic and social affairs, tourism, energy, and the environment.
- To be a united body in world affairs.
  For instance, under the Lomé Convention, the EC gives favourable trading terms and financial assistance to most countries in Africa, the Pacific, and the Caribbean.

Figure 4 Institutions of the European Community

The Council of Ministers
The main decision-making body of the EC, it plays a vital role in conducting EC policy. Made up of representatives of the governments of the member states

The European Commission
Responsible for both proposing and implementing EC policy. It manages the common policies, implements the budget, and directs the administration. Based in Brussels, it comprises seventeen commissioners nominated by member states. Commissioners are obliged to act in the Community's interest and not in the interest of their own country.

The European Parliament
The representative assembly of the EC, directly elected since 1979. It has a say in Community legislation and the budget and is the EC's supervisory body. Its powers were extended by the Single European Act in 1986. Meets in Strasbourg.

The Court of Justice
Meets in Luxembourg and comprises thirteen judges. Ensures that EC law is observed in the interpretation and application of EC treaties. It can decide whether the conduct of any member state breaches Community law. The Court also gives rulings on relevant points of law referred to it by the domestic courts of member states.

5th March 1975 European Regional Development Fund established

10th May 1975 The Lomé Convention signed between EEC and 46 developing countries

6th June 1975 In referendum on the UK's countinued membership of EEC, 67.2 per cent vote in favour

6th June 1979 First direct Euro-elections to European Parliament, but only 1 in 3 Britons vote

1st January 1981 Greece becomes tenth member state (EUR 10)

1st January 1986 Portugal and Spain join, making it 12 member states (EUR 12)

February 1986 Single European Act signed. Gave the EC wider powers and prepared the way for the single European market (1st January 1993)

3rd October 1990 Unification of Germany

December 1991 Maastricht Summit. Agreement on political union and economic and monetary union

Figure 5 Basic information about the EC countries

	Capital	Seats in European Parliament	Area Km^2	GNP per capita US$	Population	Population density per Km^2	Currency
France	Paris	81	551 500	19 490	56.1	103	French Franc
UK	London	81	244 880	16 100	57.2	237	Pound Sterling
Italy	Rome	81	301 270	16 830	57.1	196	Lire
Germany	Bonn/Berlin	81	356 910	20 750	77.5	229	Deutsch Mark
Spain	Madrid	60	504 780	11 020	39.2	78	Peseta
Netherlands	The Hague	25	37 330	17 320	15.0	440	Guilder
Belgium	Brussels	24	33 100	15 549	9.8	311	Belgium Franc
Greece	Athens	24	131 990	5 990	10.0	77	Drachma
Portugal	Lisbon	24	93 390	4 900	10.3	115	Escudo
Denmark	Copenhagen	16	43 070	22 080	5.1	121	Krone
Irish Republic	Dublin	15	70 280	9 550	3.7	51	Punt
Luxembourg	Luxembourg	6	2 590	24 860	0.4	144	French Franc

A world superpower?

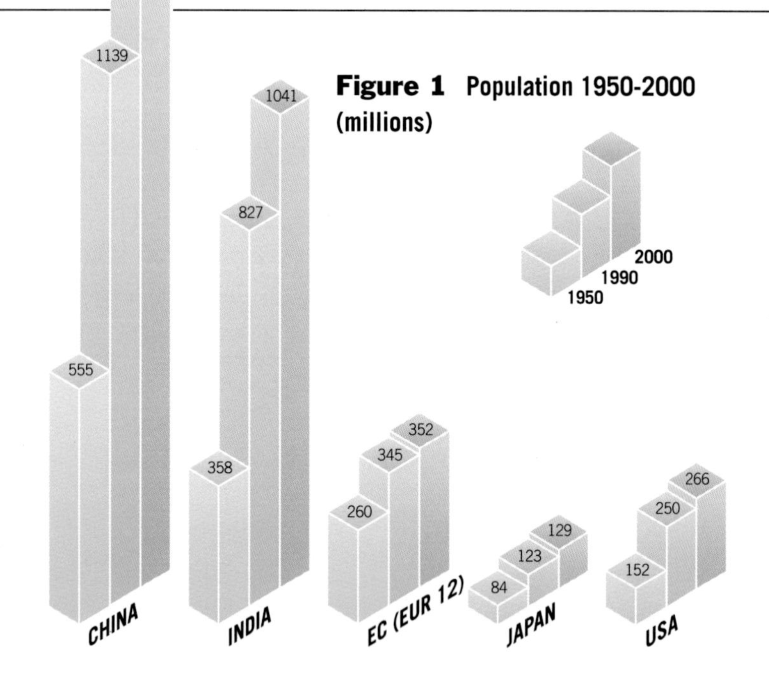

Figure 1 Population 1950-2000 (millions)

Figure 2 Some information about EC Gross Domestic Product (GDP)

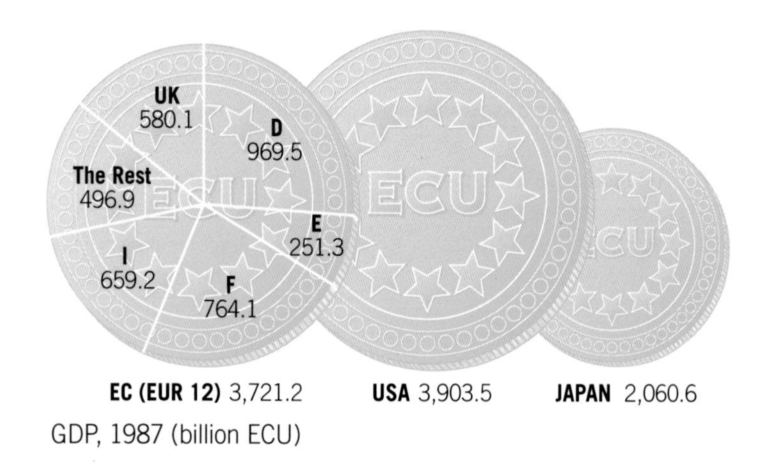

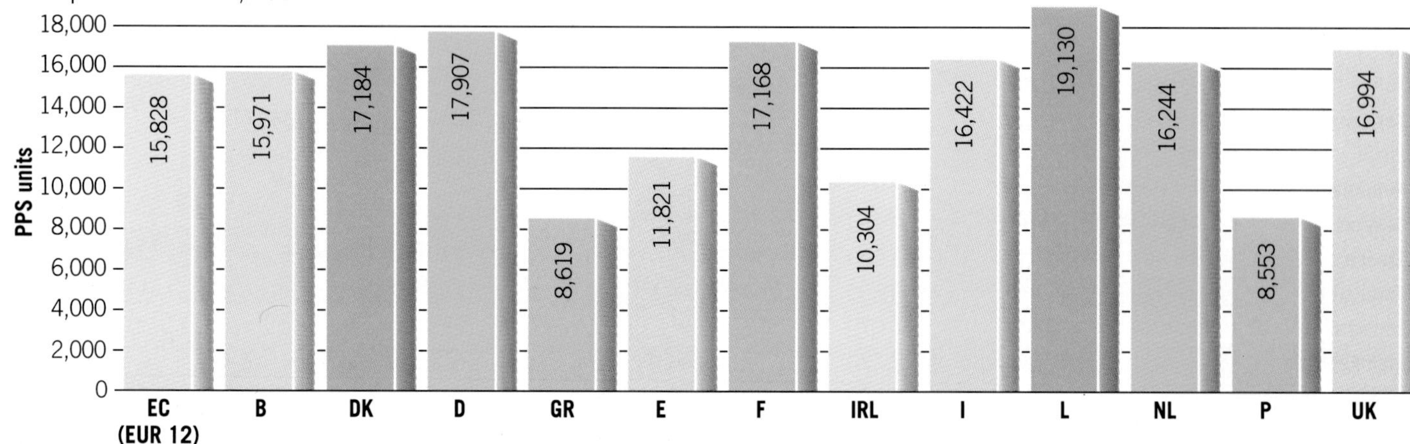

The time since the late 1980s has seen remarkable change in Europe. Most dramatic was the break-up of the USSR and the overthrow of communist regimes in the countries of Eastern Europe - the former Communist Bloc. It was also a time of increasing power and influence for the European Community. Many people now think that the EC has achieved the status of 'superpower'. Is this the case? Let us consider three aspects of the 'EC superpower': its population, its economy, and its role in world affairs.

The population of the European Community in 1990 stood at 345 million. This was about 6 per cent of the world's population. The population of the European Twelve is thus greater than that of both the USA (250 million) and Japan (123 million). However, in population terms, the EC is dwarfed by the huge population of both China and India. Figure 1 shows that the growth of the EC's population is very slow. Several member countries are actually experiencing a decline in their population. For example, German women have an average of only 1.3 children each, compared to 2.2 in the USA and 3.4 in the world as a whole (2.1 would be required to maintain a constant population). Some people question whether this is good or bad for Europe.

During the last twenty-five years the average European family has doubled its income, and now has twice as many goods and services at its disposal. In the same period, the average American family has had only a 60 per cent increase, whilst in Japan it multiplied by four. The relative size of the major world economies is given in Figure 2.

The consumption of goods and services by a society can be expressed by a PPS (purchasing power standard). The EC average is 15 828 units per person which is higher than Japan (9500 units) but below the USA (16 400 units). The growth of the PPS for the EC is greater than that for either Japan or the USA.

Some people argue that if the EC wants to be seen as a world power, it must act in a unified way towards foreign affairs, such as the war in Yugoslavia or the moves to protect the world's environment.

In its dealings with many of the poorer countries of the South, the EC has been working as a whole for many years through the Lomé Convention. This is explained in more detail in Figure 4.

Figure 4 **The Lomé Convention**

Through this Convention the EC provides financial support to development schemes. It now covers 69 African, Caribbean, and Pacific (ACP) countries.

Purpose

- To finance projects which increase food supply, mainly through rural development.
- To promote regional cooperation through programmes aimed at problems such as disease and desertification.
- To give food aid.
- To encourage trade by guaranteeing export prices and providing free access to the EC for most exports.

How the money was used in 1990	
Rural production	25.8%
Industrialisation	20.9%
Transport and communications	17.6%
Education	6.9%
Water supply	6.3%
Health	1.9%
Trade	1.4%
Tourism	0.6%
Other	18.6%

Figure 3 **The location of the EC**

Activities

1 Look at Figure 1. Give as many reasons as you can to explain why the population of the EC is rising slowly.

2 Use an atlas to find out about population growth in other parts of the world and draw a graph of your findings.

3 *Research idea:*
What other criteria could be used to identify a superpower?
Using the criteria that you have chosen, find out how the EC compares with the USA, Japan, and other countries. Show your findings as a series of graphs and diagrams.

4 *Essay:*
Write an essay of about 500 words in answer to the question 'Is the EC a superpower?'

Figure 5
EC monitors played a major role in organising casesfires between Serbs and Croats during the fighting in the former state of Yugoslavia

Regional variations

Figure 1
An abandoned farm in the Massif Central, France

People's prosperity and way of life differ greatly across the EC.

It is the peripheral regions that have the most serious economic and social problems. To try and identify the parts of Europe facing the most serious problems, the EC has produced a table of 'regional prosperity'. This gives an index measuring the relative intensity of regional problems in each administrative region of the twelve member states. Two criteria were used to produce this index - how much is produced in the region and the level of unemployment.

The EC average of this index is 100; regions with many problems are below this value whilst regions with fewer problems are above it (Figure 2). The regions with the lowest index include the Irish Republic, Northern Ireland, the Mezzogiorno in Italy, Corsica, Merseyside, Strathclyde, Tyne and Wear, Gwent, Devon and Cornwall, Hainaut and Limburg provinces in Belgium, eastern Germany, central Spain, and much of Greece and Portugal. The majority of the regions with an index above the EC average are to be found in northern Italy, eastern France, and western Germany. It must be remembered that they also have their share of problems and difficulties - congestion and pollution, for example.

But why is it that such considerable regional differences exist? 'Core areas' benefit in the following ways:

- They have the largest markets and the most services (schools, shops, and hospitals).
- They have most government and administration functions.
- They have more cultural and social attractions.
- Their good communications and transport networks attract investment.

'Peripheral areas' are hindered by:

- Greater distance and remoteness from markets and centres of population.
- A lack of investment in infrastructure, such as roads and hospitals.
- A decline in the traditional sectors of their economies such as heavy industry and agriculture.
- Poor development of their services, which encourages people to move away.

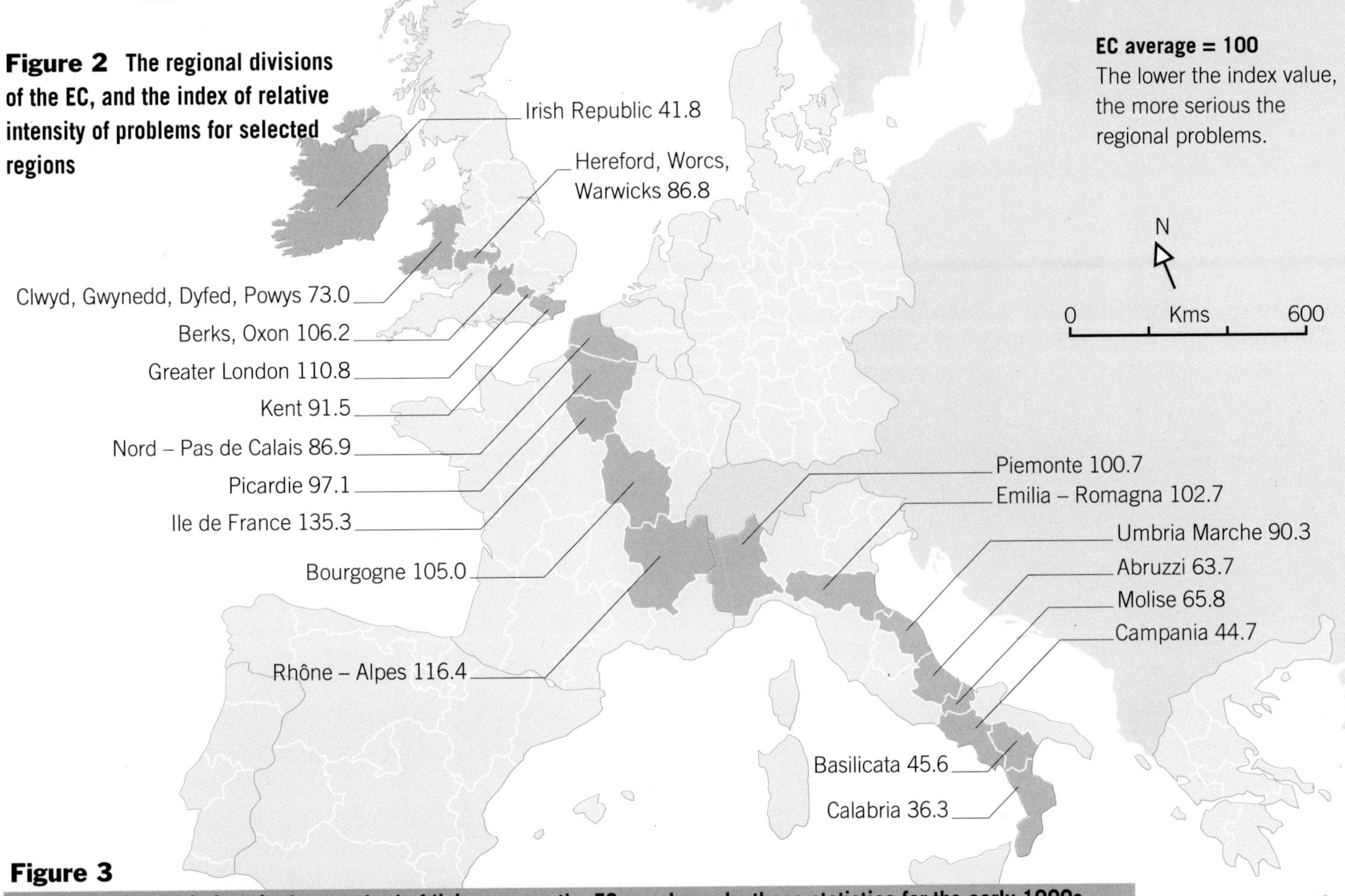

Figure 2 The regional divisions of the EC, and the index of relative intensity of problems for selected regions

Figure 3

There are large variations in the standard of living across the EC, as shown by these statistics for the early 1990s

	Telephones (per 100 people)	Cars in use (thousands)	Energy use per person per year (tonnes of coal equivalent)	Average farm size (ha)	Urban population (% of total)
UK	60	18859	5.1	64	93
France	66	21970	4.0	29	74
Germany	55	31500	5.9	17	82
Greece	41	1433	3.2	4	63
Belgium	48	3453	5.8	15	97
Spain	40	10219	2.5	14	78
Portugal	20	1947	1.8	5	33
Netherlands	64	5118	6.8	15	89
Italy	49	23496	3.8	6	69
Luxembourg	-	169	14.8	30	83
Irish Republic	28	743	3.8	23	59
Denmark	86	1602	4.5	32	86

Activities

1 Suggest reasons why the farm shown in Figure 1 might have been abandoned.

2 a) Describe the pattern shown by the sample of shaded regions in Figure 2.

b) How does this information suggest the idea of a core and periphery in Europe?

3 a) Study Figure 3. Choose one of the variables shown and draw a choropleth (shading) map of it on an outline map of the EC.

b) Compare your map with other people's. Which of the statistics show a core and periphery division of the Community? Write a paragraph to describe your findings.

Helping the regions

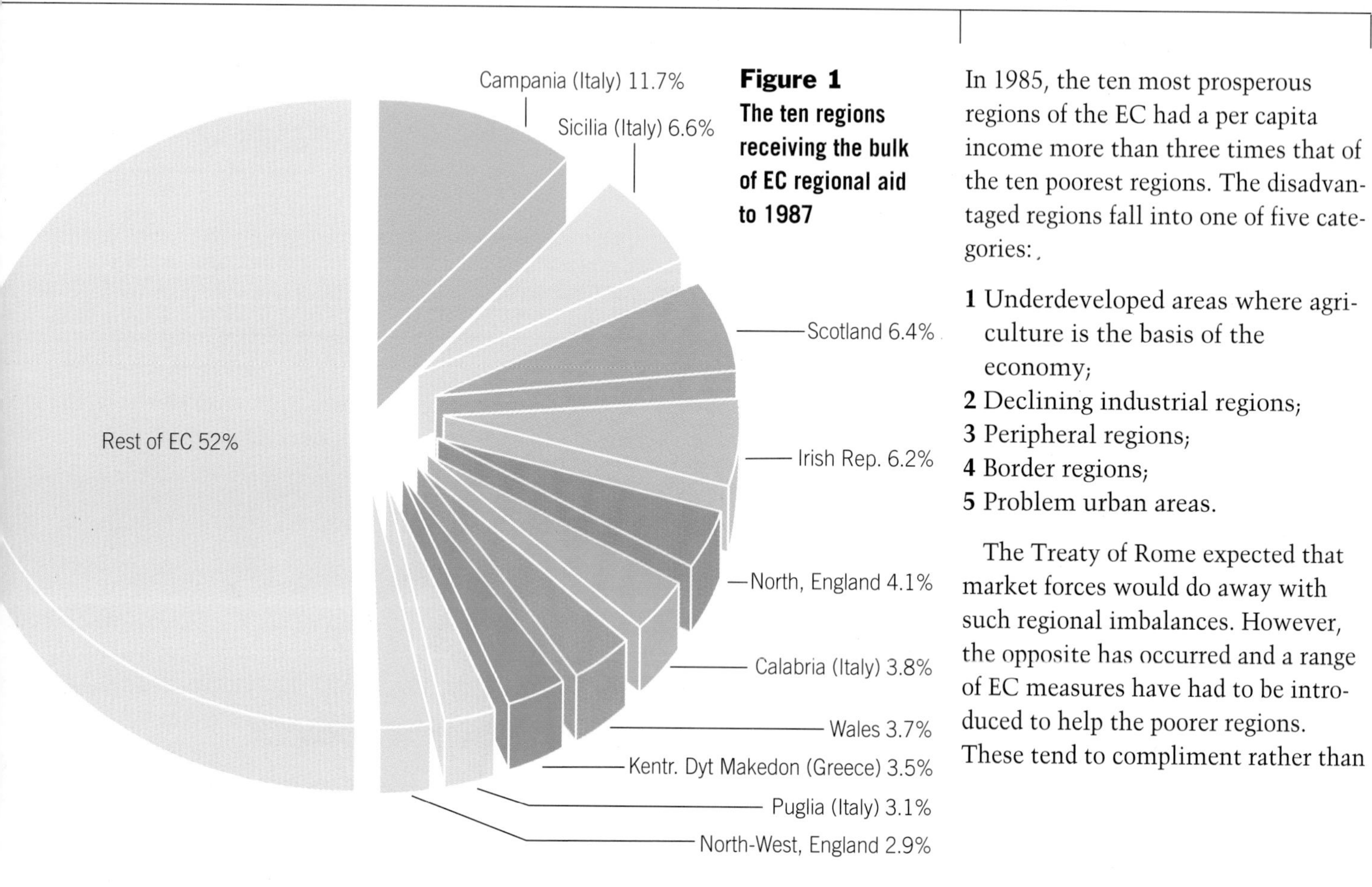

Figure 1 **The ten regions receiving the bulk of EC regional aid to 1987**

In 1985, the ten most prosperous regions of the EC had a per capita income more than three times that of the ten poorest regions. The disadvantaged regions fall into one of five categories:

1 Underdeveloped areas where agriculture is the basis of the economy;
2 Declining industrial regions;
3 Peripheral regions;
4 Border regions;
5 Problem urban areas.

The Treaty of Rome expected that market forces would do away with such regional imbalances. However, the opposite has occurred and a range of EC measures have had to be introduced to help the poorer regions. These tend to compliment rather than

Figure 2 **The European Regional Development Fund (ERDF)**

The ERDF was set up in 1975. It accounts for almost 10 per cent of the EC budget.

Objectives

1 To help underdeveloped regions.
2 To redevelop regions affected by industrial decline.
3 To fight long-term unemployment.
4 To provide for the employment needs of young people.
5 To promote agricultural development.

Eligibility

To be eligible for help under Objective 1, a region must have a per capita income of less than 75 per cent of the EC average.

To be eligible for help under Objective 2, a region must have a GDP lower than the EC average, plus at least one of the following: more than 20 per cent of the population employed in agriculture or a declining industry; a rate of unemployment higher than the EC average for the last three years; out-migration of over 10 per 1000 over a long period.

Criticisms

Available funds only small.

Inflation and recession have made them less effective.

Measures of the intensity of problems vary between countries making it difficult to be fair.

replace national regional development policies.

The European Investment Bank (EIB) provides grants and loans for a variety of projects in the more underdeveloped parts of the Community. It helps particularly with industrial projects that the national government cannot afford itself.

The European Social Fund helps to stimulate training and employment for women, the young, the handicapped, and migrant workers. It aims to help people who want to set up their own businesses. In particular, it assists those people who have lost their jobs in a declining industry such as textiles and the steel industry.

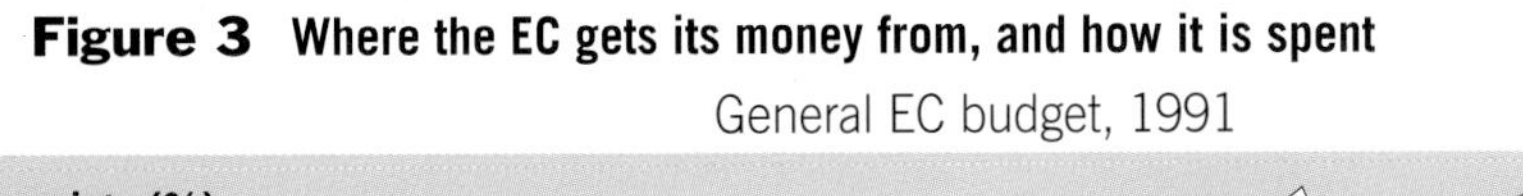

Figure 3 Where the EC gets its money from, and how it is spent

General EC budget, 1991

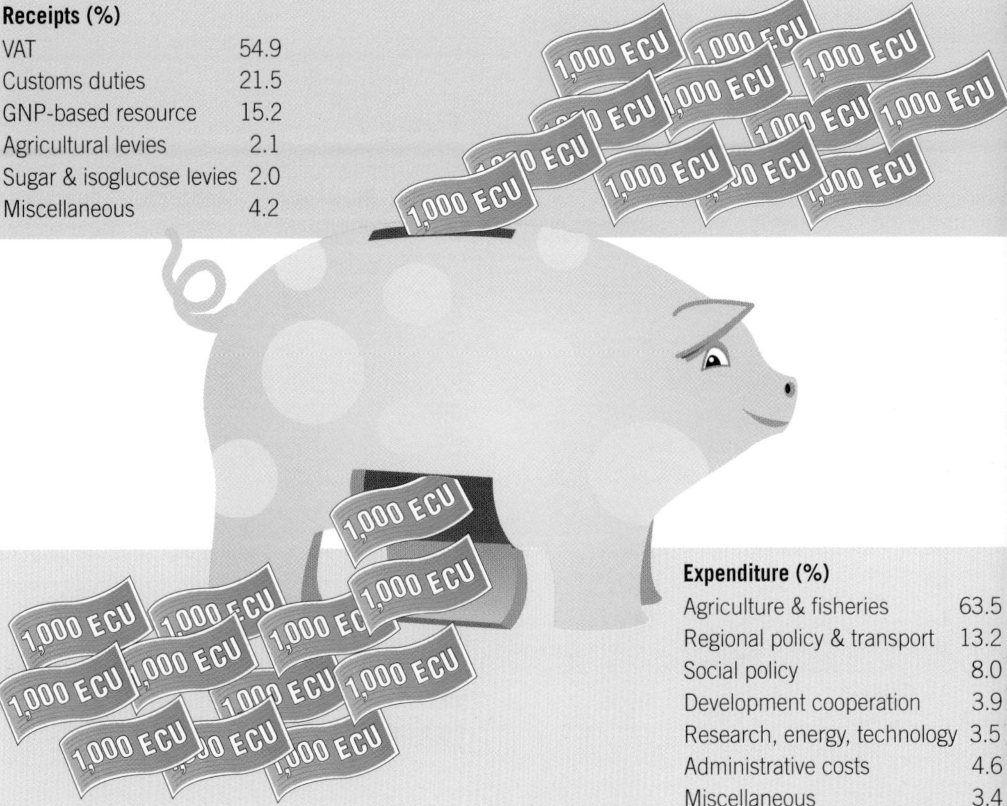

Receipts (%)	
VAT	54.9
Customs duties	21.5
GNP-based resource	15.2
Agricultural levies	2.1
Sugar & isoglucose levies	2.0
Miscellaneous	4.2

Expenditure (%)	
Agriculture & fisheries	63.5
Regional policy & transport	13.2
Social policy	8.0
Development cooperation	3.9
Research, energy, technology	3.5
Administrative costs	4.6
Miscellaneous	3.4

Figure 4 How the money is shared out

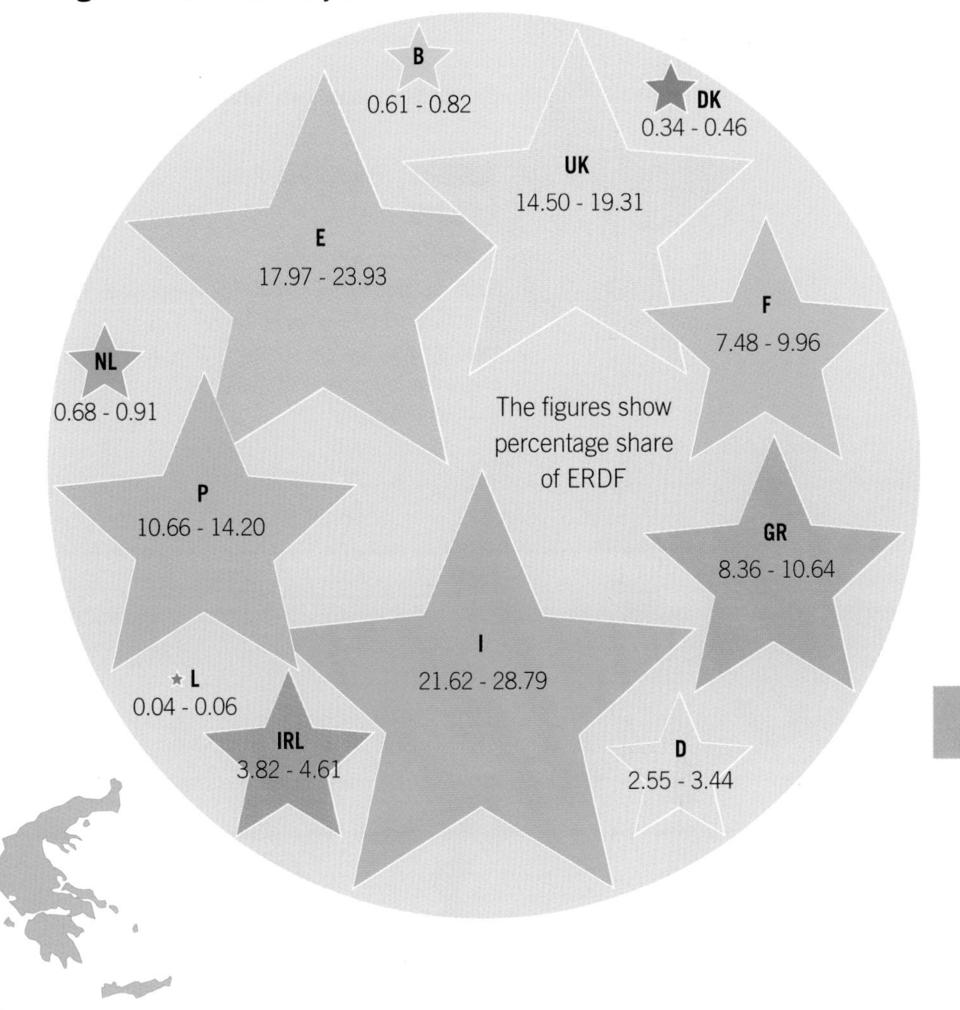

Activities

1 a) Look at Figure 1. Name the four regions receiving the highest percentages of EC regional aid.

b) What do you notice about the location within the EC of the ten regions named in Figure 1?

2 a) Look at Figure 2. How does the EC define an 'underdeveloped region'?

b) Write a paragraph to describe the pattern shown on the map.

3 Look at Figure 3.

a) Where does over half of EC money come from?

b) What is by far the largest use to which EC funds are put?

c) Can you suggest reasons why so much is spent in this way?

4 Using Figure 3 on page 11 and Figure 4 on this page, investigate whether there is a link between the aid given to a country and its standard of living.

European agriculture

Resource Bank

Figure 1

Changing income of Europe's farmers

1980 = 100

	1985	1990
B	112.9	109.3
DK	149.5	121.1
D	97.8	102.6
GR	112.7	110.3
F	103.0	97.9
IRL	118.5	146.5
I	95.5	92.7
L	134.4	143.6
NL	117.0	120.1
UK	96.8	90.8
E	104.6	140.7
P	-	-
EC (EUR12)	106.3	105.7

Figure 3

Farm size and land use

	No. of holdings *(thousands)*	Average size *(ha)*	Distribution of holdings *(per cent)*			Land use *(per cent of agricultural land)*		
			<2ha	2-<20ha	≥20ha	Arable land	Permanent crops*	Permanent grassland
B	93	15	23.6	51.2	25.2	52	3	45
DK	87	32	1.5	42.5	56.0	92	0	8
D	705	17	15.9	54.7	29.3	60	2	38
GR	953	4	46.3	51.4	2.2	51	31	18
E	1792	14	33.3	53.5	13.2	57	19	24
F	982	29	13.2	39.6	47.2	56	5	39
IRL	217	23	4.7	55.7	39.6	19	1	80
I	2784	6	51.8	43.5	4.7	52	20	28
L	4	30	14.2	32.1	53.8	43	2	55
NL	132	15	19.5	52.3	28.2	42	3	55
P	635	5	61.5	35.3	3.2	66	17	17
UK	260	64	10.6	34.5	54.9	38	0	62
EC (EUR12)	8644	13	37.0	46.5	16.4	51	9	40

*Orchards, vineyards, olive groves

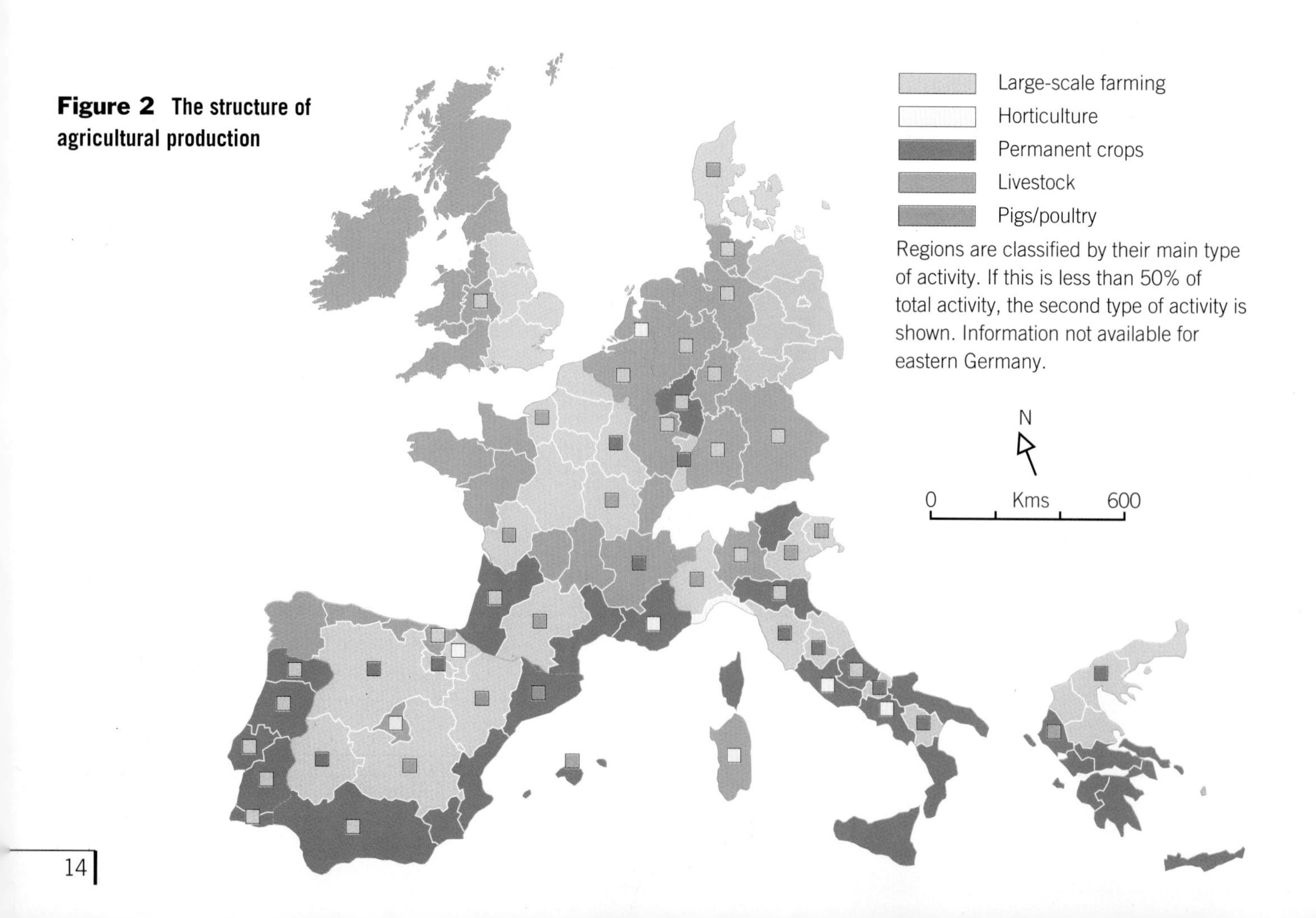

Figure 2 The structure of agricultural production

Figure 4 Agriculture's changing share of the workforce

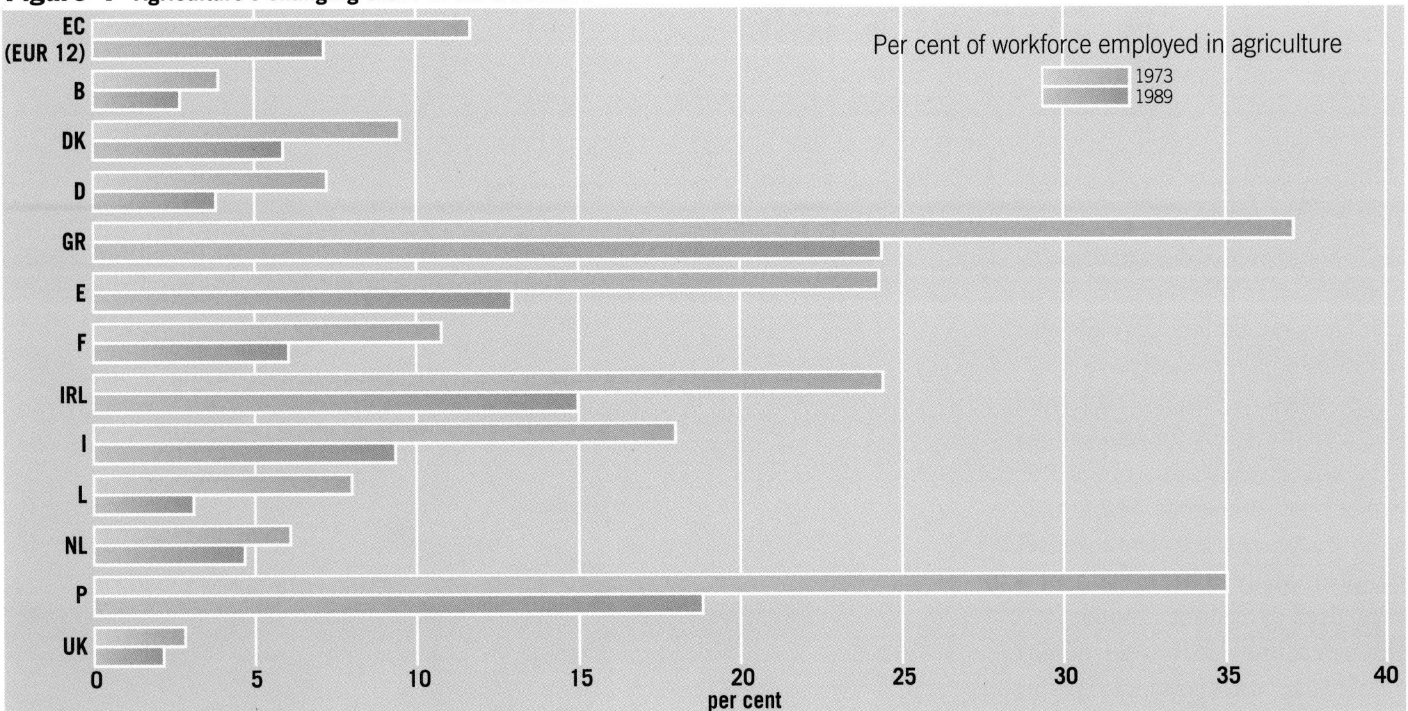

Figure 5 The Common Agricultural Policy (CAP)

Since the Treaty of Rome in 1957, the objectives of the CAP have been:

- to increase agricultural productivity
- to raise farm incomes and ensure a fair standard of living for farmers
- to stabilise markets, making them independent of world price and volume fluctuations
- to ensure food supplies
- to ensure that consumers pay fair and reasonable prices
- to protect the environment

Results and achievements:

- increased production
- reasonable consumer prices ensured
- markets stabilised for most products
- higher farm incomes
- a greater degree of self-sufficiency
- average farm size and average field size increased
- rural depopulation reduced

Problems:

- increased food prices
- creation of food surpluses - the infamous 'mountains' and 'lakes'
- increased gap between core farming regions and periphery
- farms on periphery still small and often uneconomic
- high cost of subsidies - some countries, particularly the UK, object to most of total EC budget being spent on agriculture
- loss of wildlife habitat

Reform:

The EC is changing the focus of the CAP. The aim is to align agricultural production more closely to consumption and to reduce the costs of the CAP.

Figure 6 Self-sufficiency in agricultural products, 1989

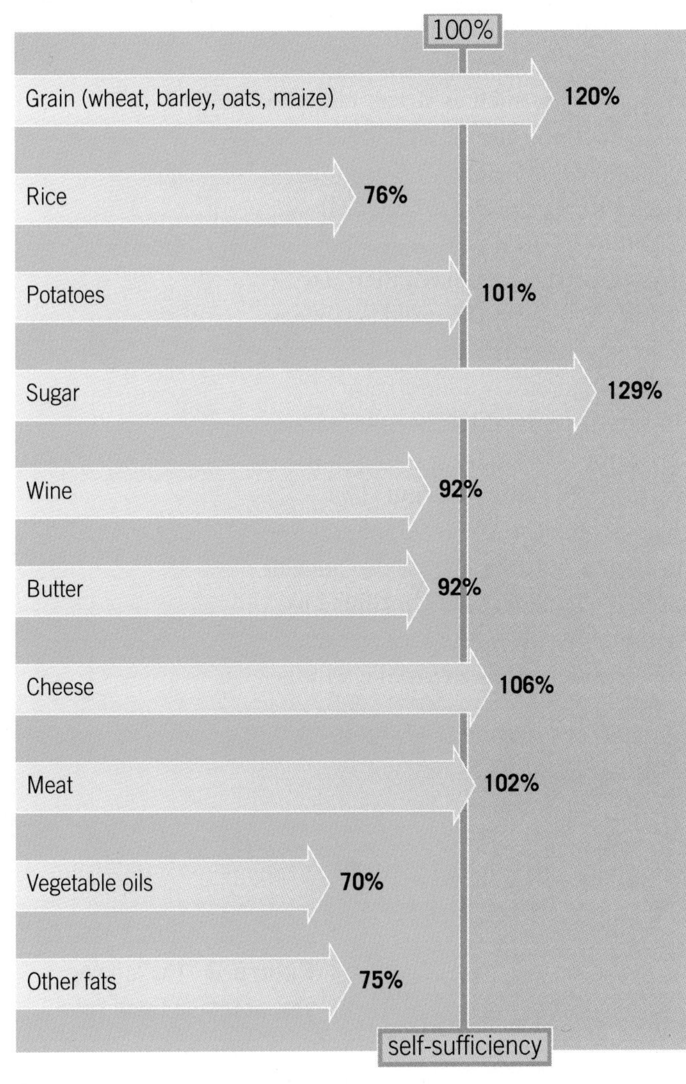

A farmer's tale

Gorfen Letch Farm is a family-run farm of 98 hectares in Northumberland, about three miles north of the county town of Morpeth. The farm is located on glacial boulder clay which does not drain very easily.

Gorfen Letch Farm has been run by the Turnbull family for four generations. It is a mixed farm, producing both animals and crops. Sheep and cattle are kept on the farm for wool and meat. Many of the crops are fodder crops, used to feed the animals, although some are also sold. Some of the fields are used permanently for grass, which in turn can be used for grazing or for silage or hay. The other fields on the farm have their use varied through a process of crop rotation. Crops such as wheat take the nutrients from the soil which must be replaced by fertilisers. Mr Turnbull changes the use of the fields to allow the soil to recover. The fields of permanent grass also have their use rotated as the animals could easily eat all the grass, leaving the soil bare and open to erosion.

In recent years, it has been increasingly difficult to make a living from farming in Northumberland. The prices obtained at the local market for animals have fallen, whilst the price of inputs to the farm have continued to rise. Many farms in the area are up for sale as farmers decide to make a living by other means.

Figure 1 Gorfen Letch farm - the buildings

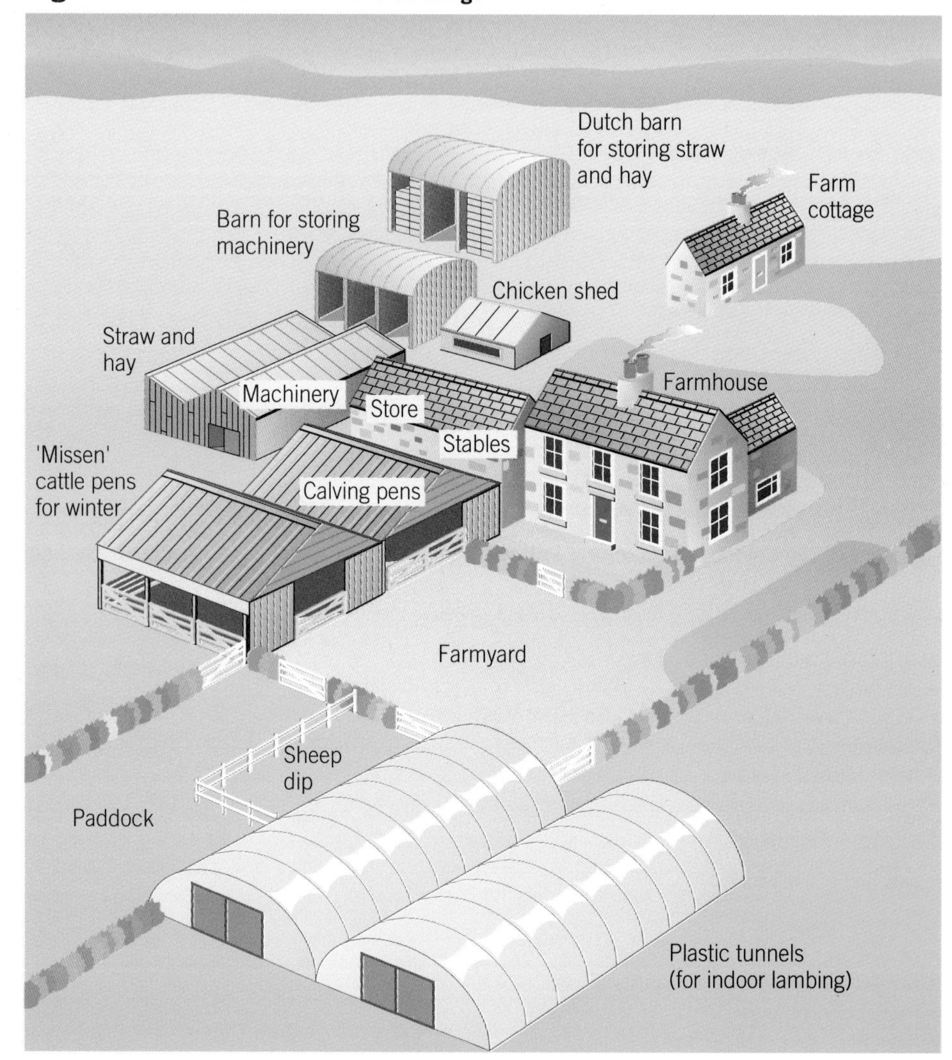

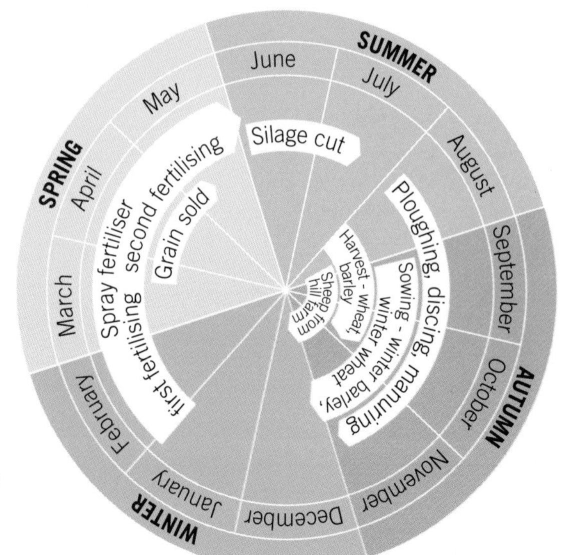

Figure 2 The farming year at Gorfen Letch Farm

Figure 3 Gorfen Letch Farm - the fields, showing crops in year 1 of rotation

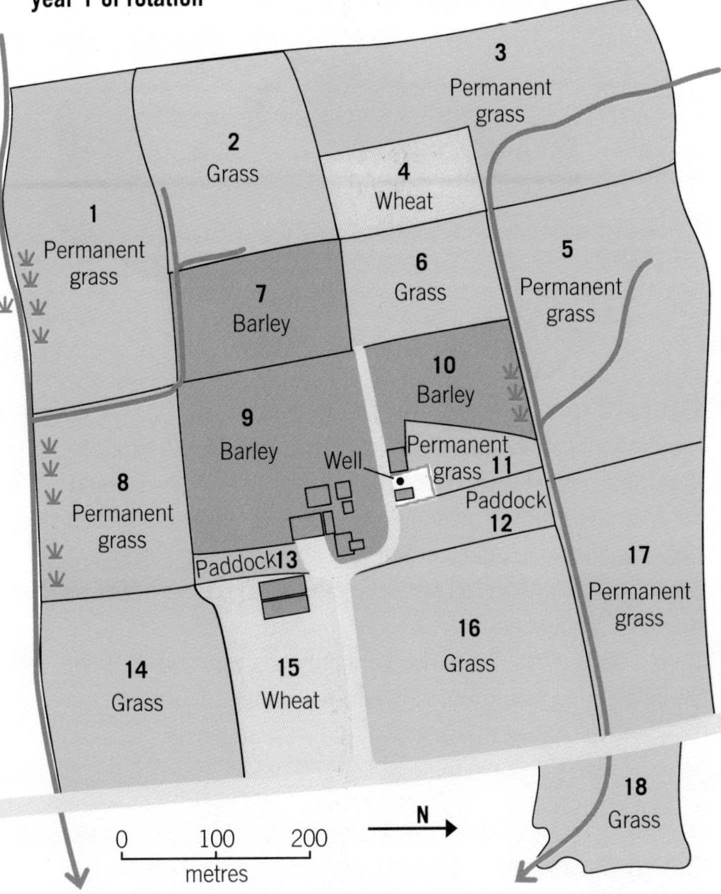

Figure 5 Mr Turnbull says...

"In recent years it has become increasingly difficult to farm profitably in areas like Northumberland. We're near the edge of the EC, a long way from the main areas of population and without good roads to link us either. The weather is unpredictable, we're continually fighting a battle with the cold, the rain, and the snow."

"Both the government in London and the EC should be doing everything that they can to keep farmers profitable in remote areas like this. Without us the local economy would collapse. Yes, they do give subsidies, but they are too small and frequently for crops and animals ill-suited to the environment. These subsidies mainly seem to help big farmers in more favourable parts of Europe. The markets get flooded by subsidised produce that nobody wants to buy."

"European bureaucracy? The bane of my life. I've never had so many forms to fill in. Forms for this, forms for that. The latest EC scheme designed to improve my farm is the completion of a map of the farm showing all sorts of details about the fields. I know what my farm's like! How will this scheme possibly help me?"

Figure 4 Crop rotation on Gorfen Letch Farm

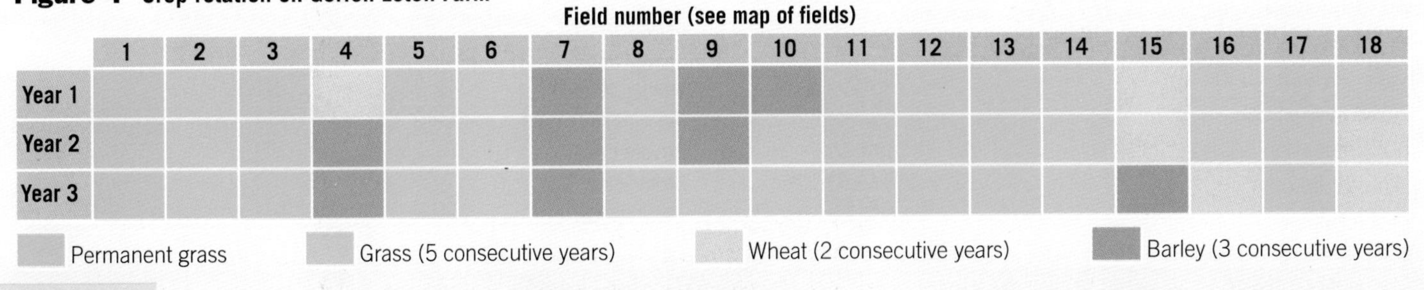

Activities

1 a) Study the sketch of Gorfen Letch Farm in Figure 1. Draw a map of this part of the farm showing all the farm buildings. Label each building.

b) Classify the buildings according to their function, using these categories: human - red, animals - blue, fodder storage - yellow, other storage - green, other functions - brown. Shade the buildings accordingly.

2 Look closely at the information about land use at Gorfen Letch Farm.

a) Why are some fields put permanently to grass?

b) Make a copy of the map in Figure 3. Colour and label the fields according to the land use you would expect for year 4 of the rotation pattern shown in Figure 4.

c) Why is it necessary to rotate crops in this way?

3 Explain why Mr Turnbull believes the local economy 'would collapse' without farmers like himself.

4 a) Write a letter from Mr Turnbull to his MEP (Member of the European Parliament). Express his views on EC agricultural policy. You should also outline three things that he believes would improve his situation at Gorfen Letch Farm.

b) Exchange your letter with a partner. Take on the role of the MEP and write a reply to your partner's letter. Try to address each of the points it raises.

Eastern Germany, EC newcomer

On 3rd October 1990, the EC gained another 15 155 000 citizens. After forty-one years, East and West Germany were reunited. The people of both East and West declared that they were 'one people', and their governments prepared a 'plan for German unity'.

The road to unity would not be easy. The two parts of Germany belonged to totally opposite social systems. The West is a parliamentary democracy, with highly productive and efficient industry and agriculture, in accordance with EC regulations. East Germany was a socialist economy based on central planning, state ownership of industry, and collectivisation of agriculture. The two countries had different currencies, passports, armies, and alliances.

Figure 2
The Trabant car was typical of East Germany's economic ills. Unreliable, polluting, and with huge delays in delivery, it could not compete in a free market. It quickly went out of production after unification. In addition, with the collapse of the Soviet Empire, East Germany lost the markets for 40 per cent of its industrial production.
In the 1980s, West Germany's economy was very strong. It had low inflation, high employment, and few debts. Unification threatens to change this. In 1992, the western lander or provinces gave those in the east DM180 billion. This is 6 per cent of Germany's GNP or about 25 per cent of all public expenditure.

Figure 3 Changes in industrial production, East Germany

(1985 =100)	**1989**	**June 1990**	**Oct 1990**
TOTAL	111.8	96.2	55.3
of which:			
Energy and energy products	103.9	81.1	61.2
Building materials	109.0	111.8	37.0
Private cars	102.1	27.1	0
Precision engineering	120.2	101.9	93.7

Figure 1
People all over the world rejoiced when the Berlin Wall came down in November 1989, but unification has brought its own problems

We Westerners are known as 'Wessis'. We have worked very hard for over forty years earning the opportunities afforded by our free enterprise society. We have achieved a higher standard of living than the East. We also have greater skills than the Ossis who are slow, lacking in initiative, and always complaining.

The Wessis are like schoolteachers, they think that they can do everything better than the Ossis. They should remember that we've had no chance to live as we wished. It was not our fault that our government was corrupt and inadequate. Anyway, I've heard that many Wessis are con-men out to make lots of money from our situation and inexperience.

Figure 4 **Personal wealth in Germany's sixteen lander**

		GDP per capita 1990 (DM thousands)
1	Schleswig-Holstein	32
2	Mecklenburg-West Pomerania	13*
3	Hamburg	68
4	Bremen	48
5	Lower Saxony	33
6	Brandenburg	13*
7	Saxony Anhalt	13*
8	Berlin	27
9	Saxony	13*
10	Thuringia	13*
11	North Rhine-Westphalia	37
12	Hesse	44
13	Rhineland-Palatinate	34
14	Saarland	33
15	Baden-Württemberg	40
16	Bavaria	39

*Average GDP per person for East Germany

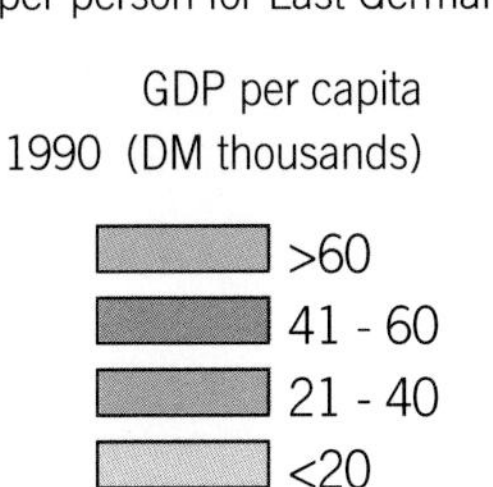

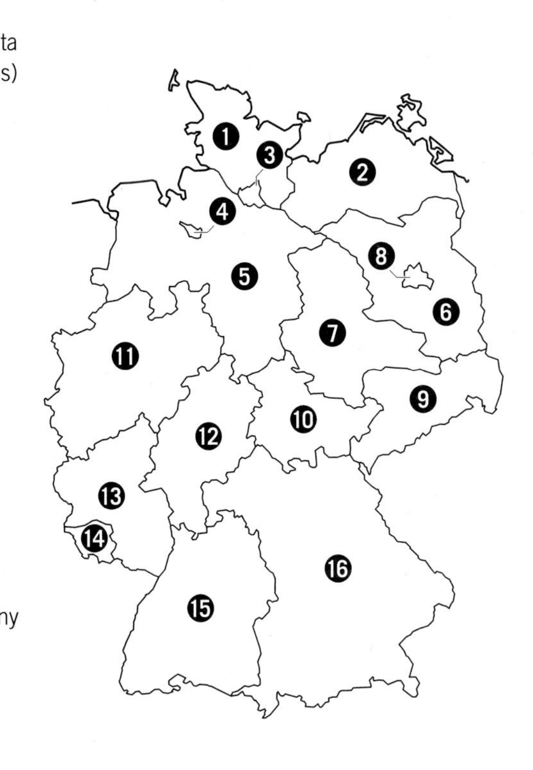

Figure 5 **Some of the measures taken to help the eastern lander**

- Low interest government loans
- Town twinnings between east and west
- Encouragement of private investment
- The new lander will not be fully taxed until 1994
- A 'German Unity Fund' has been set up to provide DM 100 billion up to 1994
- The Federal government has contributed to infrastructure projects such as schools and hospitals
- Job creation and retraining schemes
- DM 30 billion has been raised on the world money markets to help privatise eastern industries
- The EC will provided funds:
  DM 3 billion from Regional Fund
  DM 1.8 billion from Social Fund
  DM 1.2 billion from Agricultural Structure Fund

Figure 6 **Issues the EC must face as a result of German unification**

- Germany pays 28 per cent of the EC budget. Can it still afford to do this?
- Germany has the same number of seats in the European Parliament as the UK, France, and Italy. It is now a much bigger country, so how should the seats be redistributed?
- Should the EC give more help for the reconstruction of eastern Germany? In 1991, it gave only DM 1 billion.

- Now that their country is unified, will the Germans go 'cool' on European integration?
- How should Germany and the EC respond to growing right-wing nationalism in eastern Germany? Much of this is a result of Germany's constitution which guarantees asylum to victims of oppression (250 000 in 1991). The Ossis feel that they need help before refugees.

Activities

1 Write about what some different German people might have been thinking the night the Berlin Wall was finally brought down.

2 a) Draw a series of line graphs to show East German industrial production as shown in the table in Figure 3.
b) Explain why the drop in car production was much greater than in precision engineering (which includes things like cameras and binoculars).

3 Imagine that you are a German government official who is very much in favour of unification. Write a reply to each of the opinions stated in Figure 1.

4 a) Make a copy of the outline map of the German lander in Figure 4.
b) Using the key provided, shade it in to show the relative wealth of the different parts of Germany.
c) Describe and attempt to explain the pattern that is shown by your map.

5 In small groups, discuss the issues set out in Figure 6. What do you think the EC should do?

Eastern Germany's legacy of pollution

Figure 1 Jobless Jorg Kuba used to work at Chemiewerke, Bitterfeld

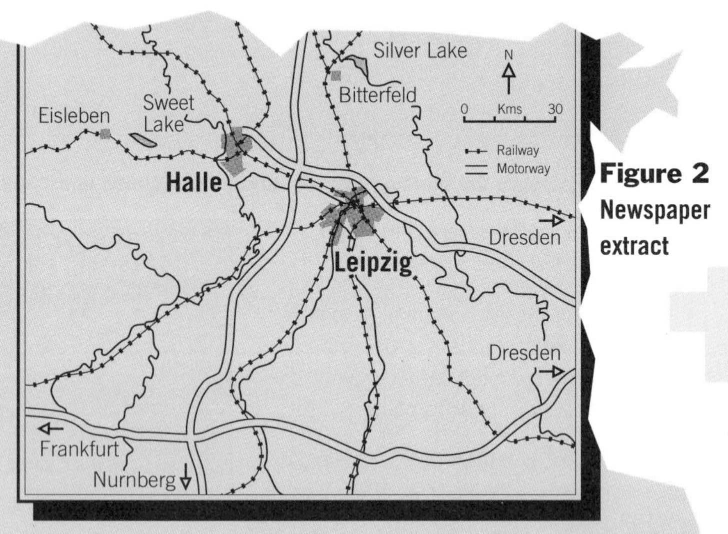

Figure 2 Newspaper extract

Counting the cost of cleaning up

It seems like an almost impossible task. By the start of the next century, Germany hopes to bring its economically ailing and underdeveloped eastern states up to the environmental standards of those in the west.

Some experts say it just cannot be done. Others are confident that the necessary financial, industrial and political muscle will be brought to bear on the problem and that east Germany will become an environmental showcase.

The end result is likely to be somewhere between the two. Germany's unification treaty stresses the importance of raising environmental standards in the east both to improve the quality of life and as part of the whole economic reconstruction process. More than DM60m (£21m) has been spent on studies alone to assess what needs to be done and what is feasible.

What the experts do not dispute is that the whole process will be extremely costly; the Ifo economic research institute in Munich estimates around DM200bn, though others go much higher. The old East Berlin government treated the issue of pollution with notorious disdain, forbidding concerned citizens to seek out the real facts. The environment was a taboo subject. What was important was economic success and self-sufficiency. 'Nature was exploited', says Karl Eugen Huthmacher, an environment ministry official.

Two of the worst industries in pollution terms were chemicals and metal processing. Bitterfeld, the town which housed one of east Germany's biggest chemical complexes, became a byword for the industrial fouling of the land, air, and water. The name symbolised east Germany's environmental ills all too aptly; as well as the mouldering chemical plant, a factory producing lignite briquettes also contributed to the stench and dirt.

Bitterfeld lies in the heart of the industrial complex between Leipzig and Halle, both historic cities which suffered from the weight of industrial development. Not far outside Leipzig is an opencast lignite mine, which devastated a vast area of landscape as the coal was brutally scooped off the ground by huge excavators. From the air, it looks like an arid moonscape where life never existed.

Centred on Halle is a huge chemicals complex, which accounted for half of east Germany's toxic waste and 30 per cent of its water and air pollution. Slightly to the west is Eisleben, the headquarters of the Mansfeld metals complex. Scattered around the countryside are big slag heaps.

Ironically, notes Ifo, east Germany did specify the protection of nature in its constitution, one of the few countries to do so. But it is only in the past two years that environmental consciousness has been allowed to develop. Because of past neglect, the clean-up job looks forbidding.

Air

- East Germany had the worst air pollution in Europe.
- 80 per cent of electricity was produced by burning lignite, which gave off vast amounts of sulphur-rich smoke.
- Nearly 280 large power plants will have to be fitted with filters.
- By 2005, the aim is to cut CO_2 emissions by 40 per cent.
- By 1996, the government wants to cut SO_2 pollution by 4.2m tonnes.

Water

- Only 75 per cent of the population is connected to a sewerage system and only 60 per cent to a sewage treatment works. Several thousand miles of new sewers will have to be built to reach the standard of the West.
- Only 1 per cent of lakes are suitable for drinking purposes. Sweet Lake and Silver Lake are examples of beautiful, yet very heavily polluted lakes.
- Like many rivers, the River Elbe is heavily polluted with chemicals such as mercury, although industrial closures have improved the situation.

Ground

- Contamination has come from industry, mining, dumping of waste, and military activity.
- 28 000 sites have been identified as possibly contaminated.
- The closed nuclear site at Greifswald will need demolishing and decontaminating.
- High levels of arsenic, cadmium, and zinc have been found at an old lead smelter near Bittefeld.
- The Soviet army occupied 280 000 ha of land which will need redeveloping and in some areas decontaminating.

Figure 3 Pollution in East Germany. The photo shows acid rain damage in the Harz Mountains

Progress is being made in cleaning up the environmental mess in eastern Germany. For one thing, the air smells cleaner. The extensive use of brown coal or lignite has been substantially reduced, and with it some of the worst levels of air pollution. Throughout eastern Germany heavily polluting factories have been closed, further reducing pollution. However, this has not been due to environmental concerns, but rather because the old factories were unable to compete in a free market. Many sites have been cleared ready for new industrial development, helping to provide much needed employment. The investing companies do not want to have to clean up the environment before they can open their new factories, so it has fallen to the German government and those of the lander to carry out the clean-up operation. They cannot afford the DM 200 billion that it might cost - they can only tackle the areas of highest priority. The clean-up is going to take a long time. But at least things should improve.

Activities

1. Using Figure 3 to help you, write a list of the causes of pollution in the former East Germany.
2. Draw a map of the area shown in Figure 2. Mark on it the incidents of pollution mentioned in the newspaper article.
3. Suggest reasons why pollution was so bad in East Germany.

Fishing Europe's seas

Resource Bank

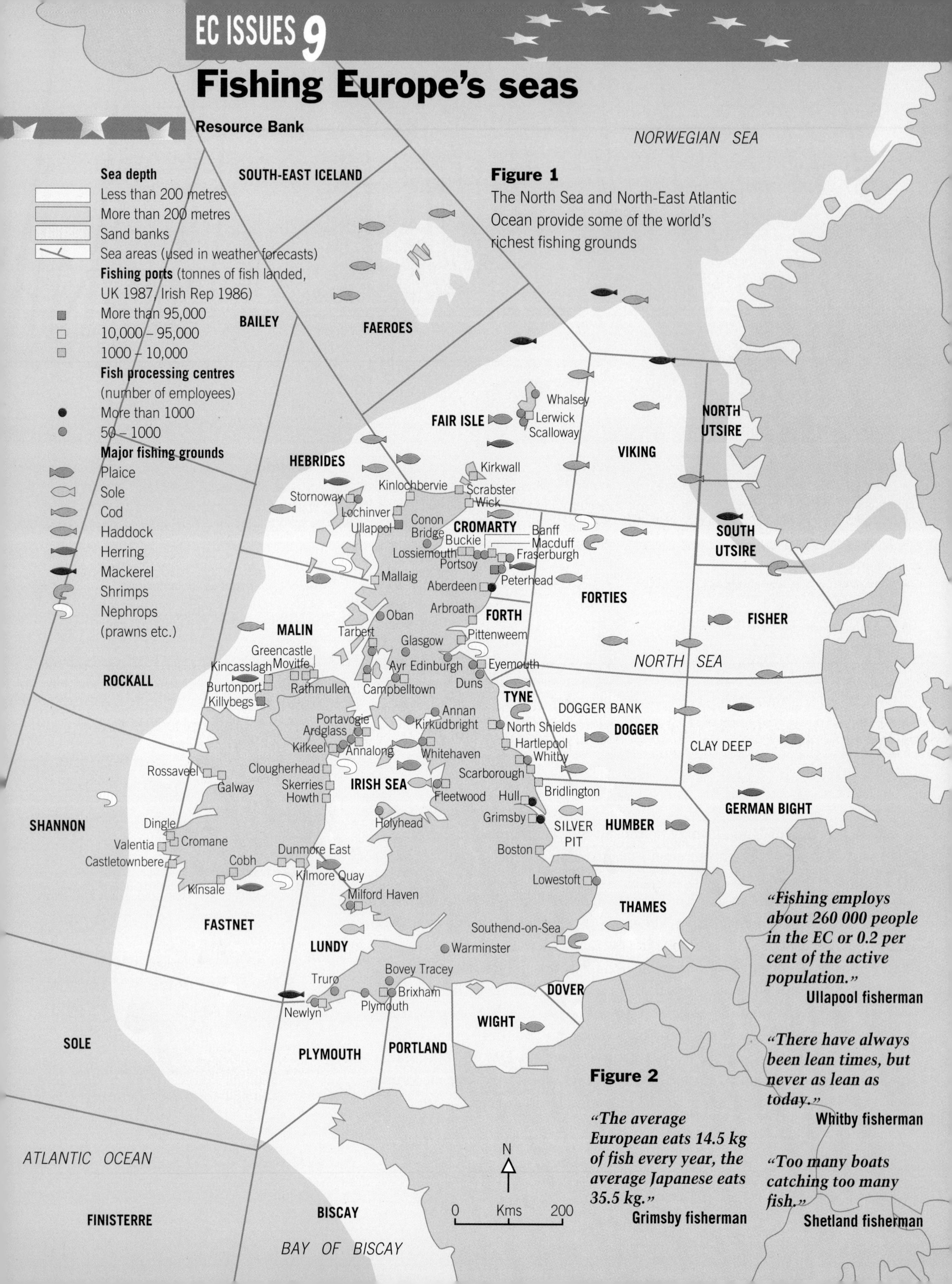

Figure 1

The North Sea and North-East Atlantic Ocean provide some of the world's richest fishing grounds

Sea depth
- Less than 200 metres
- More than 200 metres
- Sand banks
- Sea areas (used in weather forecasts)

Fishing ports (tonnes of fish landed, UK 1987, Irish Rep 1986)
- More than 95,000
- 10,000 – 95,000
- 1000 – 10,000

Fish processing centres (number of employees)
- More than 1000
- 50 – 1000

Major fishing grounds
- Plaice
- Sole
- Cod
- Haddock
- Herring
- Mackerel
- Shrimps
- Nephrops (prawns etc.)

Figure 2

"The average European eats 14.5 kg of fish every year, the average Japanese eats 35.5 kg."
Grimsby fisherman

"Fishing employs about 260 000 people in the EC or 0.2 per cent of the active population."
Ullapool fisherman

"There have always been lean times, but never as lean as today."
Whitby fisherman

"Too many boats catching too many fish."
Shetland fisherman

Figure 3
Fishing has never been an easy way to make a living, but modern boats and equipment has made it slightly less dangerous and much more efficient

- A new fishing boat can cost up to £750 000.
- A ship must make at least £7500 a week just to repay its loans.
- Satellite navigation available that can locate the ship to within a few metres.
- Echo-sounders can detect a single fish at 500 metres.
- Average crew size is 5.
- A typical fishing trip can last several days.

Figure 4 Who can fish where?
The waters up to 200 miles from the coast of the European Community, in theory at least, are open to all EC fishing boats. But there are exceptions. Waters within 12 miles of the coast are controlled by that country. Newer members of the EC, such as Spain, are restricted until 1996, when new quotas will have been negotiated.

Figure 5 The Common Fisheries Policy
The Common Fisheries Policy is cheap by EC standards. In 1989, it was allocated 280 million ECU from Community funds, or about 0.6 per cent of the total budget.
The policy concentrates on four main areas:

1. Accessibility, conservation, and management of fisheries resources. In turn, these are achieved by a system of quotas, limiting fishing in certain areas, and controlling the size of nets allowed.
2. Common organisation of markets and prices.
3. Providing EC subsidies to improve the productivity of the fishing industry.
4. Concluding fishing agreements with countries outside the Community and participating in international attempts to conserve fish stocks.

Figure 6 The species caught in the largest quantities

	Thousand tonnes per year
Sand eel (for industrial use)	900
Cod	450
Herring	400
Mackerel	350

Figure 7 Fish catch, 1990 (thousand tonnes)

Country	Total	NE Atlantic	Mediterranean
B	42	41	–
DK*	1971	1947	–
D	209	175	–
GR	128	–	105
E	1430	593	135
F	889	642	46
IRL	252	252	–
I	559	–	435
L	–	–	–
NL	398	379	–
P	346	239	–
UK	946	919	–
EC (EUR 12)	**7182**	**5191**	**723**
Turkey	627	–	583
Norway	1826	1823	–
Sweden	251	246	–
Finland	121	113	–
Soviet Union**	11332	781	347
World	**97985**	**10509**	**2012**

**The Danish fleet concentrates mainly on species for industrial use (fish meal and fish oil).*
***It is unclear how the break up of the Soviet Union will affect its fishing fleets.*

Figure 8 Fishing fleets, 1986

	Number of vessels	Tonnage*
B	172	20695
DK	3186	120593
D	672	58408
GR	3081	195405
E	14418	421401
F	13955	214301
IRL	-	-
I	26730	284631
NL	1059	150892
P	-	-
UK	-	-

**Gross registered tonnage*

Do European fisheries have a future?

Assignment

Background information

Controversy and dispute increasingly surround Europe's fishing industry. Against a background of naval vessels stopping and boarding fishing boats, fishermen blockading harbours, and endangered fish stocks, many fishermen claim they are struggling to survive.

Your assignment

- Investigate the conflicting views that are held about the future of the fishing industry in EC waters.
- Consider the effects that a decline in the industry would have on fishing communities throughout Europe.

The framework for doing this is set out in the Work Programme.

Figure 3

The British government's view

The government sees a crisis in fishing stocks and believes that drastic action must be taken now. If not there may not be a fishing fleet at all in a few years time. One-quarter of all the fish in the North Sea are caught each year. A fish is now twenty times less likely to reach adulthood than it was sixty years ago. Furthermore, birds and sea mammals suffer from food shortages due to overfishing. Government restrictions aimed at conserving stocks mean that each fishing boat has to be tied up in port for at least 130 days each year. Each boat is also given a quota of each type of fish that it can catch for that month. The government wants to cut the fishing fleet by 25 per cent, but will probably only be able to compensate about a fifth of the owners.

Figure 4

The EC's viewpoint

The Common Fisheries Policy may not be perfect, but it is the best that we have at the moment. The policy will mean that boats have to go to the scrapyard, but it could be an economic and environmental disaster if they do not. All the fishermen seem to look to somebody else to make the sacrifices. The EC relies upon individual governments to compensate fishermen who stop fishing. In Denmark, the fleet has been cut by 20 per cent since 1985 and nearly everyone has been fully compensated for their loss.

Figure 1

Policing the fishing grounds

Each EC country is charged with policing its own section of EC waters. Aeroplanes are used to monitor fishing boats. Patrol ships make random searches of fishing boats at sea. They check the size and type of catch against the log book, as well as measuring the size of the nets. Inspectors onshore note the fish that each boat lands. They also watch out for undersize fish in the markets. A box of undersized fish carries a heavy fine. Skippers caught landing fish over their quota can be fined up to £50 000. UK inspectors are the most rigorous in the EC. But it is a tough and expensive business, with one inspection at sea costing around £2000. In some other countries, skippers get word of an inspector's visit and quickly leave port before they can be checked.

Figure 2 French fishermen dump fish in Lille in February 1993 in a protest against low prices due to cheap imports

Figure 5

Fishing in the Shetland Islands

Twenty per cent of the people in the islands make a living from fishing either directly or indirectly. The way of life of the islanders depends on protecting and conserving the fish which remain. Skippers have invested very heavily in new boats, and many of the younger ones have huge mortgages to pay on them. They want a 'Shetlands Box' to limit the number of 'foreign' fishermen who can fish their waters. They want EC help that would be cheap for Brussels but would do a great deal for their communities.

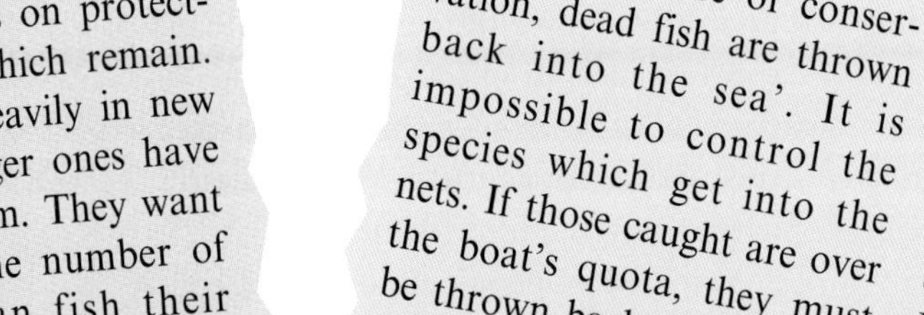

Figure 6

Fishing the East Coast of England

Fishermen are angry that 'in the cause of conservation, dead fish are thrown back into the sea'. It is impossible to control the species which get into the nets. If those caught are over the boat's quota, they must be thrown back. Many think that this is immoral and land them illegally - so called 'black fish'. East Coast fishermen have suffered greatly since the Cod Wars in the 1970s. In Grimsby alone, 53 000 jobs have been lost. Often, the compensation available was not fairly distributed, meaning that some skippers got nothing. They are angry with Spanish fishermen who have bought up British-registered boats, together with their quotas. In this way, 20 per cent of the UK quota is landed in Spain, making it even harder for British skippers to make a living.

Figure 7

Fishing from La Coruna in Spain

Spain's fleet is the largest in the EC, three times the tonnage of the British fleet. The bulk of it operates from La Coruna in Galacia. Fishermen there are facing a bleak future as catches are down by 50 per cent. They have to fish seven days a week to repay the loans on their boats. A favourite fishing ground is the 'Grand Sol' to the west of Ireland. The number of boats allowed there is limited to 300, but many more go there for the rich catches. Fifty boats were caught and fined by the Irish authorities in 1989.

Work Programme

- Work in groups of eight. You have been commissioned by a local broadcasting company. Your task is to produce a documentary about the future of the EC fishing industry. It can be for either radio or TV, the choice is yours. Use the information here and in the Resource Bank on pages 22-23 as well as your own knowledge, research, and ideas.
  Your documentary should consist of:
  - A scene-setting introduction.
  - Background information.
  - A series of interviews.
  - A concluding section.
- Study all the information that is available to you.
- Decide who will take the following roles:
  The documentary-makers
  - Presenter
  - Sound engineer / camera operator

  The interviewees
  - Mary Delany, UK government fisheries spokesperson
  - Manuel Gonzalez, EC Commissioner with responsibility for fisheries
  - Hamish MacDonald, a young Shetland fisherman
  - Luis Cardona, Spanish fisherman from La Coruna
  - Peter Brown, captain of UK fisheries inspection patrol
  - Sam Tate, a Whitby fisherman considering retirement
- As a group you must plan:
  - the key points that you wish to make in the documentary;
  - how the documentary will begin;
  - the questions to ask each interviewee;
  - how to end the documentary.
- Once your planning is complete, record your documentary.

Tourism - a growth industry

Tourism is one of the fastest growing industries in Europe today. It is a major source of revenue for most countries, although some countries spend more on tourism than they earn (Figure 5). It is also an important source of jobs and has been encouraged in areas which have little economic value beyond their natural environment. Travel, for leisure as well as business, has been part of the lives of many people throughout history. However, tourism, as we know it today, has more recent origins. The spa towns of Europe grew up in the eighteenth century, while the 'Grand Tour of Europe' became popular with the wealthier classes in the nineteenth century. Mass tourism dates from the mid-twentieth century. Most people now take an annual holiday as well as short-term visits to tourist centres.

The locations of some of the major tourist centres in Europe are shown in Figure 2. They can broadly be classed as coastal resorts, mountain resorts, historic and cultural centres, areas of outstanding natural beauty, and spa centres.

Figure 1
Some tourist destinations: Italian ski slopes; the Black Forest, Germany; a resort on Spain's Mediterranean coast; the Roman Baths at Bath, UK

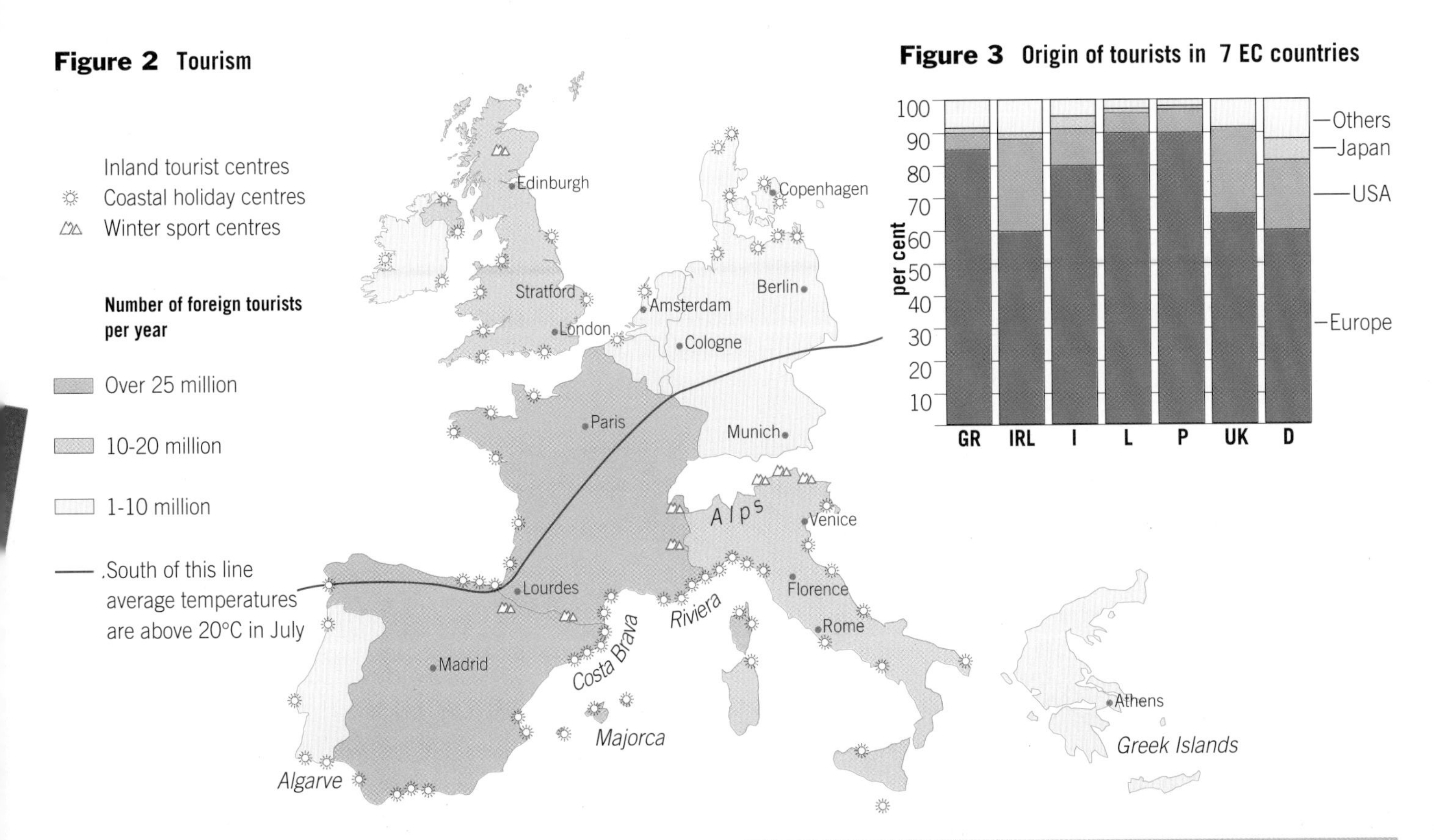

Figure 2 Tourism

Figure 3 Origin of tourists in 7 EC countries

Figure 4 Reasons for the growth of tourism

Greater mobility -the increase in car ownership has resulted in more freedom and the convenience of being able to go from door to door.
Greater accessibility - the improvements in road and rail quality has reduced travelling times and encouraged more people to travel.
Mass air travel - since the 1960s, charter flights and new airports at tourist centres have enabled large numbers of tourists to travel greater distances.
Package holidays - cheaper holidays are possible with block bookings and deals where travel, accommodation, and meals are all included in the price.
Greater education - more people have developed a desire to experience other cultures.
Advertising - people are now more aware of the holiday opportunities that are available to them.
Self-catering holidays - more of these facilities have enabled families, especially those with young children, to have holidays for less cost.
EC policies - the Community has provided financial encouragement for areas to develop their tourist potential.

Figure 5 Earnings from, and expenditure on, tourism

Country	Earnings from tourism *(million ECU)*	Expenditure on tourism *(million ECU)*
B	2585	3370
DK	1922	2478
D	6693	20455
GR	1906	439
E	12852	1693
F	10295	7368
IRL	724	1210
I	10539	3927
L	130	624
NL	2348	5577
P	1834	340
UK	8886	10339

Activities

1 Study the photos in Figure 1. How would you classify the different types of holidays that people could take in Europe?

2 a) Which are the two most-visited European countries?
b) Study Figure 3. What does it tell you about the origin of tourists staying in different countries? Give reasons for the observations that you have made.

3 Look at Figure 4. Which reasons do you think have been most important? Explain your answer.

4 a) Look closely at the data in Figure 5. Plot this data on a bar graph. Use black bars for tourism earnings and red bars for expenditure.
b) Decide and explain which country is the biggest net loser from tourism and which country is the biggest beneficiary.
c) Is there a division between northern and southern Europe with respect to the net benefit of tourism? If so, can you give an explanation?

The Alps - winter wonderland

Resource Bank

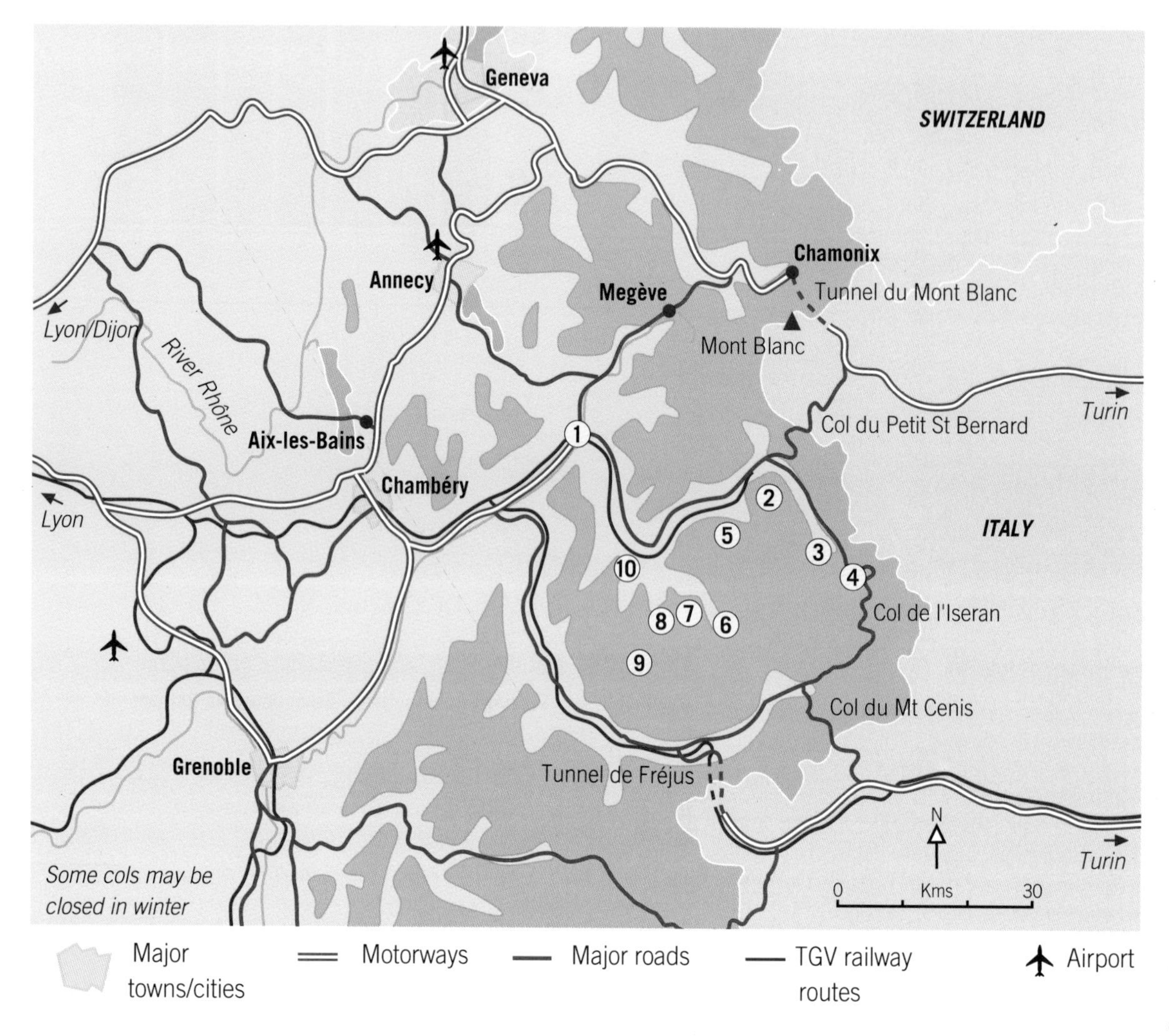

Figure 1 Olympic sites

1. **Albertville*** - skating
2. **Les Arcs** - speed skiing
3. **Tignes** - freestyle skiing
4. **Val d'Isère** - men's downhill skiing
5. **La Plagne** - bobsled and luge
6. **Pralognan la Vanoise** - curling
7. **Courchevel** - ski jumping
8. **Méribel** - ice hockey and women's skiing
9. **Les Menuires** - men's slalom skiing
10. **Les Saisies** - cross-country skiing and biathlon

* No one resort was large enough with enough facilities to host the Winter Olympics in 1992. Albertville was chosen as host town, but the events were held in 10 centres across 1500 km² of the Alps. Albertville usually has a population of 18000 – the new stadium built can seat 36000! The French government saw the Olympics as a vehicle for economic development in the province of Savoie.

Figure 2 Some information about the French tourist industry

Percentage of tourist beds occupied through the year in one French Alpine resort	
January	100% (full)
February	65%
March	57%
April	67%
May	65%
June	100% (full)
July	100% (full)
August	100% (full)
September	82%
October	63%
November	45%
December	100%(full)

Origin of tourists in one French Alpine resort	
France	42%
UK	15%
USA	11%
Germany	8%
Netherlands	5%
Switzerland	4%
Belgium	4%
Sweden	2%
Spain	2%
Others	7%

Figure 3 (opposite page) **Extract from a holiday brochure**

Val d'Isère

High Altitude Skiing

Guaranteed Snow

Ski Guide

Village height: 1,850m (6,105 ft)
Highest Lift: 3,656m (12,064 ft)
Approx. Transfer Times:
Geneva 4 hrs, Lyons 4 hrs, Ski Train (Bourg St Maurice) 45 mins, Chambery 2 1/4 hrs

Flights from Gatwick, Bristol, Birmingham, Glasgow, Heathrow, Luton, Manchester, Newcastle and the Snow Train.

Accom	La Daille		La Daille	
Code	10085		10085	
Price Includes	Studio 4 pers Self Catering		Apartments 5 pers Self Catering	
No. of Nights	7	14	7	14
Departures on				
Dec 19	249	355	256	375
Dec 26	289	339	296	359
Jan 2	169	219	176	239
Jan 9	179	235	186	255
Jan 16	195	269	199	289
Jan 23	225	289	232	309
Jan 30	249	345	256	365
Feb 6	295	425	299	445
Feb 13	335	469	342	489
Feb 20	324	455	331	475
Feb 27	305	395	312	415
Mar 6	289	375	296	395
Mar 13	275	359	282	379
Mar 20	265	345	272	365
Mar 27	255	364	262	384
Apr 3	269	364	276	384
Apr 10	255		262	
Supplements per person per night	3 pers occ £3.00 2 pers occ £9.00		4 pers occ £2.40 3 pers occ £6.00	

OLYMPIC NOTE

Val d'Isère was the proud host of the Men's Downhill event at the 1992 Winter Olympics. Visit an Olympic resort and ski the pistes of the Champions.

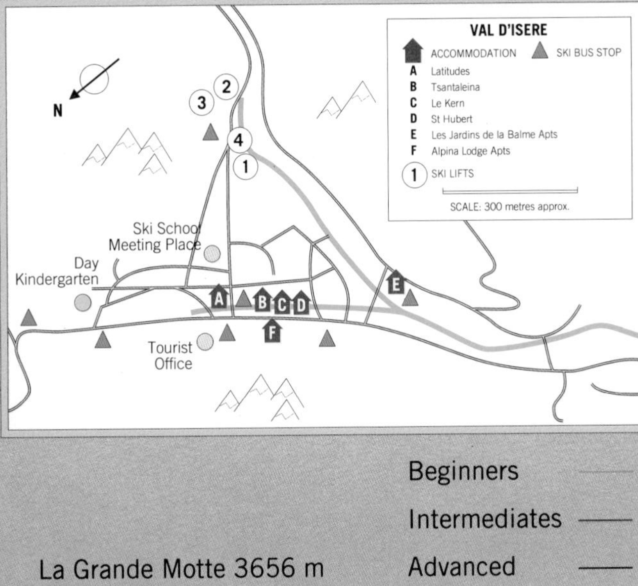

Total kms of Piste: 300kms

Piste Type	No. of Runs
Easy	32
Intermediate	91
Difficult	12

Direction of Slopes: N, S, E, W
Approx no. of snow cannon: 125
Longest Run: 10kms
No. of Mountain restaurants: 13
No. of cross country trails: 9
Total No. of Lifts: 101
No. of Ski School Instructors: 22 Snowfun (all English speaking)
Usual hours of instruction: 1030-1330, 1415-1645, Sun-Fri

Children's Ski School: French school holidays only with Snowfun. ESF all season, 5-12 years - 0900-1600, Sun-Fri, approx £30 for six half-days, lunchtime supervision available.

Kindergarten: Petit Poucet 3-8 years, 0900-1730 every day approx. £20 per day including lunch or £110 for the week, English spoken, lunchtime supervision available.

Babysitting: Available through tourist office or ask a chalet rep.

EATING OUT: Over 50 restaurants all categories * 3-course French meal around 130FF * Fondue for 135FF including wine * Pizza from 50FF. Recommended: Au Bout de la Rue for traditional French cuisine, La Perdrix Blanche for the best pizzas and the best value in town. The Alamo for great Mexican food.

APRES SKI: Lively right through to the early hours. Recommended: "Gingermen" for excellent cocktails. "E" Jays for their happy hour, Dicks T-Bar for the best laser show and videos, Bar d'Alsace - pub atmosphere, The Pub for a lively atmosphere with live bands and karaoke.

ACTIVITIES: * Cinema with regular films in English * Skidoo riding * Indoor swimming-pool free with 7-15 day lift pass * Fitness centre with English tuition * Parapente * Children's ice-skating rink.

OTHER RESORT AMENITIES: * Weekly open-air market * Supermarkets * Wide range of boutiques * Art exhibitions

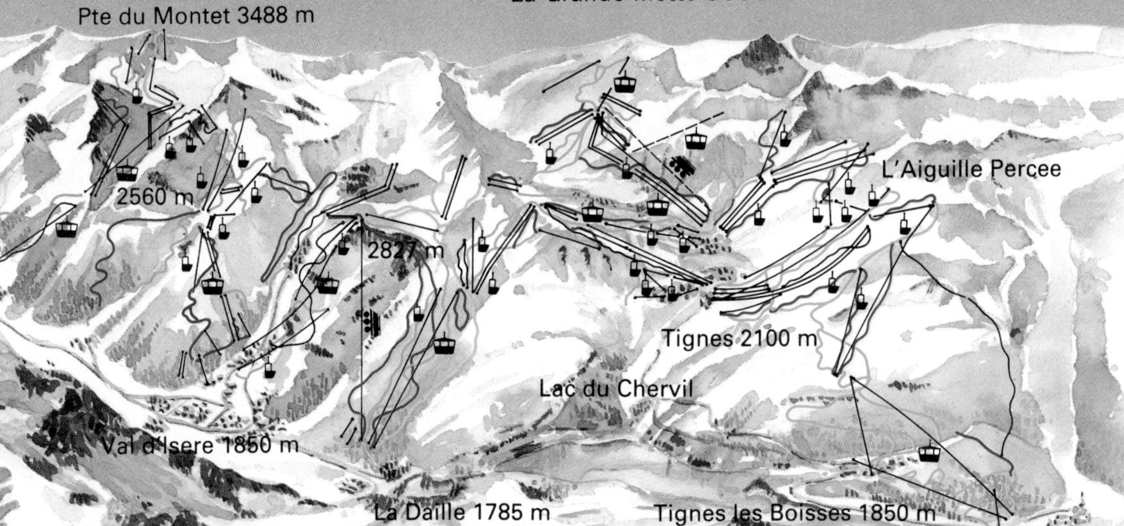

Skiing damages the environment

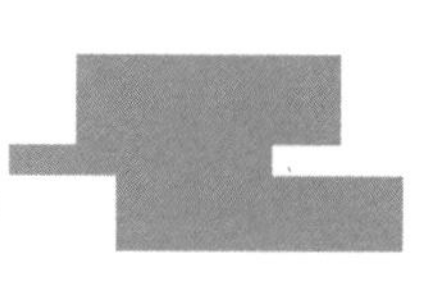

Figure 2 Avalanche damage. The risk of flooding in the Alps has also increased due to tourist developments. Large-scale deforestation and soil compaction in an already vulnerable mountain environment have resulted in erosion and rapid runoff into the valleys, causing flash floods

Figure 1
During the summer months, ski-runs look very different. Once the snow has melted, the effects on the environment are obvious: bare and barren slopes, isolated concrete structures, and redundant chair lifts

French mud disast[…] 'could have been prevented'

Twenty-four people are missing or de[…] twelve more are wounded, after a m[…] buried a campsite last week in the French[…] Another victim of the catastrophe was the remna[…] France's former Ministry of Environmenta[…] Technological Risk. The director of the Delegati[…] Major Risks resigned, saying that the disaster should have been prevented.

The meteorological office in Chamonix, in the French Alps south of Geneva, recorded 3.5 times as much rain in June than usual. On the night of 14 July, a violent thunderstorm battered soils that were already saturated. A violent mudslide tore down the valley of the Borne. It formed waves a metre high before it hit the crowded riverside campground at Grand-Bornand.

The French Prime Minister, Jacques Chirac, last week announced compensation for the victims. He called the disaster 'unforeseen'. Renaud Vie le Sage, director of the Delegation on Major Risks, promptly resigned. He described Chirac's statement as 'an insult to the dead'.

In July 1936, he says, a similar mudslide buried exactly the same location. The dangers at Grand-Bornand may have been raised by excavations on nearby mountain slopes to accommodate tourist facilities. This could have loosened soils. No one should have been allowed to set up a campsite on the river. However, there is strong pressure not to limit development in the depressed mountain regions of France.

Last week's disaster will cost £500 000 in compensation.

Figure 3 Newspaper extracts

Ski deaths as avalanches sweep Alps

Avalanches killed at least 21 people over the weekend as heavy blizzards continued in many of Europe's most popular ski resorts.

The most dramatic accident, where two giant avalanches 400 yards wide claimed 10 lives, occurred shortly before 7am yesterday morning. The final death toll may well be higher. On Saturday three people were killed in further avalanches. Poor communications hampered the search for further victims and survivors. By yesterday afternoon over 200 volunteers had joined the rescue operation, which was encountering great difficulties.

Large areas remained on an alarm footing as meteorologists claimed that further avalanches could not be ruled out. People have been warned not to make any journeys.

In the Italian Alps. avalanches killed at least six over the weekend - two Germans and an Italian skier died yesterday, and two Swiss and one German on Saturday.

In Germany, the heaviest snowfalls in the Black Forest for six years at the weekend brought chaos to the country's most popular skiing region.

A 40-year-old man was trapped by an avalanche and killed while cross-country skiing, while in the Bavarian Alps a two-year-old boy was killed by a huge block of snow sliding down from the roof of a barn.

Figure 4 **Some effects of the growth in winter sports holidays**

- Hotels, shops, restaurants intrude on the landscape
- Destruction of traditional way of life
- Hotels run by outsiders, employing non-locals, especially in managerial jobs
- Much employment is seasonal
- Most food and other necessities must be imported
- Services such as sewerage and water must be provided in a difficult physical environment
- Recreational activities result in increased erosion
- Less water held in soil and vegetation, leading to increased risk of flooding
- Deforestation exposes the soil
- Snow-moving vehicles compact soil; snow melt runs off quickly as a result
- Vehicles and skis damage fragile Alpine flora, reducing the rate of growth during the summer
- Runoff increased by impermeable surfaces like roads and car parks; one result is a reduced lag time between snow melt and water reaching river channels
- Increased risk of rock falls from exposed slopes
- Loss of wildlife habitats
- Risk of avalanches increased
- New building work for hotels and roads affected by landslides

Activities

1 Look at the information on these pages.

a) Make a list of the ways in which the Alpine environment is being damaged.

b) For each way, link the damage done to possible causes.

2 Design a poster to be displayed in ski resorts to encourage skiers to be more aware of the ways in which they can limit damage to the environment.

3 Prepare a report outlining the methods that a ski resort could employ to reduce the risk of flooding and avalanches.

Changing Alpine communities

Figure 1
The traditional economy of the Alpine valleys. Alpine scenes may look like something from the lid of a chocolate box, but in reality they are living and working landscapes

1 The alpage pastures where cattle, sheep, and goats are grazed during the long days of summer. The grass is thin so care must be taken not to overgraze. Huts are built to house the shepherds, who stay with the animals all summer. Other huts are used to milk the cattle and turn it into cheese which will keep throughout the winter.

2 The north-facing slopes or l'ubac are frequently forested and not used for agriculture. This is because even in summer they do not receive much sunshine. In spring the snow lies much longer and it returns earlier in the autumn than on the more favoured south-facing slopes.

3 Some patches of forest may be found on the south-facing slopes if the gradient is too steep for agriculture.

4 Some small communities may be found on the bench or mayen on the side of the valley. These are usually on the south-facing or l'adret slopes. The pastures here will be grazed in spring and autumn each year as the animals are taken to and from the alpage. Large areas of the pastures will be used to grow hay as winter fodder.

5 Most people live in villages on the valley floor. Barns provide winter accommodation for the livestock, often forming the ground floor of houses, with the people living upstairs. The land is flat and can be cultivated. Even today, this is sometimes still done using hand tools by the women of the family.

The traditional economy of the Alpine valleys has changed little for hundreds of years. It is based around a system of agriculture called transhumance involving seasonal migrations of mainly cattle, but with some sheep and goats, to the available pastures. Irrigation of the cultivated fields of the valley floor has been practised for hundreds of years. Water is brought down from the high streams by earth ditches, wooden sluices, and more recently concrete pipes. This system is very much in harmony with the environment, adapting throughout the year to the prevailing climatic conditions, as shown in Figures 1 and 3. It is a relatively hard way of life, susceptible to the unpredictability of the weather. Traditional Alpine communities tend to be close-knit and self-contained. Modern technology was slow to arrive in these valleys. Even mechanical cultivators did not begin work here until the 1960s. However, by this time these communities had begun to experience problems. Most of these arose from the migration of young people away to the towns and cities of the lowlands. They were attracted by the chance of paid employment with regular hours and a higher standard of living.

Figure 2 Questions and answers

Q What started the changes in Alpine valleys?

A A new kind of 'transhumance'. It was the summer and winter migration of people from the crowded cities of lowland Europe to the peace, fresh air, and recreational activities that are only available in the high Alps.

Q But how did they get into the remote valleys?

A Many of the valleys had new roads built into them when large HEP schemes were built in the 1960s and 1970s. Others had roads built simply to open them up for tourism.

Q How many tourists?

A Most valley communities experienced at least a four-fold increase in the number of tourists between 1970 and 1985.

Q What did this mean for the villages?

A The construction industry boomed! Hotels, apartment blocks, and chalets began to spring up. New facilities such as swimming pools, tennis courts, and ski-lifts were built. Many settlements on the mayen became permanent, and new ones were established on alpage pastures as ski stations (like Arc 2000).

Q How was all this paid for?

A In Rhône-Alpes, grants from the government and investments from outside the region covered 42 per cent of the expenditure, local funds 38 per cent, and commercial loans 20 per cent.

Q What jobs were created?

A In the district around La Plagne in 1984, 28 per cent of jobs were in construction, 22 per cent tourism, 18 per cent services, 16 per cent industry, 12 per cent commerce, and just 4 per cent in agriculture.

Q What other effects were there on agriculture?

A Surprisingly, it started to do better. It was greatly modernised. More animals were kept and land was brought back into production.

Figure 3 The Alpine farming year

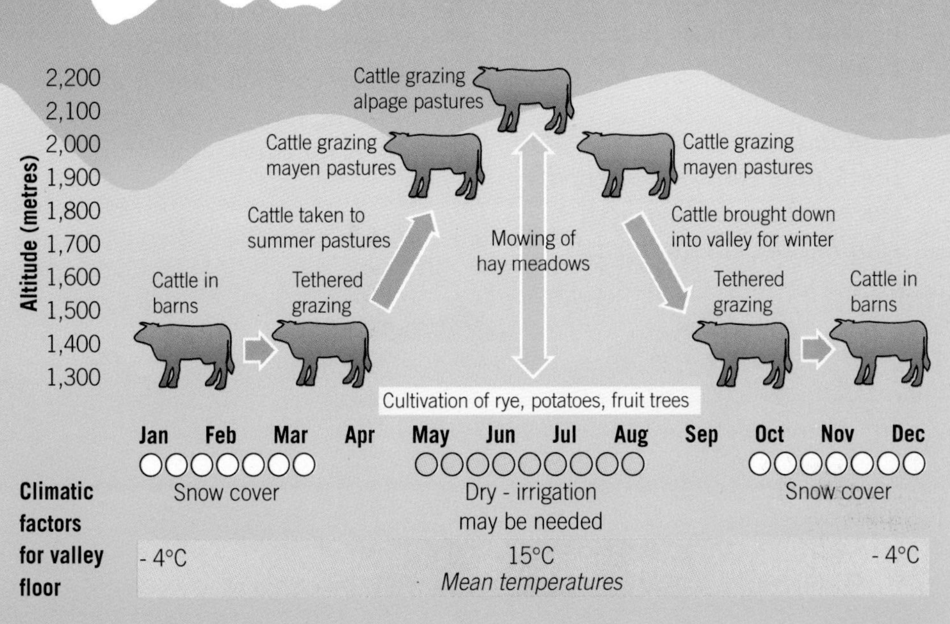

Activities

1 a) Write a definition of the term 'transhumance'.
b) In the old days, when transhumance was widely practised, how would a farmer spend a typical day in summer and in winter?

2 Make a sketch copy of Figure 1. Mark on and label the changes that have occurred due to tourism.

3 How might old-style farmers, now retired, feel about all the changes they have seen in their lifetimes? Write some quotes to illustrate your ideas.

4 Use the information from all the pages about the Alps to complete a table to show all the environmental, social, and economic problems facing the region.

Managing the Alpine future

Alpine resorts attract people in summer as well as winter. During the summer months, people come for walking, climbing, and sports such as golf and tennis, as well as for sailing and cruising on the beautiful lakes. Problems occur during the peak seasons. The sheer numbers of people and cars cause congestion and pollution. The amenities are overused and the crime rate rises. There are also problems out of the main summer and winter peak seasons. Trade falls away and the income of the local people falls with it. Many amenities actually close with the loss of facilities for the local people and a rise in the unemployment rate. The resort takes on a closed feel which is unattractive for those tourists who are present.

Resorts can minimise their closed seasons by offering 'minibreaks' and 'out of season deals'. These might take the form of reduced rates for OAPs or free accommodation for children. Special festivals and sporting events help to attract visitors in spring and autumn.

In places, the expansion of tourism has irrevocably changed the Alpine environment. The more successful development schemes have featured the following:

1 Developments planned with the participation of the local people, to minimise their impact on the traditional values of the valley.
2 Majority of developments non-speculative in nature.
3 Land use plans devised to retain the existing character of villages. Zones for the construction of chalets, hotels, and apartments set out, as well as zones where existing buildings, some over 200 years old, protected.
4 Infrastructure such as roads, parking, sewers, and water supply installed before building allowed.
5 Vehicle-free zones established in older sectors of villages.
6 All building work harmonised with existing architectural styles so not to detract from the Alpine environment.
7 Many roads in valley widened to two lanes.
8 Villages connected by ski-lifts to expand network of ski trails.

Figure 1
A number of problems continue to challenge even the best-managed Alpine communities

How can agricultural activity be maintained so that traditional values will be preserved?

How will the land be protected against fire, erosion, and avalanches?

Will the beauty of the Alpine environment be preserved for both the inhabitants and the tourists?

What can be done to help villages without skiing potential that have not benefited from the tourist boom?

Can industry be attracted into the Alpine valleys to diversify the economy, but without spoiling the environment?

Is it possible to maintain the flow of tourists to the region without spoiling its unique character?

Are there too many jobs in the construction industry, an industry which cannot go on building new apartments and hotels for ever?

Figure 2 Tourism comes to Val Caporoni

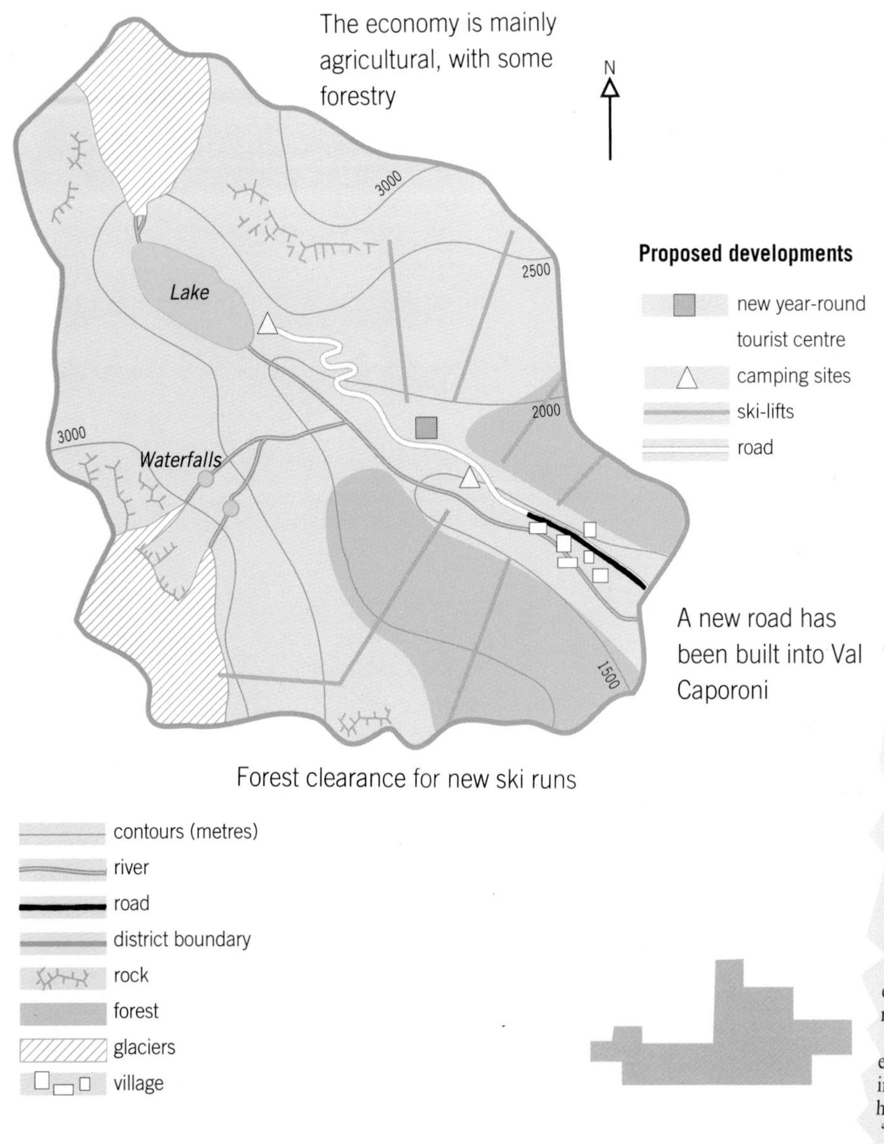

Figure 3 Newspaper extract

Alps ailing, says prince

Prince Sadruddin Aga Khan, one of the richest men in the world, is fed up with pollution, developers and thousands of tourists destroying his skiing holidays in the countryside near his home.

But unlike many who just shrug and lament the despoliation of their countryside, he has decided to do something about it. He has persuaded European governments that what is happening on his doorstep could have serious consequences for us all.

Last February the prince, uncle of the present Aga Khan, who is spiritual leader of the world's 15m Ismaili Muslims, assembled a panel of 21 experts to discuss environmental problems in the Alps after seeing the effects near his chateau on the shores of Lake Geneva.

The panel, funded by the prince's private think-tank, the Bellerive Foundation, has produced a report showing that Europe's climate and river systems could soon be drastically changed by pollution and over-development of the mountainous playground favoured by thousands of British holiday-makers.

The prince, who has spent many years working to help the Third World, believes the situation is so serious in Europe that immediate action is needed. He is calling for the creation of an international agency to manage and conserve the Alps in the same way that the International Whaling Commission and the International Tropical Timber Organisation have been set up to conserve whales and tropical rain forests.

Leaders of the seven nations that govern the Alps, including President Francois Mitterrand of France, have given a cautious welcome to the proposal, which would involve severe restrictions on further expansion of tourism and funding for conservation programmes.

Prince Sadruddin is heartened by their response, but still concerned about the future of his home if they decide to do nothing.

"I think the consensus among all the experts is that, whatever the cause of the problems in the Alps, the people developing the area are killing the goose that lays the golden egg," he said.

"This is the most threatened mountain system in the world and I see this as a test case, a test of whether man can save his environment."

Activities

1 Study the map of the proposed developments in Val Caporoni. Make a list of all the infrastructure that would be required to be built for the development.

2 If you were the Mayor of Val Caporoni, what would you have to think about when planning how to manage the proposed tourist developments? Write a report giving some suggestions for a management strategy.

3 Read the newspaper article in Figure 3. Suggest reasons why a Europe-wide strategy for managing the Alps is urgently required.

4 a) Work in groups of four. Choose three of the challenges given in Figure 1 and discuss what issues are involved.
b) Decide what Alpine communities could do to meet these challenges.
c) Present your ideas to the rest of the class.

5 *Essay:*
Discuss whether you think that further tourist development should be allowed in the Alps.

The traditional British seaside resort

Figure 1 British seaside resorts and holiday areas

Figure 2 Scarborough's tourist industry

Spending in seaside resorts like Scarborough as a percentage of total tourist spending	
1973	45%
1980	41%
1986	34%
1989	33%

Visitors to Scarborough	% from different parts of Britain
Yorkshire/Humberside	18.6%
North-West	16.5%
North	13.4%
East Midlands	12.5%
Scotland	10.9%
South-East	9.9%
West Midlands	9.8%
South-West	3.3%
East Anglia	2.9%
London	1.8%

Scarborough's income from tourism in 1989	(£000s)
Hotels and accommodation	43484
Food and drink	25016
Leisure and recreation	4404
Shopping	25344
Transport	3139
Indirect	33860
TOTAL	135247

Jobs generated by tourism in Scarborough in 1989	
Hotels and accommodation	3393
Food and drink	1927
Leisure and recreation	410
Shopping	786
Transport	97
Indirect	1958
TOTAL	8571

One of the most popular types of holiday in Britain is the sun, sea, and sand holiday taken at one of the country's seaside resorts. These coastal towns have high average daily sunshine figures in summer and are easily accessible by road and rail from most parts of Britain. A survey by the English Tourist Board in 1989 revealed that about a quarter of holidays were taken to seaside resorts. These trips accounted for nearly a third of all domestic tourist expenditure (16 per cent of all expenditure if foreign holidays are included).

Each resort has its own unique features, but they have many attractions in common and have similar land use patterns. The natural attractions often include a sandy beach, attractive coastal scenery and, of course, lots of bracing sea air! In these resorts whole areas have been developed for recreation for visitors. These include hotels, guest houses, cafes, amusements, piers, funfairs, and theatres. The 1989 survey found that 26 million trips were made to the seaside resorts, of which 21.3 million were for holidays of over five days.

The British seaside resorts experienced a decline in their share of the

Figure 3 Scarborough

tourist market from the 1970s until 1988. This was largely due to the increased availability of cheap foreign package holidays. However, crowded European skies are expected to cause a return to more traditional types of holiday.

The resorts share two main problems: the unpredictable British weather and the seasonal pattern of holidays. To overcome the second problem, some of the larger resorts have developed conference facilities to encourage business throughout the year, but especially in the winter.

Scarborough is Yorkshire's most popular seaside resort and has been attracting visitors for nearly 400 years. It is often described as a typical British seaside resort and is also one of England's oldest spa towns.

The town itself stands above two large, sandy bays which are separated by a headland, on which stands a Norman castle. The majority of tourists in Scarborough are either families with young children or older people, perhaps retired. They have been attracted by the many facilities that the town has to offer. These include a miniature railway, a sealife centre, and Water Splash World as well as many of the more customary seaside attractions. The town's position makes it possible to combine a seaside holiday with visits to places of interest inland, such as the North Yorks Moors, historic York, and stately homes like Castle Howard. Scarborough has also become a major conference centre, hosting over 250 major conferences every year. The Police Federation, trade unions, and political parties have all held annual conferences in the town.

Scarborough is aiming to expand its tourist industry by improving road and rail links, developing non-weather-dependent activities of all types, and extending the programme of events into May and September.

Activities

1 a) Make a copy of Figure 1.
b) Using an atlas, label the 15 most popular resorts in their correct locations on the map.

2 Using the photo, describe the features that could attract tourists to Scarborough.

3 a) Draw a bar graph to show the number of jobs created by tourism in Scarborough.
b) Think of some examples of jobs to fit each category.

4 Are seaside resorts like Scarborough more or less popular than twenty years ago? Give reasons for your answer.

5 Using an atlas and data from Figure 2, draw a map showing where Scarborough's tourists come from. It is up to you to decide exactly how best to map the information.

Fieldwork in Scarborough

Assignment

Background information

Julie and her class from Headland School went on a geography fieldtrip to Scarborough. Their geography teacher gave them the fieldwork sheet shown in Figure 1. Some of Julie's results are given in Figure 3.

Your assignment

Your assignment is to analyse and present the findings and then draw some conclusions about tourism in Scarborough. Work with a partner.

Work Programme A

- Draw a diagram to illustrate the way buildings are used along Foreshore Road (see result sheet A).
- What percentage of the buildings have uses directly linked to tourism?
- Do your results tend to prove or disprove hypothesis (a) in Figure 1?

Work Programme B

- Use the data in result sheet B, and your atlas, to map where this sample of tourists came from.
- Do your results tend to prove or disprove hypothesis (b) in Figure 1?

Work Programme C

- Use attractive ways of presenting the data in result sheet C.
- Do your results tend to prove or disprove hypothesis (c) in Figure 1?

Headland School

Geography Department

Tourism Fieldwork in Scarborough

<u>Aims</u>
1. To investigate some of the land use patterns produced by tourism in Scarborough.
2. To discover the origin of tourists in Scarborough.
3. To get the views of tourists on how the town could be improved.

<u>Hypotheses</u>
In order to achieve these aims, you should try to test whether these statements or hypotheses are true or false.
a) There is no obvious pattern in the tourist functions of Scarborough.
b) The further a region is from Scarborough the lower the number of tourists who travel to the town for their holidays.
c) Most tourists believe that no improvements could be made to the town from a tourist's viewpoint.

<u>Methods</u>
a) You will each be given a part of the town in which to record the tourist functions. Use the following key to help you:

H	Hotel
G	Guest House
A	Amusements
C	Cafe
IC	Ice cream
S	Sweets
GS	Gift shop
T	Take-away

You may find it easiest to record your findings on a simple map.
b) The tax discs of cars are stamped by the post office where they were issued. This gives a good indication of where their owners have come from. You will each be given a road in Scarborough in which to record the origin of 50 cars.
c) Carry out the following questionnaire survey on 20 people chosen at random (hint: think about anything you have learned about sampling). Record your findings in the form of a table.

'Excuse me. I'm doing a survey for a geography project at school. Would you mind answering a few, simple questions?'

1. Would you agree that this area is.....?

	YES	NO
Attractive		
Clean		
Interesting		
Value for money		

2. If you have used any of the following, did you find them of a good or a poor standard?

	GOOD	POOR
South Beach		
Toilets		
Amusements		
Boat trips		
Parking		

3. Which three of the following should the Council consider and in which order?

Better:..	1st	2nd	3rd
Gardens			
Parking			
Disabled access			
Pedestrian safety			
Access to town centre			
Amenities			

'Thank you very much for your help!'

<u>Results</u>
Use maps, graphs, and diagrams to show the results of your fieldwork. Make sure that each one is clearly labelled to explain what it shows.

<u>Conclusions</u>
i) Decide whether each hypothesis is true or false.
ii) Use evidence from your fieldwork findings to back up your decision.
iii) Give some suggestions as to how the fieldwork could have been improved.

Figure 1
Fieldwork sheet

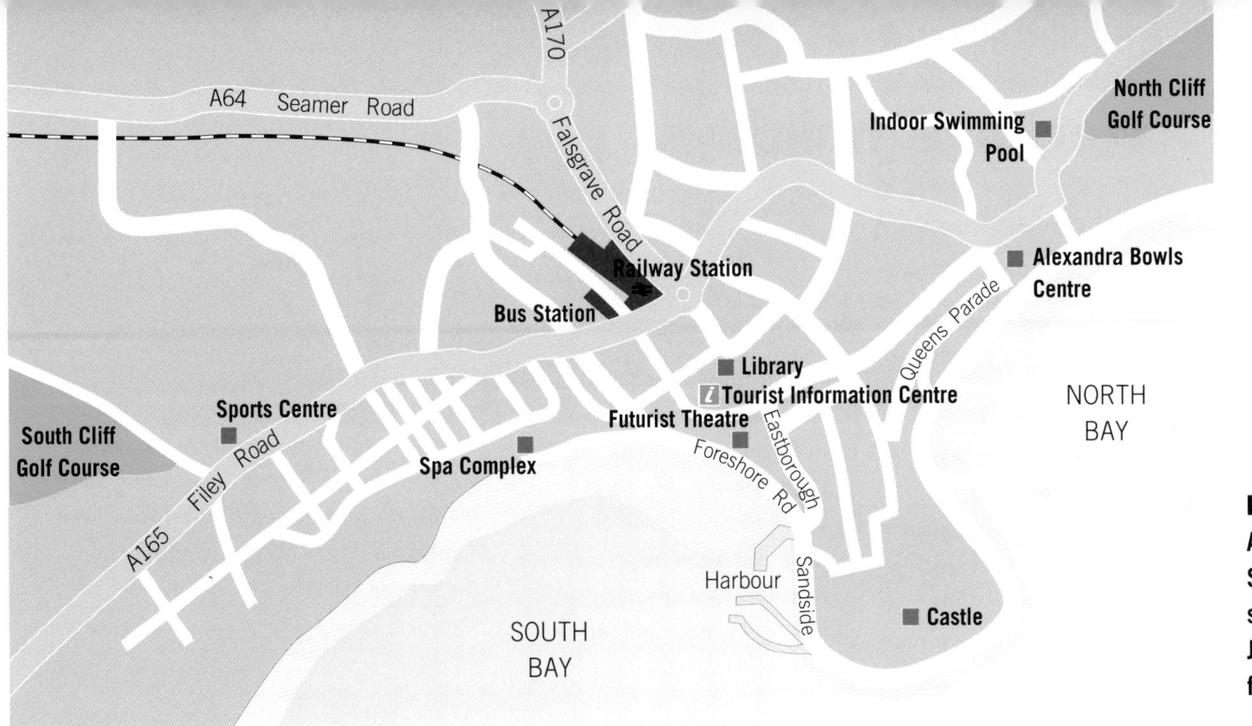

Figure 2 A street map of Scarborough showing where Julie did her fieldwork

Figure 3 Julie's result sheets

A

Survey of tourist functions,
Foreshore Road, Scarborough

arbour End ... East Sandgate Road

ub C
S
C + IC
GS + IC
A

Eastborough Road

C	T	GS
A	C	A
Pub	IC	A
IC	A	5 vacant retail units
A	C + IC	Hologram Shop
GS	S	A
Rock Shop	T	T
GS	Flight Simulator (A?)	

Bland's Cliff

Fish + Chips	GS	Bowling Alley
Pub	IC	A
Fortune Teller	A	
A	Cliff gardens	
Theatre		

Cliff railway to town

B

Car tax disc survey, Queens Parade, 10.00 a.m. 11 July

Region	Number
London and South-East	
South-West	
East Anglia	1
North	4
Yorks/Humberside	18
Wales	
Scotland	3
North-West	6
East Midlands	6
West Midlands	3

Not sure about......
Luton
Bourne
Morpeth
Wrexham
Consett
Shanklin
Milton Keynes

C

Results of questionnaire survey carried out on Foreshore Road

(number of responses to each answer)

1

	YES	NO
Attractive	6	14
Clean	9	11
Interesting	15	5
Value for money	16	4

2

	GOOD	POOR
South Beach	17	3
Toilets	10	10
Amusements	19	1
Boat trips	11	9
Parking	2	18

3

	1st	2nd	3rd
Gardens	1		1
Parking	13	15	9
Disabled access			2
Pedestrian safety		1	2
Access to town centre	6	4	6
Amenities			

Heritage holidays

Figure 1 Some of Europe's heritage sites that have become tourist attractions

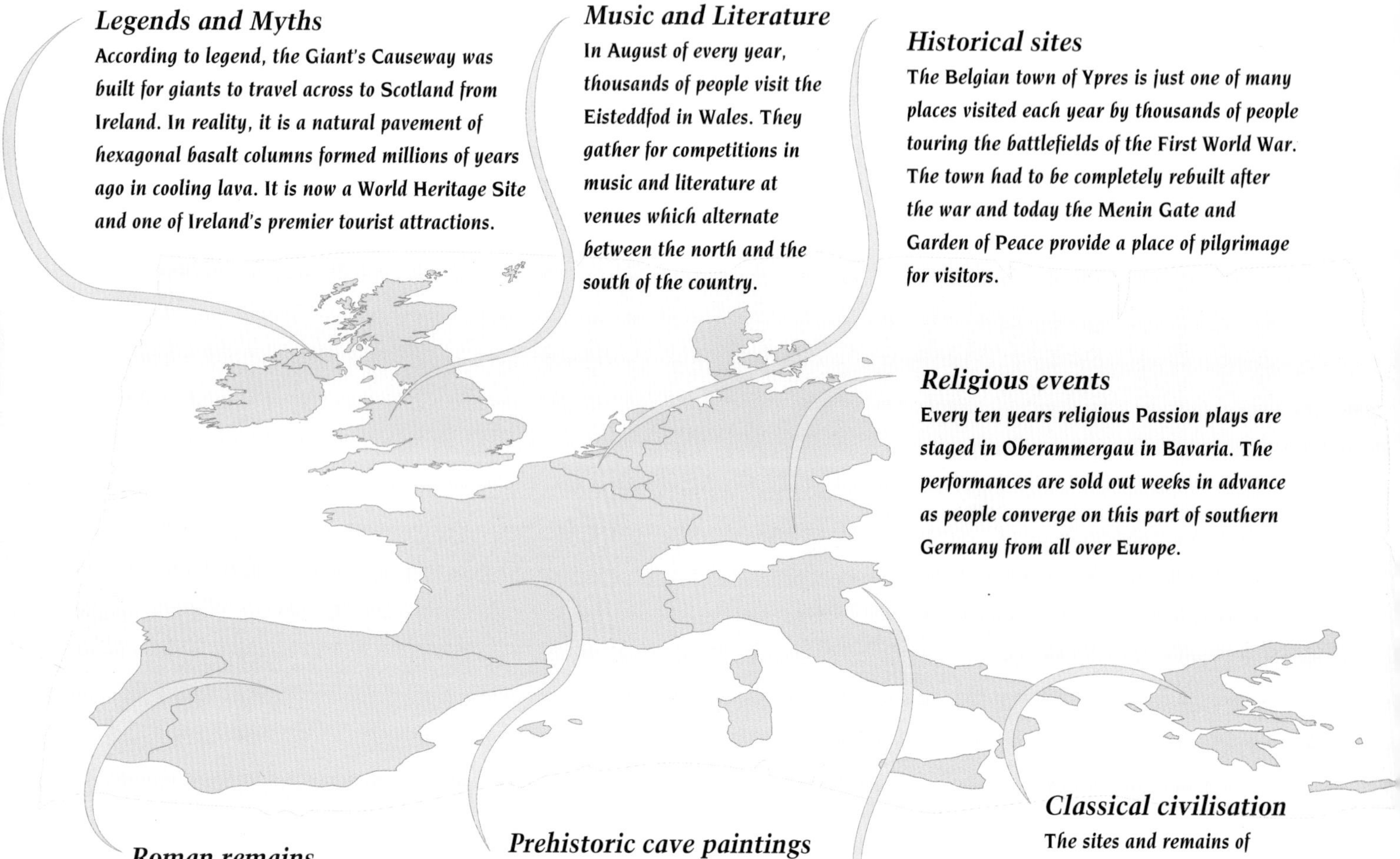

Legends and Myths
According to legend, the Giant's Causeway was built for giants to travel across to Scotland from Ireland. In reality, it is a natural pavement of hexagonal basalt columns formed millions of years ago in cooling lava. It is now a World Heritage Site and one of Ireland's premier tourist attractions.

Music and Literature
In August of every year, thousands of people visit the Eisteddfod in Wales. They gather for competitions in music and literature at venues which alternate between the north and the south of the country.

Historical sites
The Belgian town of Ypres is just one of many places visited each year by thousands of people touring the battlefields of the First World War. The town had to be completely rebuilt after the war and today the Menin Gate and Garden of Peace provide a place of pilgrimage for visitors.

Religious events
Every ten years religious Passion plays are staged in Oberammergau in Bavaria. The performances are sold out weeks in advance as people converge on this part of southern Germany from all over Europe.

Classical civilisation
The sites and remains of Ancient Greece.

Roman remains
Today it is the capital of Extremadura, but 1800 years ago Merida was one of the most important towns in Roman Spain. Its present-day Roman attractions include one of the best preserved classical theatres in the world, an amphitheatre, and two aqueducts.

Prehistoric cave paintings
Lascaux is a small cave in the Dordogne region of France. It is renowned for its paintings and engravings of animals thought to be 17 000 years old. It was opened to the public in 1948, but had to be closed again in 1963 as humidity changes threatened the paintings. A replica cave was opened nearby to tourists in 1984.

Architecture and Art
Florence in Italy is a World Heritage Site famed for its many religious buildings, palaces, and other wonders such as the Ponte Vecchio. People visit the city to marvel at its Renaissance art, by such masters as Leonardo da Vinci and Michelangelo.

Many people like to have the chance to learn about and experience the history, music, and other aspects of various cultures. The places that people visit vary greatly in size, from a small standing stone that might have five visitors a month, to whole cities such as Venice that cater for the needs of thousands of tourists every week. There are different kinds of heritage site, as shown in Figure 1. Heritage holidays tend to attract people on day trips and touring holidays. They also have a more even distribution throughout the year.

Figure 2
Extract from a holiday brochure

LIVE ANCIENT GREECE!

ke a luxury short break around the ajor sites guided by an expert in lassical Greek studies.

DAY 1: ATHENS

Visit the Acropolis, dating from the 5th century BC. Rising high above the city on a fortified outcrop, the site once contained the National Treasury and many other buildings and shrines. Afternoon free to explore this fascinating city. Cruise overnight along the coast and through the Corinth Canal.

DAY 2:
(A.M.) CORINTH

This town originated as a city state that was often at war with Athens. There are extensive remains to be seen, including the world-famous Temple of Apollo

(P.M.) MYCENAE

Explore this fortified town associated in Greek tradition with Agamemnon, the conqueror of the city of Troy. Cruise overnight across the Gulf of Corinth.

DAY 3: DELPHI

Tour the ancient sanctuary of Apollo and visit the seat of his Oracle. The remains lie on the slopes of Mount Parnassos and were excavated in the 19th century.

Figure 3 **The impact of tourism on heritage sites**

- Footpaths and steps are worn away by overuse.
- Air pollution can discolour and damage stonework and statues.
- Traffic vibration damages historic buildings.
- Tourist facilities such as car parks and souvenir shops, together with litter, can spoil the visual appeal of heritage sites.

World Heritage Site A site (natural or cultural) recognised by the international community, through *UNESCO*, as possessing universal value and therefore requiring collective responsibility. In 1989, there were 119 countries party to the scheme and 317 sites on the list.

Figure 5

Figure 4 **Heritage sites in Britain**

A number of organisations, including the National Trust and English Heritage, work towards the conservation and preservation of all types of heritage sites in Britain. Management of such sites is not easy. It must try to take into account the needs of nature conservation, archaeology, agriculture and forestry, public access, leisure and recreation, and change, both natural and human.

Activities

1 a) Write your own definition of a 'heritage site'.
b) Working with a partner, think of some examples of what you would consider heritage sites - make separate lists for the UK, the rest of Europe, and the rest of the world.

2 a) Use an atlas to help you draw a map of Greece. Mark on your map the route taken by the holiday in Figure 2.
b) Label the attractions of each site visited.
c) Find out more about Ancient Greece, so that you can add a fourth day to the tour.

3 a) Why do many heritage sites now need special protection?
b) What are the arguments for and against preserving heritage sites?

4 *Research idea*:
Find out as much as you can about the National Trust or English Heritage.

Venice - a World Heritage Site

Most people have heard of Venice, if only in relation to gondolas! But Venice is much more than a city 'afloat'. Its many historical, architectural, and cultural attractions make it one of the world's famous tourist cities, now designated a World Heritage Site. Venice consists of 118 islands, crossed by many canals, like the Grand Canal. These canals are the main traffic arteries. The buildings have been built on a limestone foundation which rest on piles driven into the lagoon bed. The islands are linked by numerous bridges and to the mainland by a road and rail causeway. This century an industrial complex at Porto Marghera and a commercial centre at Mestre have been developed on the mainland. This has contributed to the depopulation of the lagoon, with Venice's population falling from over 180 000 in 1950 to just over 80 000 in 1991. Venice has long been a popular tourist centre. Its festivals (such as the Venetian Festival held in February/March, the Gondola Race, and the Festival of Modern Art held in September), palaces, and exhibitions became part of the 'Grand Tour of Europe' in the nineteenth century. The museums, galleries, and the famous piazzas still attract thousands of tourists every year.

Figure 1
The Grand Canal

Figure 2 **The plight of Venice**

Very few of Venice's tourists realise the future of this historic city is uncertain. As a consequence of many environmental problems Venice can be said to be 'sinking' and its beautiful buildings decaying. Since 1908, Venice is estimated to have subsided 22cm - 10.4cm as a result of well extraction, 2.9cm due to natural geological sinking, and 9.1cm because of global sea-level rises.
So much damage has been done that careful future management is essential. Even so, the battle may already be lost.

Management strategies employed to date include:

- Building movable barriers to keep out flood tides. But their success is limited because they must not interfere with normal tides or shipping.
- Employing traditional methods such as raising canal edges and waterproofing buildings.
- Continue an international campaign (first started after flooding in 1966) to raise the huge sum of money required to restore buildings and art treasures.
- The industries of Porto Marghera have been subjected to strict pollution controls.

Continued depopulation will mean that houses in Venice will fall into disrepair and services will decline. Tourists will probably still come. However, they will stay in modern hotels in Mestre, leaving those in Venice to decay. The solutions both tried and proposed can only be effective for a limited period due to the rising level of the sea and natural subsidence.

Figure 3 Decaying buildings

Figure 4 **The environmental problems facing Venice**

1 The Po Basin has been sinking geologically at a rate of 1.3cm per year ever since the end of the Pleistocene period.
2 Worldwide sea-levels are rising. A tide only 80cm above normal would flood Venice to a depth of 20cm.
3 The shape of the Adriatic Sea encourages storm surges, especially between November and April.
4 Vast quantities of water were abstracted during the building of Porto Marghera, causing the ground below Venice to subside.
5 Land reclamation on the edges of the lagoon for aluminium, steel, and chemical works has meant that the marshlands can no longer act as a natural buffer against the tides.
6 In the 1980s, disposal of industrial and human waste reached very high levels. Bacteria and chemicals help to weaken foundations during flooding.
7 Traditional gondolas have been replaced by motor boats, whose wakes have eroded the sides of the canals.
8 Ninety per cent of Venice is built of porous bricks which are susceptible to disintegration by saltwater.
9 Large numbers of tourists spoil the visual beauty of the city, cause congestion, and leave litter.
10 Acid rain and the droppings of thousands of pigeons have contributed to the disintegration of the buildings.

Activities

1 Make a list of the reasons why you think that Venice is a World Heritage Site.

2 a) Make a large copy of this table.

Causes of problems facing Venice

	People	Industry	Nature	Building construction
Unsolvable				
Controllable				
Solvable				

b) Look closely at Figure 4.

c) Fill in the table with the various problems facing Venice, placing them in the correct box according to their cause and degree of solvability.

3 Working as a small group, discuss the likely success of each management strategy given in Figure 2. Taking into account all the information about Venice, write a detailed report explaining what you think should happen to this World Heritage Site.

Tourism - the future

Assignment

Background information

Cheviot Leisure Group PLC are proposing to extend their interests by building a new holiday complex on the coast of Northumberland.

Your assignment

Your assignment is to determine whether or not the holiday complex should go ahead. You should attempt to:

- Consider some of the criteria used when siting a new holiday complex.
- Examine the possible effects that such a complex would have on the local community and environment.

Figure 1

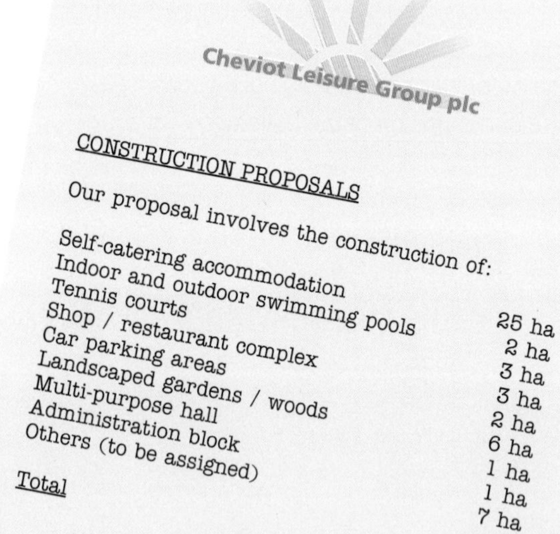

Cheviot Leisure Group plc

CONSTRUCTION PROPOSALS

Our proposal involves the construction of:

Self-catering accommodation	25 ha
Indoor and outdoor swimming pools	2 ha
Tennis courts	3 ha
Shop / restaurant complex	3 ha
Car parking areas	2 ha
Landscaped gardens / woods	6 ha
Multi-purpose hall	1 ha
Administration block	1 ha
Others (to be assigned)	7 ha
Total	50ha

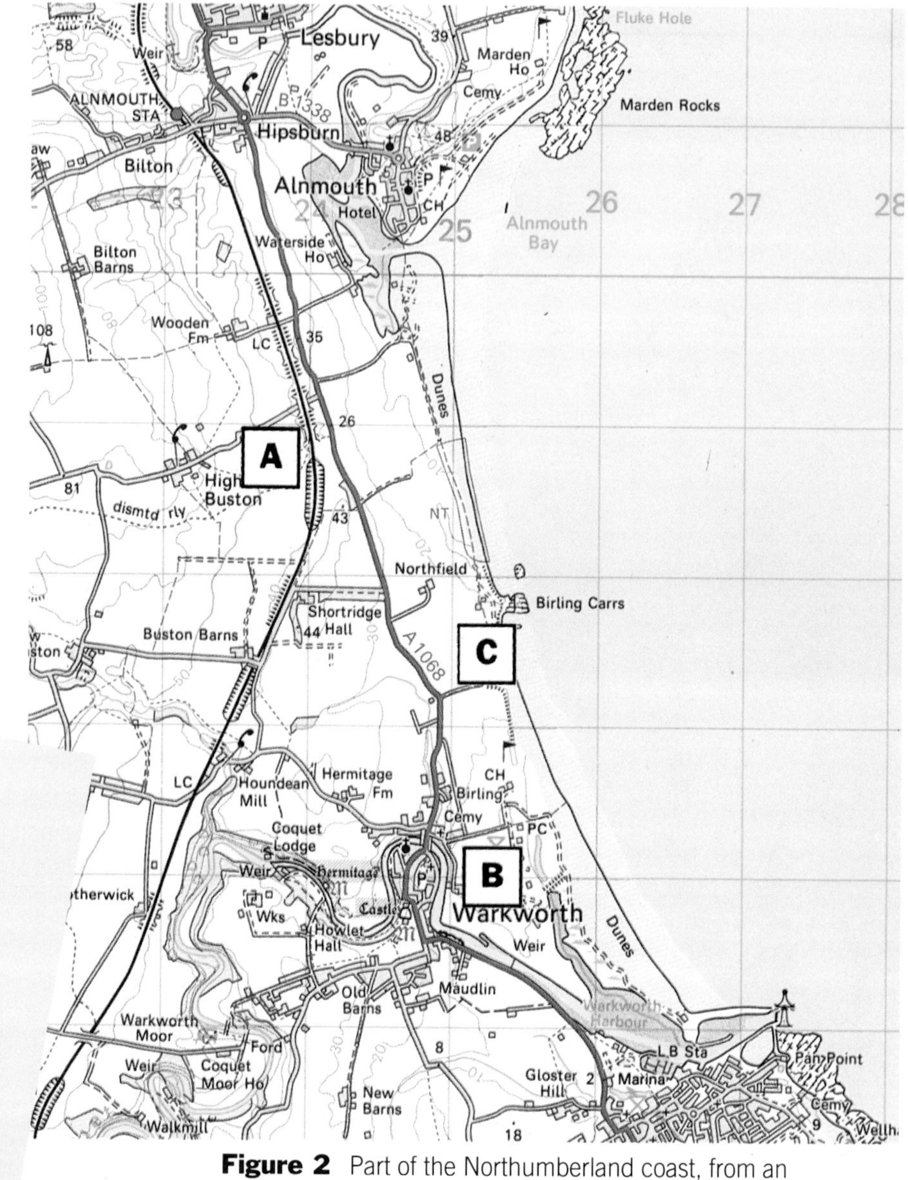

Figure 2 Part of the Northumberland coast, from an Ordnance Survey 1: 50 000 map

Figure 3

North-East Coast
Northumberland

Britain Factfile

Population:	300,900
Area:	5032km ^{2}
Major rivers:	Tyne, Blyth, Wansbeck, Coquet, Aln
Major towns:	Morpeth (county town), Berwick-upon-Tweed, Ashington, Cramlington, Alnwick, Hexham
Economic activities:	Sheep, barley, fishing, forestry, coal mining, light industry

Places of interest:	Kielder Water, Holy Island, Farne Islands, Hadrian's Wall, castles (e.g. Alnwick), Bamburgh, Cheviot Hills

Other tourist attractions:

Golf:	Links courses along the coast
Fishing:	Excellent river and sea fishing available
Boating:	Kielder Water and at sea
Bird-watching:	Uplands famous as refuge for birds such as Merlin and Golden Plover. Coast noted for millions of sea birds and rare migrant

Figure 4

BIG TOURIST PROJECT GETS COUNCIL GO-AHEAD!

Alnwick District Council last week gave the go-ahead to Cheviot Leisure Group's new all-year holiday centre on the coast between the villages of Warkworth and Alnmouth. Three possible sites for the centre have been proposed and a survey commissioned to look into the impacts of each site. It will recommend which site best fulfils the requirements of both the council and the company. A spokesperson for the Council said that the centre would give a big boost to the local economy. The increased numbers of tourists would use local services and visit the many tourist attractions in the area. The company already has two other successful holiday centres in Devon and the Lake District and believes that Northumberland has not yet realised its true tourist potential.

Concern has already been expressed by members of Warkworth Parish Council about the likely effect of construction traffic, and they fear that the increase in both people and cars might spoil the character of this historic village. Environmental groups have pointed ou the wildlife value of this part of the coast. However, the proposal has been welcomed by many people, most notably traders in both Warkworth and Alnmouth, who see the centre as providing a much needed increase in cu tom. The proposed holiday centre is in its f stage of planning.

Figure 5 EC Tourism Policy

The aims:

- To stimulate trade and business.
- To create jobs.
- To integrate transport routes.
- To encourage rural craft industries and so reduce rural depopulation.
- To improve local service provision.
- To protect the cultural and physical environment.
- To stimulate areas which have little other economic importance.
- To provide funds for tourism projects from the European Investment Bank and European Regional Development Fund.

Work Programme A

- Imagine that you are the chief planning officer for Alnwick District Council. Use the information on these pages to assess the potential of each of the three proposed sites. You should rank each site according to the criteria in the table below. The site with the lowest total score will be the most suitable.

Criteria	Rank of each site		
	A	B	C
Nature of site			
Access roads			
Proximity of beach			
Access to water sports			
Provision of local services			
Total score			

- You should now complete your recommendation to the Council. It should comprise:
  1 your recommendation for the site of the centre;
  2 a map to show why you have chosen this site;
  3 an assessment of the good and bad effects that the centre will have on the local economy and on the environment. This might best be shown in the form of a table.

Work Programme B

- Work in groups of six. Each member of the group should take on the role of one of the following people:
  - Chairperson of Warkworth Parish Council
  - Craftshop owner in Warkworth
  - Farmer of Wooden Farm
  - Spokesperson for the Royal Society for the Protection of Birds (RSPB)
  - Unemployed teenager from Alnmouth
  - Licensee of Red Lion public house in Alnmouth

  Having decided how your role would feel about the proposed new holiday centre, discuss the proposal within the group. Each group should then report its discussion to the rest of the class, stating whether or not the proposal should be given the go-ahead.
- Working on your own, write an account of the discussion about the proposal. You should give the outcome as well as the reasons for the decision that was reached.

1 Ranging in size from the vast global scale to the smallest micro scale, the earth's environments are all fragile. Some are more fragile than others. Human activity can do immense harm to them. But does it matter? Won't the planet just repair the damage that we inflict upon it?

What makes an environment

2 Unfortunately, we are all too familiar with this kind of damaged environment. But at least rivers can start to clean themselves within days if the source of pollution is stopped. Many other environments take a great deal longer to repair. Can you think of any examples? Why do some environments take so long to repair?

3 Some damage to the Antarctic environment is very visible. But some is not so easily seen and can be far more harmful in the long run. What kinds of invisible damage to the environment can you think of? What effects can it have?

6 Not all environments have come about totally as a result of natural processes. Chalk downlands, for example. Find out how they have developed. However, they are also fragile and are coming under great pressure for change. Should only natural, fragile environments be protected? Can urban environments be fragile?

fragile?

7 Before the twentieth century, even the most fragile environments were reasonably safe. What has happened to change this? What is likely to happen in the future?

5 Some environments are more fragile than others. In this photograph, low temperatures mean that the environment only develops slowly. It also makes repair of the environment a very slow process. What other conditions do you think give rise to particularly fragile environments?

4 Many environments can be harmed even if they are not directly damaged. For example, pollutants can be passed up through the food chain. What sort of steps can we take to ensure that environmental damage is not passed on in this way?

Donana - disappearing wetland

In the south-west corner of Spain lies the Donana National Park, the last major wetland in Western Europe. The map in Figure 3 shows that it forms part of the Costa de la Luz between Portugal and Gibraltar. The park has an area of 76 000 hectares, about the size of the Isle of Wight. It was created in 1969 with help from the World Wildlife Fund (now the Worldwide Fund for Nature). The aim was to help with the conservation of the Donana area - a fragile environment consisting of a variety of different ecosystems.

Hundreds of years ago, Donana was used as a hunting ground where the Spanish royal family and their guests chased wild boar and other game animals. Later, the land became the property of a few sherry-producing families from nearby Jerez de la Frontera. But now that the land is state owned, the locals have lost their hunting rights and National Park rangers patrol to keep them out.

Agriculture has traditionally been the mainstay of the economy in this, Spain's poorest region. However, tourism is becoming increasingly important and is just one of the factors which threaten the delicate balance in the area.

This part of Spain has low rainfall in the summer months and, consequently, fresh water is a valuable resource. At the heart of Donana lie a series of lagoons, where fresh water from deep underground comes to the surface. Fresh water is also brought in by the River Guadalquivir. It is the lagoons and the river's floodplain which provide a home for the great majority of Donana's wildlife. Around the lagoons and the river are found marshes which, although wet in winter, become dry and cracked in summer. In parts, they have been reclaimed for agriculture, but the soils are sandy and poor. The marshes give way to scrubland, which is of little use for farming. Sand dunes, up to 30m in height, separate Donana from the Atlantic Ocean. The coastline itself has wide, sandy beaches, which are becoming popular with tourists.

Figure 1
A view of Donana

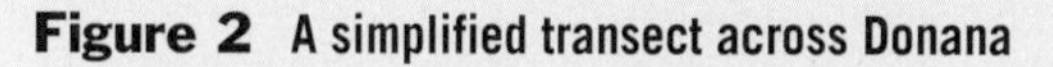

Figure 2 **A simplified transect across Donana**

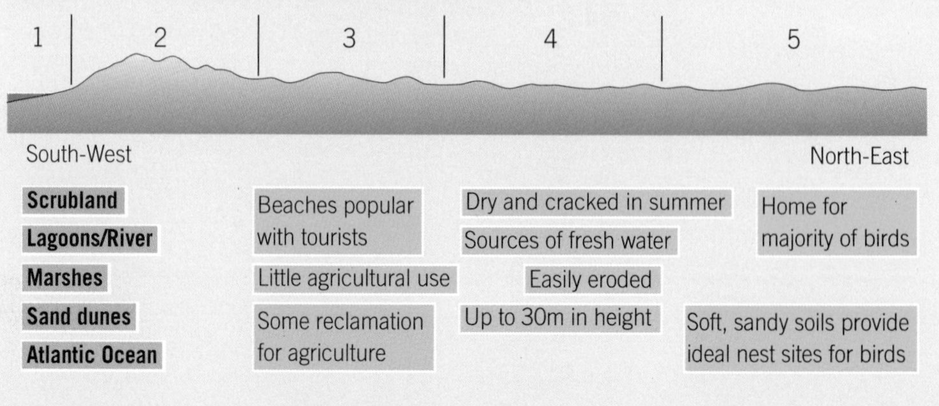

Figure 3 Donana

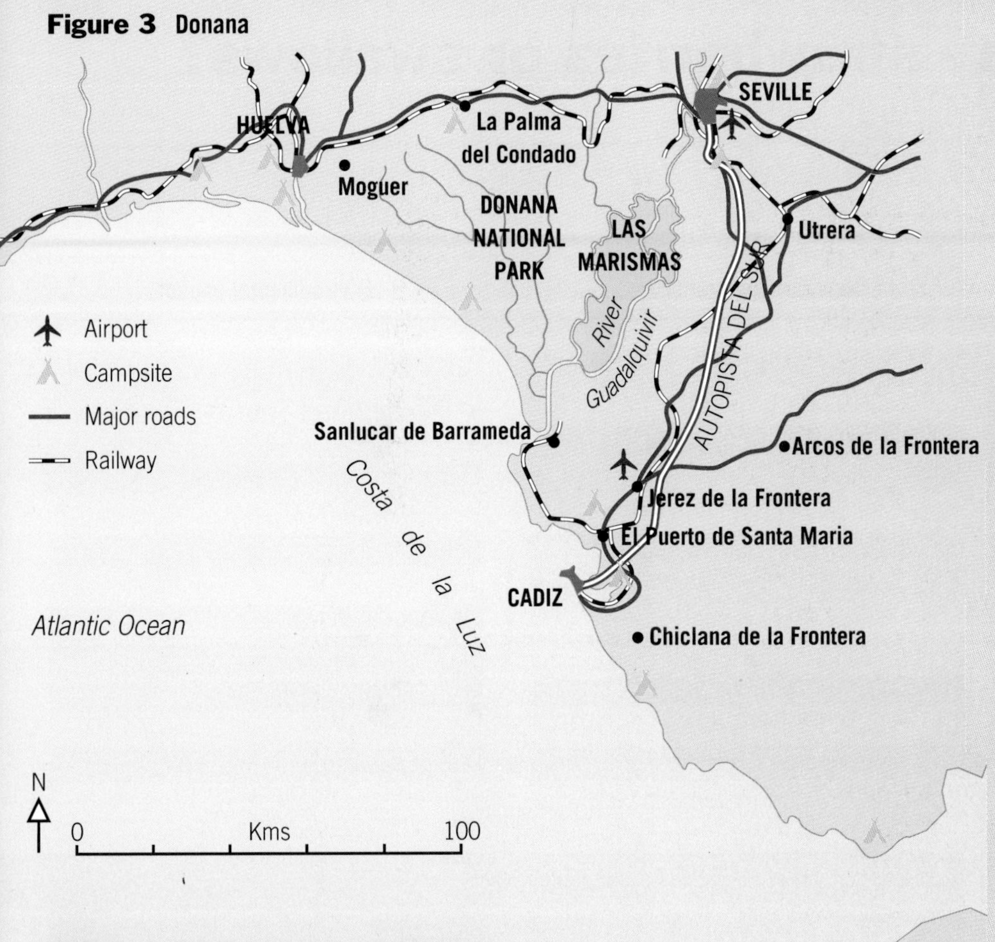

Nesting spoonbills, Donana

The largest heron colony in Europe is found in cork oak trees near the lagoons. Donana is home to a tremendous variety of wildlife. It is the breeding ground for:

8 species of fish
9 species of amphibians
17 species of reptiles
125 species of birds
28 species of mammals, including the near-extinct Iberian lynx

In addition, Donana is a stopping-off and watering place for another 150 species of birds, totalling many millions.

Activities

1 Using the map in Figure 3 and your atlas, draw a map to show the location of Donana.

2 Study and make a large copy of Figure 2. The transect has been divided into five different ecosystems, labelled 1-5. Decide which ecosystem in the red boxes goes with each section on the transect. Write them on your transect in the correct places. Do the same for the information in the green boxes. Can you add any more environmental characteristics to your transect?

3 Draw a climate graph to depict these climate figures for Cadiz. Use your atlas to compare the climate of Donana with that of your home region.

Cadiz climate

	Precipitation *(mm)*	Temperature *(°C)*
J	92	11
F	67	12
M	84	14
A	52	16
M	38	18
J	9	25
J	2	24
A	4	24
S	31	22
O	64	19
N	79	15
D	87	12
Year	609 *Total*	17.7 *Average*

4 Devise a way to illustrate the different periods in the history of Donana.

5 In small groups, discuss why Donana could be classed a fragile environment.

6 *Research idea:*
Investigate other wetland areas which share many of the same characteristics and problems as Donana. (Hint: try the Camargue.)

Donana - strawberries or swallows?

Figure 1 **How agriculture in Donana threatens the environment**

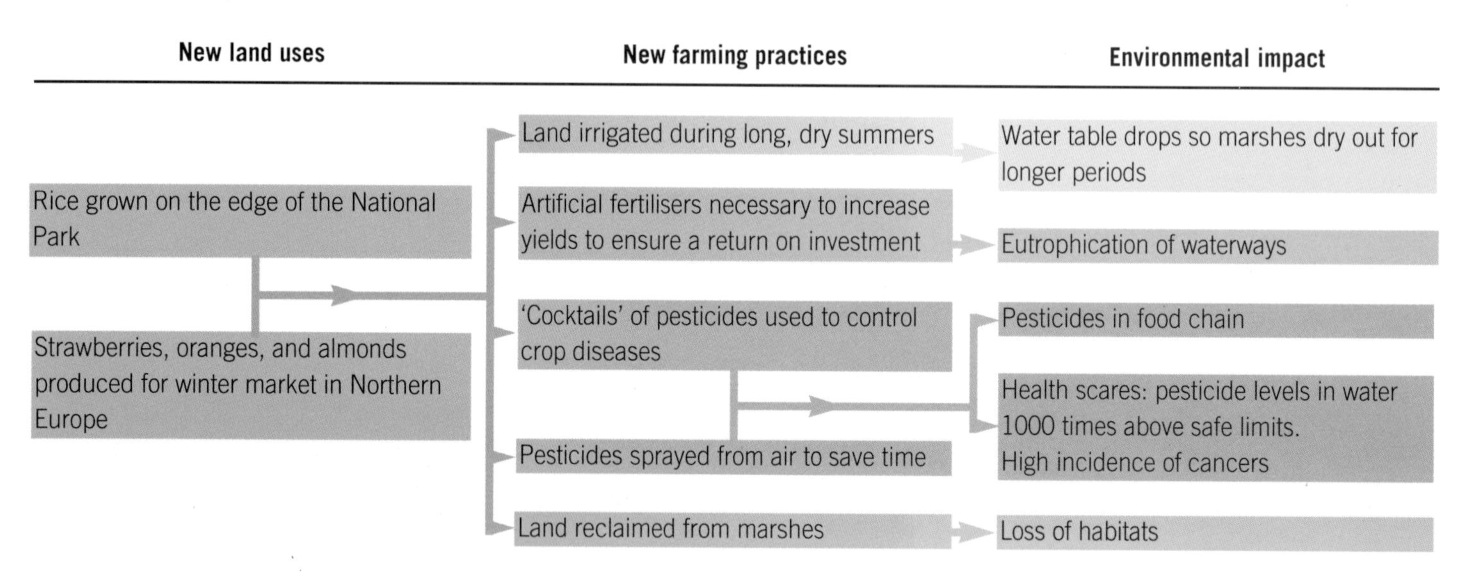

New land uses
New farming practices
Environmental impact
Rice grown on the edge of the National Park
Strawberries, oranges, and almonds produced for winter market in Northern Europe
Land irrigated during long, dry summers
Artificial fertilisers necessary to increase yields to ensure a return on investment
'Cocktails' of pesticides used to control crop diseases
Pesticides sprayed from air to save time
Land reclaimed from marshes
Water table drops so marshes dry out for longer periods
Eutrophication of waterways
Pesticides in food chain
Health scares: pesticide levels in water 1000 times above safe limits.
High incidence of cancers
Loss of habitats

Figure 2 **Some of the other threats to Donana's delicate environment**

1. Mining for lead and copper to the north of Donana results in waste being washed into the wetland. Organisms absorb toxic metals which therefore enter the food chain.
2. Pollutants and sewage from the major cities of Seville and Cordoba enter the area by the River Guadalquivir bringing them downstream.
3. Untreated sewage from 1 million local residents is discharged into water-courses.
4. Various forms of pollution enter the watercourses from local factories, including 700 grain processing plants, 49 olive oil factories, and 4 abbatoirs. A trade union report claims that the pollution harms human health, causing dermatitis, bronchitis, and various allergies.

Figure 3
Traditionally farmers in Donana tended olive trees and vines using little that was not available locally

In the past few years, Donana has seen a lot of agricultural change. The traditional crops (mainly for local use) and simple farming practices kept a balance in the ecosystem. Today, however, the main crops of strawberries, oranges, and almonds are all destined for the wider European market. These commercial crops can only be grown successfully by changing the natural environment. Large areas of marshland along the river have been reclaimed, but the soil is poor and artificial fertiliser must be used. The long, dry summers necessitate irrigation - often illegally from open wells. Some farmers who use pesticides do not know how to use them properly. In 1986, thousands of birds died due to pesticides in the food chain. These included many endangered species such as egrets and herons. A number of farmers were successfully prosecuted as a result. Ironically, this modern intensive farming is expensive and many farmers have gone bankrupt, resulting in land being left vacant!

Tourism in Donana has grown in importance in recent years, and it is said by many to be the key to prosperity in the region. However, a balance is necessary between tourist developments, which put pressure on precious water resources, and the environment. This is especially true as it is the environment which attracts tourists in the first place.

The 'Costa Donana Scheme' has been put forward to extend tourism on the coast to the north-west of the National Park. The developments are planned near sand dunes said to be of vital ecological importance, and have caused violent confrontations between locals and conservationists. At first, the Spanish government approved the scheme, but protests from across Europe have led to the scheme being shelved.

In 1991, not enough tourists visited the area and a lot of accommodation remained empty. Furthermore, visitors who are attracted to the wetland complain of having very limited access to the park and of being herded around in buses. The visitors centre and nature trails are used by more people than they were originally planned to cope with.

There remains a lot of scope for developing visitor access within Donana. Perhaps accommodation would be better sited in local villages, providing local jobs in guest houses and restaurants, without threatening the way of life of the area.

Figure 4
Modern farming is much more intensive. Here a crop of strawberries is harvested

Activities

1 Read the information on these pages. Write a paragraph which summarises the main changes in farming in Donana.

2 Study Figure 1. Make two columns in your exercise book. In the left-hand column list the impacts of new land uses on the environment in Donana. In the right-hand column list how each of these impacts affects birds and other wildlife.

3 Write two paragraphs to explain the advantages and disadvantages of tourist developments in the Donana National Park and the surrounding area.

What future for Donana?

Assignment

Background information

You will already have discovered that the Donana National Park is a beautiful, yet fragile environment, and that the pressure from modern developments is threatening its equilibrium.

Your assignment

The purpose of this assignment is for you to investigate whether or not agricultural, tourist, and industrial developments can continue without further damaging the fragile environment.

Figure 1 Views and opinions

Paco Lopez

"I poach for crayfish in the National Park and have done so for many years. Crayfish are very popular and it's worth the risk of being caught by the rangers - one sack is worth over £100 to me."

Marie-Claude Delon

"The WWF recognises Donana as Europe's last major wetland site. It is of huge importance for birds and wildlife and must be protected for future generations."

Helga Schmidt

"I'm not that interested in wildlife. *I've just come away for two weeks relaxation on the beach. We chose the hotel from the brochure and I doubt that we'll ever leave the hotel complex."*

Felipe Gomez

"As mayor of Almonte, I am very much in favour of the Costa Donana Scheme. **It would create** many vitally needed **jobs** in an area of high unemployment."

Fred Cook

*"My wife and I were **very disappointed** with our visit to the National Park. We weren't given the freedom to go where we wanted - **we were treated like children** and I didn't spot any of the birds I'd come so far to see."*

Jose Cortes

"We don't want these concrete jungles! Our heritage and way of life are threatened. The park rangers are keeping us out of our own lands! We don't get a say in what happens here. What does the government in Madrid know?"

Delores Navarro

"I am very worried by the high incidence of **cancer deaths** in this area. I would like to see more research into the effect of these **pesticides, fertilisers**, and **pollutants** on human health."

Figure 2

MEMO
FROM: The MEP for Costa de la Luz
TO: Ministry of the Environment, Madrid

I am receiving an increasing number of letters and deputations from my constituents who are concerned about the future of the Donana National Park. It is vital that we plan for the long-term development of the area. Please let me remind you of the six points of the EC Environmental Policy.

- Prevent, reduce, and try to eliminate pollution.
- Maintain a satisfactory ecological balance.
- Sound management and no exploitation of resources which may damage the ecological balance.
- Guide developments so as to improve working conditions and the quality of life.
- Ensure that more account is taken of environmental aspects of planning and land use.
- Seek common solutions to environmental problems with states outside the community.

Most experts agree that Donana has ten years left if nothing is done, but it is not too late to act! What right has the EC to preach to Brazil about its rainforest, if it cannot save its own wildernesses like Donana?

Franco Bellido

"Donana needs tourists! My company's new hotels and apartments will be built on the coast, on the edge of the National Park. They will bring much needed **money** *to Spain's poorest region."*

Pedro Alonso

"The land here is so poor that without fertilisers and the like I wouldn't be able to grow my strawberries. Of course I care about the environment, but I have loans to pay off and I have to make a living!"

Work Programme A

Hold a discussion about the problems facing Donana National Park and its future development.

- As a class, choose someone to act as chairperson for the discussion. It will be the chairperson's job to make sure that everybody can put forward their views, that nobody gets more than their fair share of time, and that questioning is conducted in an orderly manner!
- The rest of the class should divide into nine small groups. Each group takes on a different role from Figure 1.
- Each group should use their own knowledge of Donana to build on the view expressed by their 'role' about what should happen in the future. Prepare a short statement of your views.
- Each group should present their statement to the rest of the class, allowing time at the end for questions.
- Wider discussion can follow after all the statements have been presented. The chairperson should try to guide discussion towards an agreement on Donana's future development. However, do not be surprised if you cannot reach agreement!

Work Programme B

Work in a small group. You have been commissioned by the Ministry of the Environment in Madrid to prepare a report outlining a management plan for Donana National Park and its surrounding area. The report should attempt to address all of the problems facing Donana. It should also try to take into account the different views people have on the issues.
The report should have the following sections:

i) A brief introduction which summarises the problems facing Donana.
ii) Strategies for agriculture.
iii) Strategies for tourism.
iv) Strategies for industry.
v) A conclusion which links the report to the EC Environmental Policy.

Remember that in presenting your report, you should try to make it as visual as possible by using appropriate maps, illustrations, and diagrams.

The frozen Arctic environment

Resource Bank

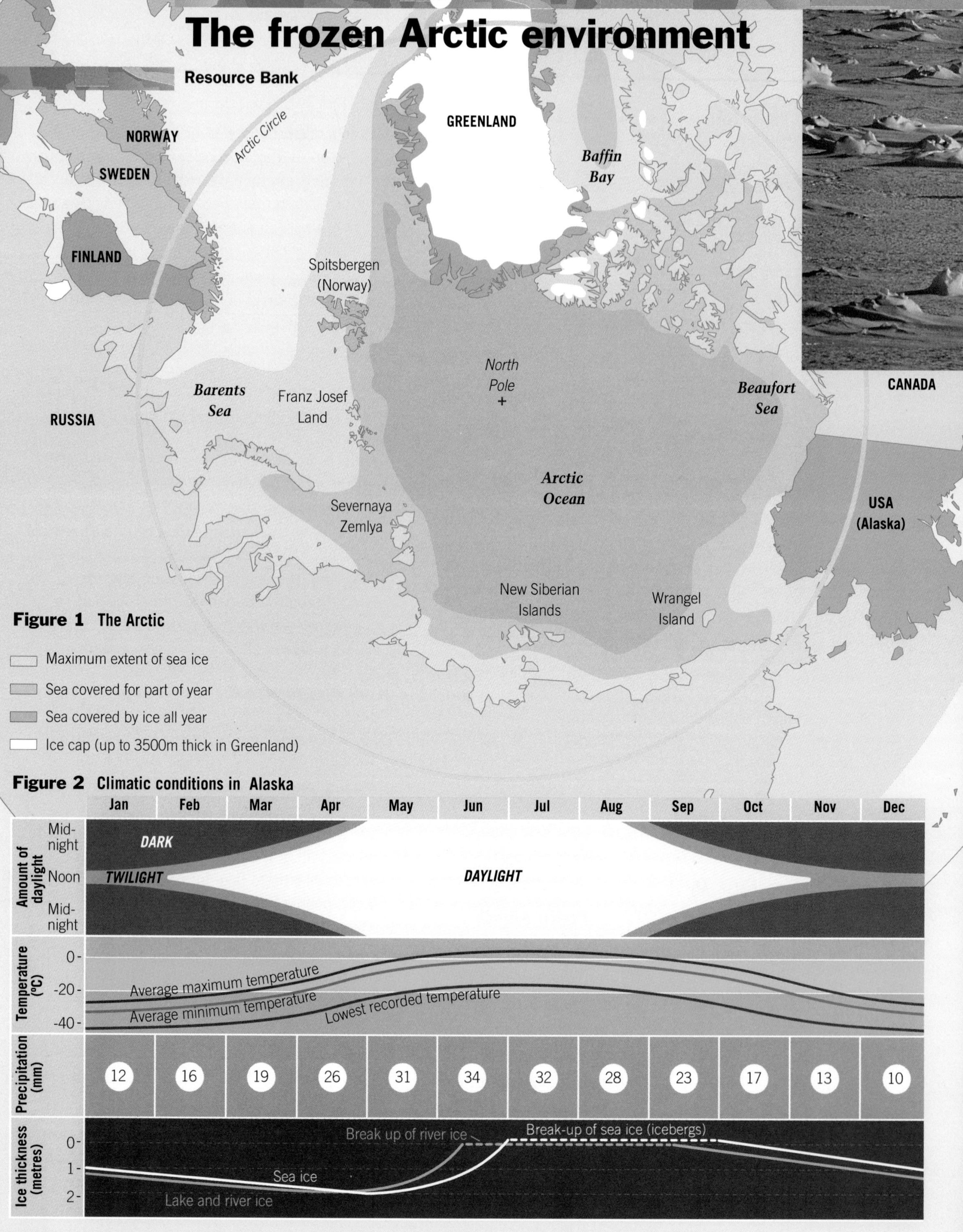

Figure 1 The Arctic

Figure 2 Climatic conditions in Alaska

Figure 3 The coral reef ecosystem

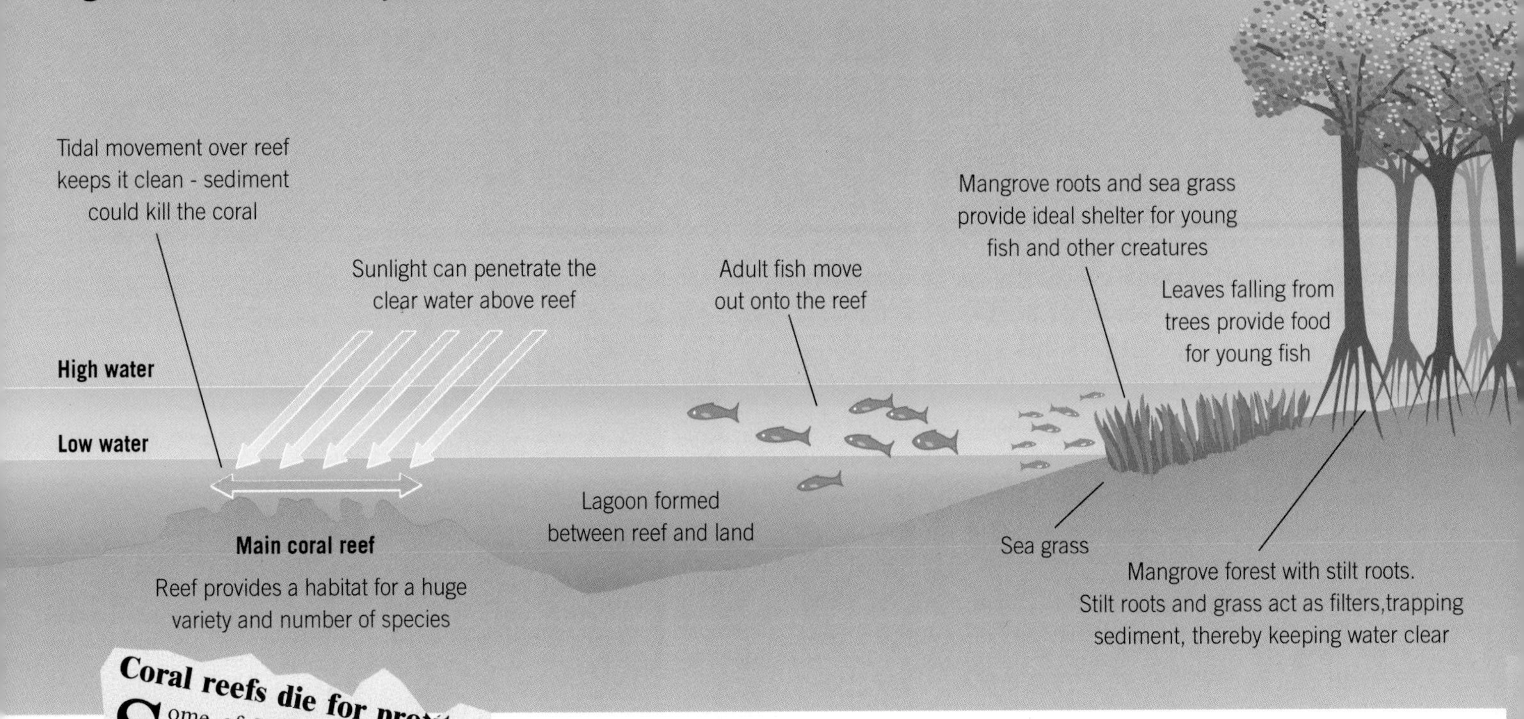

Tidal movement over reef keeps it clean - sediment could kill the coral

Sunlight can penetrate the clear water above reef

Adult fish move out onto the reef

Mangrove roots and sea grass provide ideal shelter for young fish and other creatures

Leaves falling from trees provide food for young fish

High water

Low water

Main coral reef

Reef provides a habitat for a huge variety and number of species

Lagoon formed between reef and land

Sea grass

Mangrove forest with stilt roots. Stilt roots and grass act as filters, trapping sediment, thereby keeping water clear

Coral reefs die for profit

Some of Britain's biggest high street stores are selling trinkets made from marine creatures two years after they were banned from sale because the species are endangered.

Hundreds of shops in Britain make large profits selling shells from the world's coral reefs as soap dishes, jewellery or ornaments.

Coral reefs, as important to the ecology of tropical oceans as rain forests are to the land, are suffering severe damage because of over-fishing, tourism, mining and pollution.

The threat to the marine ecosystem has meant that trading of many species of coral and shellfish has been tightly restricted since 1985.

Figure 4 Newspaper extract

Figure 5 Pressures on coral reefs

Tourism

- Coral removed for souvenirs
- Divers can damage reef
- Powerboats and jet-skis stir up sediment
- Sewage from tourist developments pollute reef
- Pleasure boats spill oil

Development

Most coral reefs are found in developing countries

- Fish and coral exported to earn foreign currency
- Land reclamation projects - for airports and hotels - damage reef
- Channels cut through reef to enable larger ships to enter harbours
- Agricultural fertilisers and industrial waste can pollute rivers entering lagoon
- Deforestation exposes soil which is then washed into lagoon

Activities

1 Make a large copy of Figure 3, but without any labels on it. Look closely at Figure 5 which shows the pressures acting on coral reefs. Decide how these pressures might affect the cross-section of reef shown in your diagram and add labels to illustrate these effects. You may find that it is necessary to add to the original diagram.

2 Imagine that you are working for the Ministry of Tourism in Seychelles. You have been asked to design an A4 leaflet which will be given to tourists as they arrive at the airport. One side of the leaflet is to introduce them to the wonders of the country's coral reefs. The other side is a reminder of the fragile nature of the coral and the things they should do to help conserve the reefs for future generations. The leaflet should be as colourful as the reefs themselves, and should also be effective at getting its message across.

3 *Research idea:*
The Great Barrier Reef is of great importance to Australia's tourist industry. Find out all you can about this reef and produce a booklet of your findings.

Kinder Scout - upland environment

The Kinder Scout plateau is part of the Dark Peak, the northern section of the Peak District. It rises to just over 2000 feet (610m) and is composed mainly of Millstone Grit. It is one of the loneliest places in England, despite the nearness of large industrial cities. It has a unique beauty of its own.

The vegetation of the high moors is mainly cotton grass with some matt grass and purple moor grass. The cloudberry is a rare type of blackberry found in only a few other areas of the country. Sheep farming and grouse shooting are the main economic uses of the moors.

The soil is very acidic because of the heavy precipitation which does not drain away easily. Up to six metres of peat has built up on the plateau, consisting of layers of sphagnum moss which has not rotted away due to the waterlogging of the soil. Deep V-shaped gullies, called groughs, now cut into the peat. The soil is very poor in nutrients, slowing the growth of the vegetation. This growth is also stunted by snow lying for 70 days a year and by frequent hill fogs, which limit sunshine to just 1000 hours a year.

Figure 1
The western slopes of Kinder Scout. Kinder Scout's vast plateau towers above the village of Edale, which marks the southern end of the Pennine Way

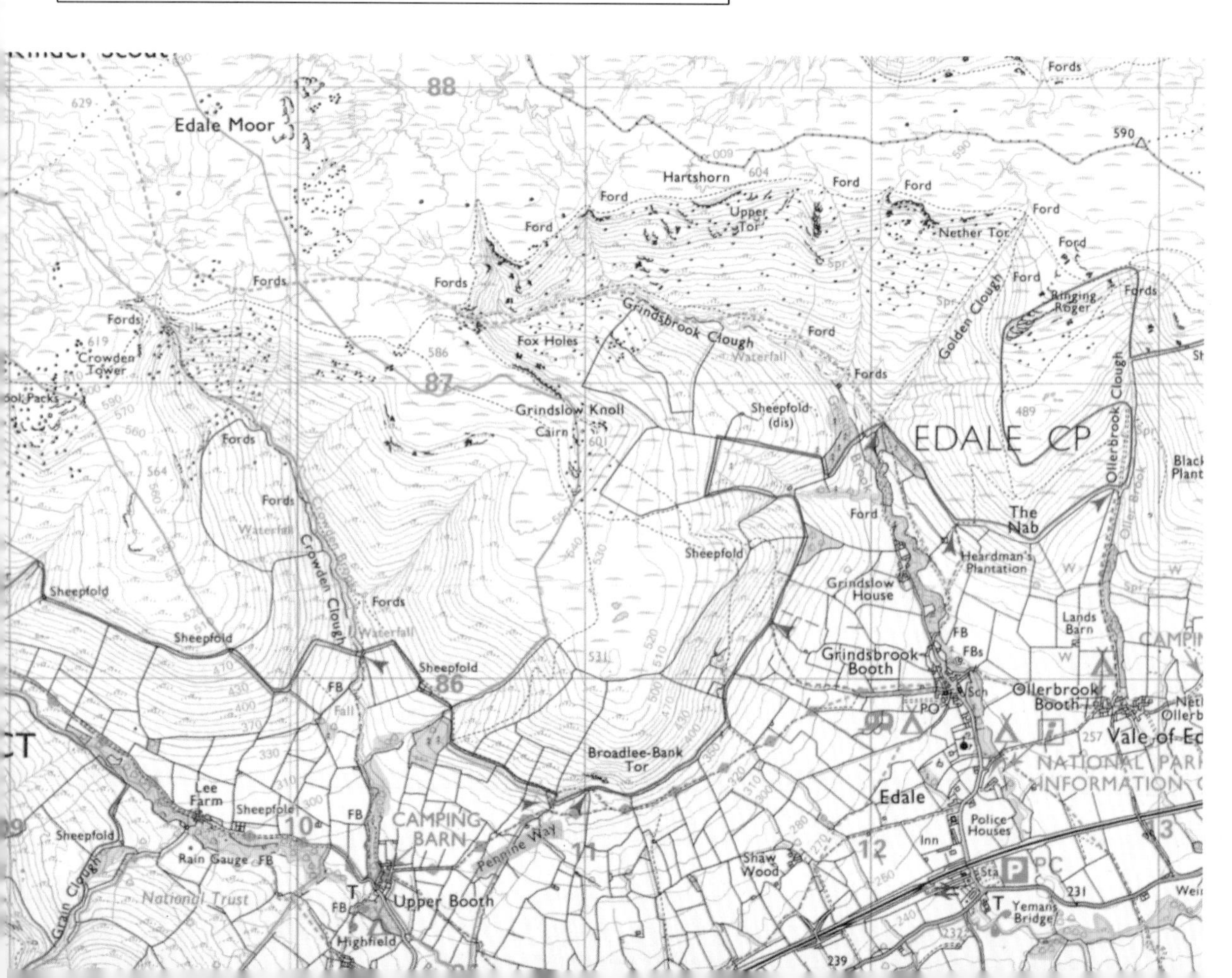

Figure 2
Kinder Scout, from an Ordnance Survey 1:25 000 map

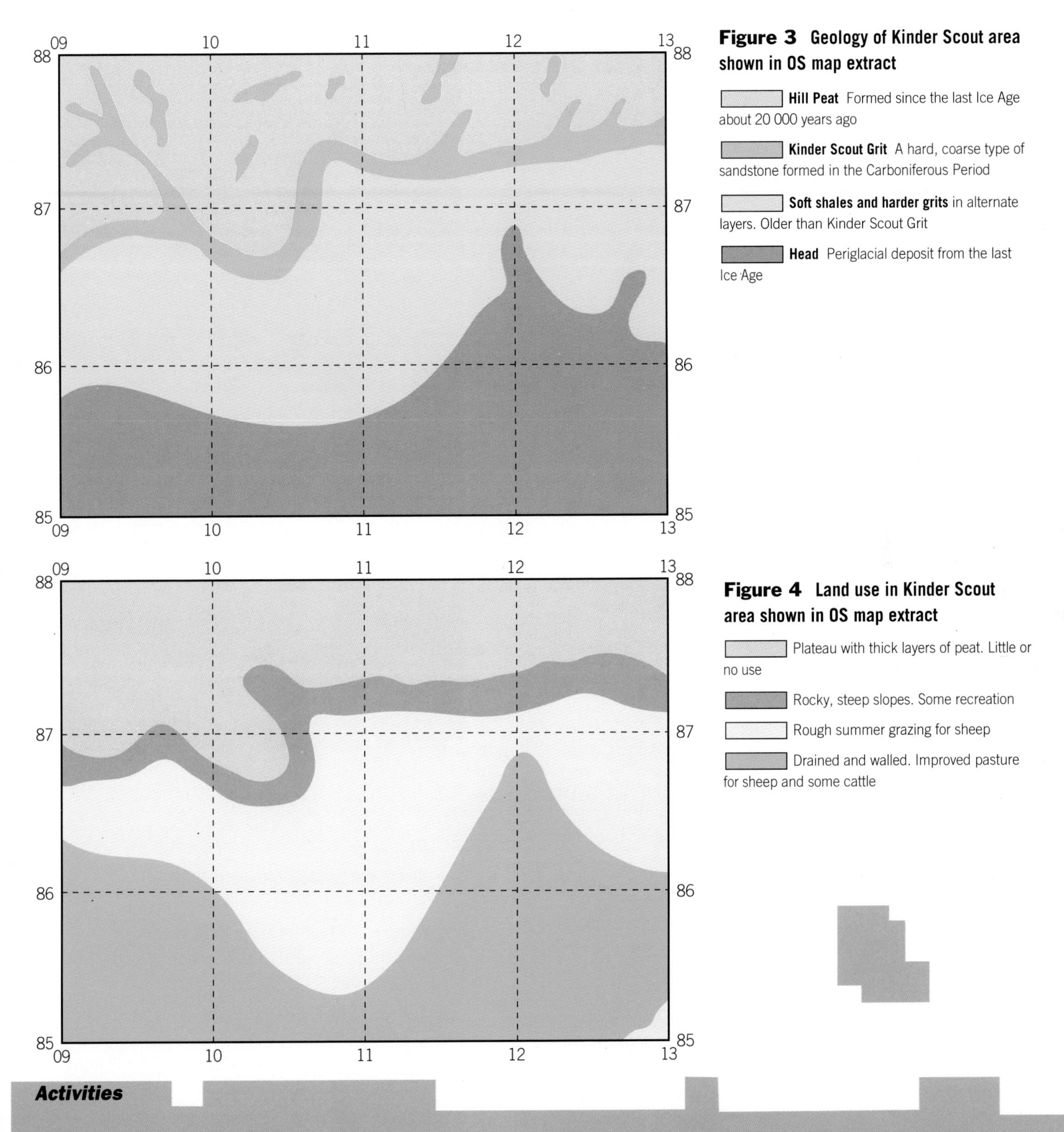
09
10
11
12
13
88
87
86
85
Figure 3 Geology of Kinder Scout area shown in OS map extract
Hill Peat Formed since the last Ice Age about 20 000 years ago
Kinder Scout Grit A hard, coarse type of sandstone formed in the Carboniferous Period
Soft shales and harder grits in alternate layers. Older than Kinder Scout Grit
Head Periglacial deposit from the last Ice Age
Figure 4 Land use in Kinder Scout area shown in OS map extract
Plateau with thick layers of peat. Little or no use
Rocky, steep slopes. Some recreation
Rough summer grazing for sheep
Drained and walled. Improved pasture for sheep and some cattle

Activities

1 Read the text and look at Figure 1. Describe the environment of Kinder Scout in as much detail as you can. Why is it such a fragile environment?

2 Using the OS map extract, draw a relief cross-section from GR 122861 to GR 105872. Name some features on your cross-section.

3 Using the geology and land use maps in Figures 3 and 4, show the rock types and land uses along the line of your cross-section.

4 Working with a partner, discuss if there is any relationship between the relief of Kinder Scout and its geology, its land use, and its soils. Can you explain any relationships?

Tourism and erosion

Figure 1
Erosion on Kinder Scout

Five men were arrested today after a 'mass trespass' in which thousands of hikers went for a walk on Kinder Scout, near Edale in the Peak District. The men were arrested after clashes with gamekeepers who were seeking to keep the hikers off private land. It was the most dramatic day yet in the increasingly bitter battle for public access to mountains and moors. Most the moors in the Peak District are privately owned. Only 1212 out of 150000 acres are open to the public

Figure 2
Newspaper extract, 24th April 1932

Recreation has not always been as welcome in the Peak District as it is today. And yet, the problems that it now causes seem to grow every year. Footpath erosion is one of the most visual and common problems. As more walkers (and increasingly cyclists) use a path the vegetation is damaged and eventually disappears. The bare areas spread and the soil is compacted. Unable to soak in as quickly as before, the rain runs down the path, eroding the soil as it goes. The path not only looks unsightly, but will get wider and wider as walkers try to avoid the muddy mess that was once a path. The soil that has been eroded in this way often ends up in the local reservoirs, reducing their capacity and shortening their economic life.

Figure 3 Tourism in the Peak District

- There are about 18.5 million visitors to the Peak District National Park every year.
- 65% of day visitors are from the surrounding conurbations.
- 80% of holidays made are short breaks of less than 7 days.
- In summer, over half of all visitors are on camping or caravanning holidays.
- Visitors are attracted to the Peak District's unspoilt open countryside and to its villages and towns.
- The major recreational activities in the Park are sightseeing and hiking.
- Each year visitor spending generates over £75 million for the local economy.
- Expenditure by visitors rose in real terms by 38% between 1971 and 1989.

Figure 4 Tourism survey of the Peak District National Park

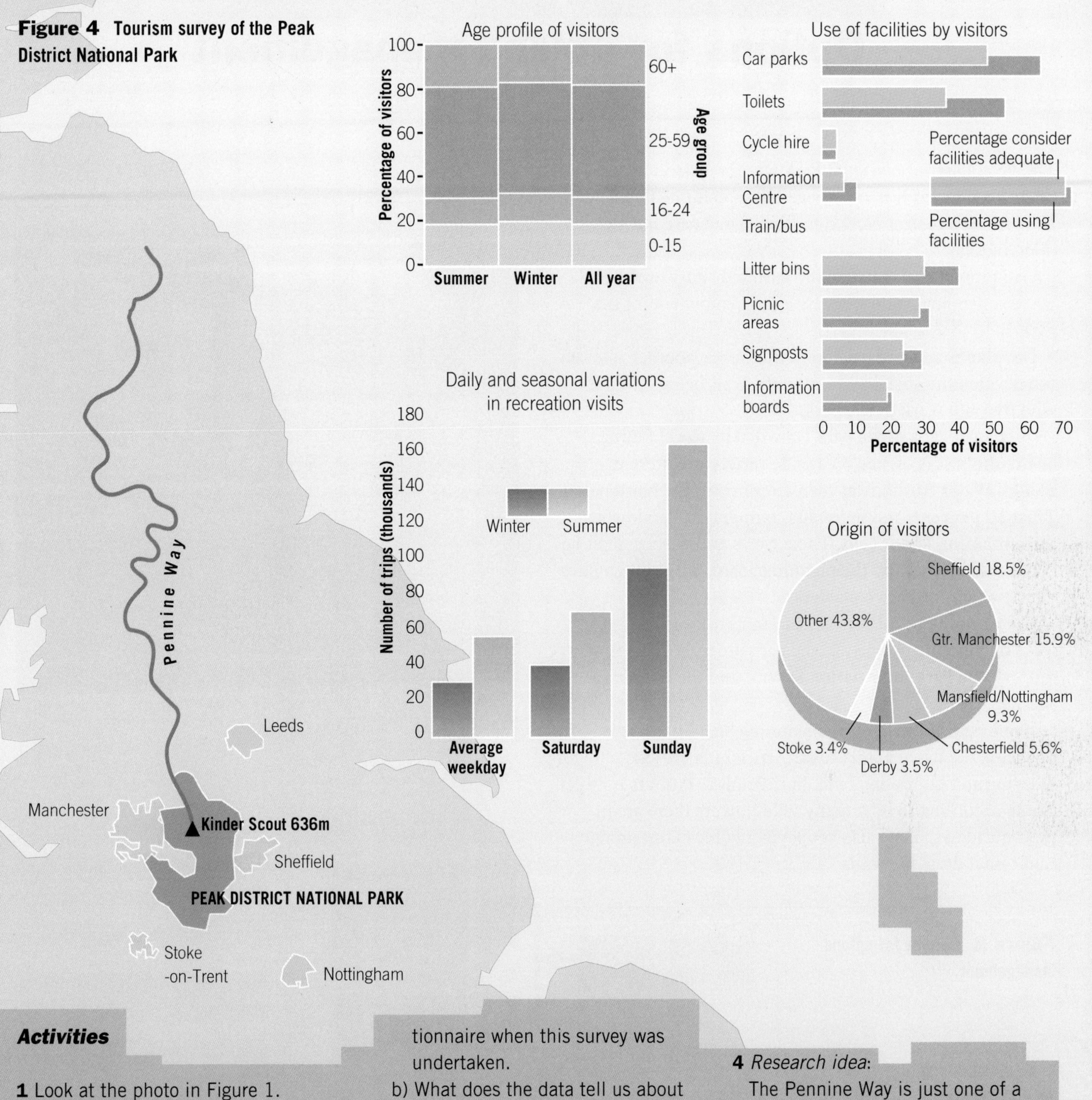

Activities

1 Look at the photo in Figure 1.

a) What particular problem is being caused by increased use of this part of the Peak District?

b) What other problems could be caused by increasing numbers of visitors?

2 Study the survey findings given in Figure 4.

a) Devise a series of questions that might have been used in the questionnaire when this survey was undertaken.

b) What does the data tell us about tourism in the Peak District National Park?

3 Increased tourism is endangering the Peak District environment. What are the arguments for and against limiting people's access to the landscape?

4 *Research idea*:
The Pennine Way is just one of a growing number of Long Distance Paths (LDPs) in England and Wales. Find out about other long distance paths. You could present your findings as a wall display in your classroom; different groups could look at different paths.

Options for upland management

The Peak District National Park was the first in Britain, designated in 1951. It is managed by a planning board. In 1989 it had a budget of £2.6 million. The board has two main duties:

- to protect and enhance the natural beauty of the park;
- to encourage public access to and enjoyment of the park.

The planning board has found that it has another role too - to develop the social and economic well-being of those who live and work in the park.

Only 4 per cent of the park is owned by the planning board, the rest is owned by a wide variety of different groups. Water Authorities own 15 per cent, the National Trust 10 per cent, and individual farmers and landowners the remaining 71 per cent. Their views and wishes must be taken into account by the planning board. Visitors too have views which must be considered.

The planning board sees education as one of the best ways of ensuring people use the park properly. This is done through the Park Information Service and the Ranger Service.

In one part of the park, the planning board has tried replacing the usual grants to farmers which are available for spraying and improving land. In their place farmers now get grants according to how many wild flowers there are in their meadows. They also get payments for maintaining traditional drystone walls.

Figure 1 The Goyt Valley, Peak District

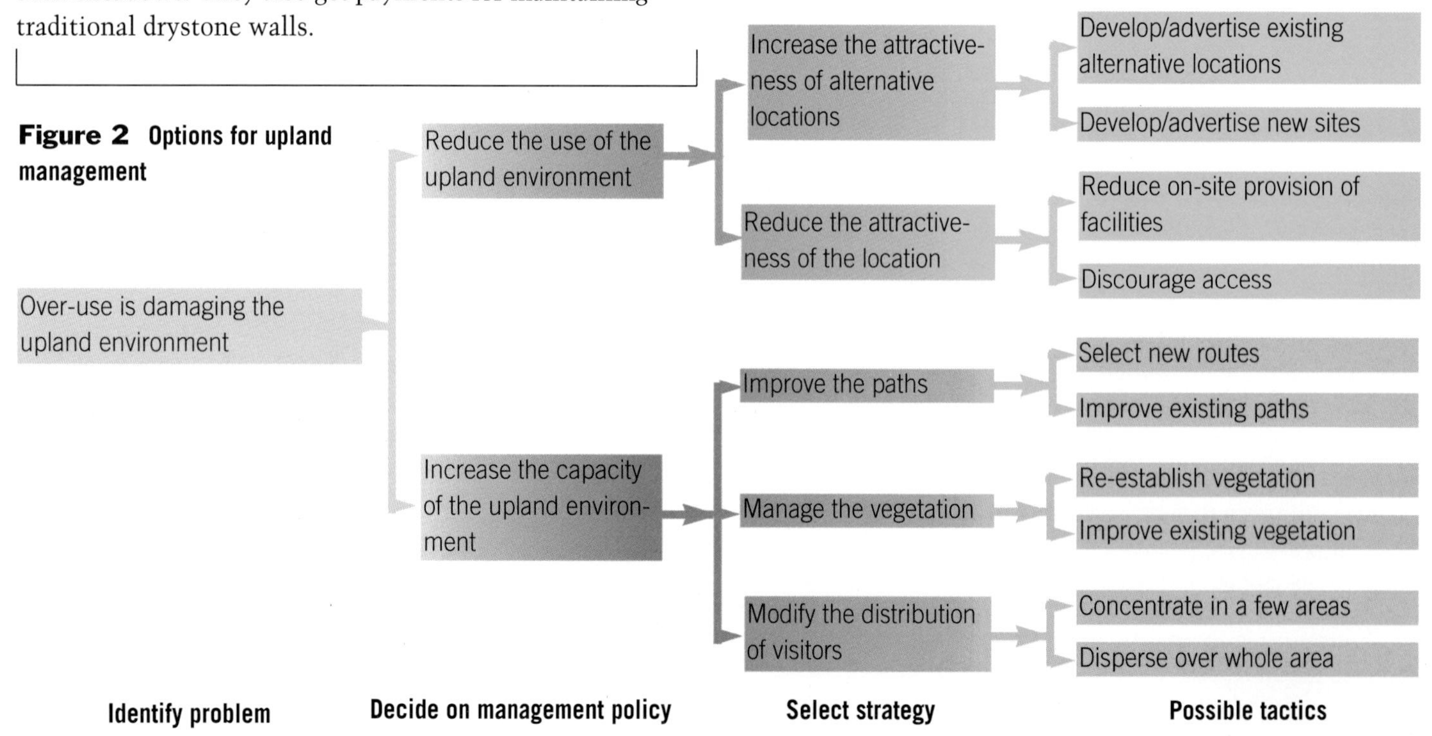

Figure 2 **Options for upland management**

Figure 3 Footpath repairs, Peak District

Figure 4 Car park, Peak District

Figure 5

Management of the fragile upland environment is made more difficult by conflicting interests like these between shooters and ramblers

Shooters

'Access to the moors has to be controlled in order to manage the upland ecosystem effectively.'

'Take the shooting away and who would provide the finance to manage and maintain the environment? How many jobs would be lost?'

'We in the Moorland Association want to keep people off the grouse moors to protect species like the curlew, the golden plover and the green plover.'

Ramblers

'We want new laws to permit more open access to the moors.'

'People should have the 'right to roam' over the moors and not be restricted to certain paths.'

'Scotland earns £750m a year from outdoor tourism, but only £35m from shooting!'

'The landowners pretend to be conservationists, but in reality they are killing many wild animals.'

Activities

1 Figure 2 gives details of ten different management tactics that can be used in upland areas like the Peak District and other National Parks.

a) Look at Figure 1. What two methods are being used to control where people go?

b) How effective do you think information boards, such as this one, are?

2 a) Look at Figure 3. What does this say about the problems of maintenance in a National Park?

b) Look at Figure 4. What problem is illustrated? What has been done to try and deal with the problem? Why have the actions not been completely successful?

3 a) Think carefully about the views expressed in Figure 5. Decide which views are nearest to your own.

b) Write a letter to your local MP asking for his or her support.

Are fragile environments doomed?

Assignment

Background information

Twyford Down - a beautiful corner of England, rich in wildlife and archaeological remains. It is also the scene of a twenty-year struggle to stop the building of a new motorway. There has been court action, four public inquiries, and intervention by the European Commission.

It is an issue typical of many throughout Britain and around the world where people are campaigning to save fragile environments from developments carried out in the name of progress. The final decision lies with politicians, but they must assess the importance of social, economic, and environmental factors.

Figure 2 **The importance of completing the M3 motorway**

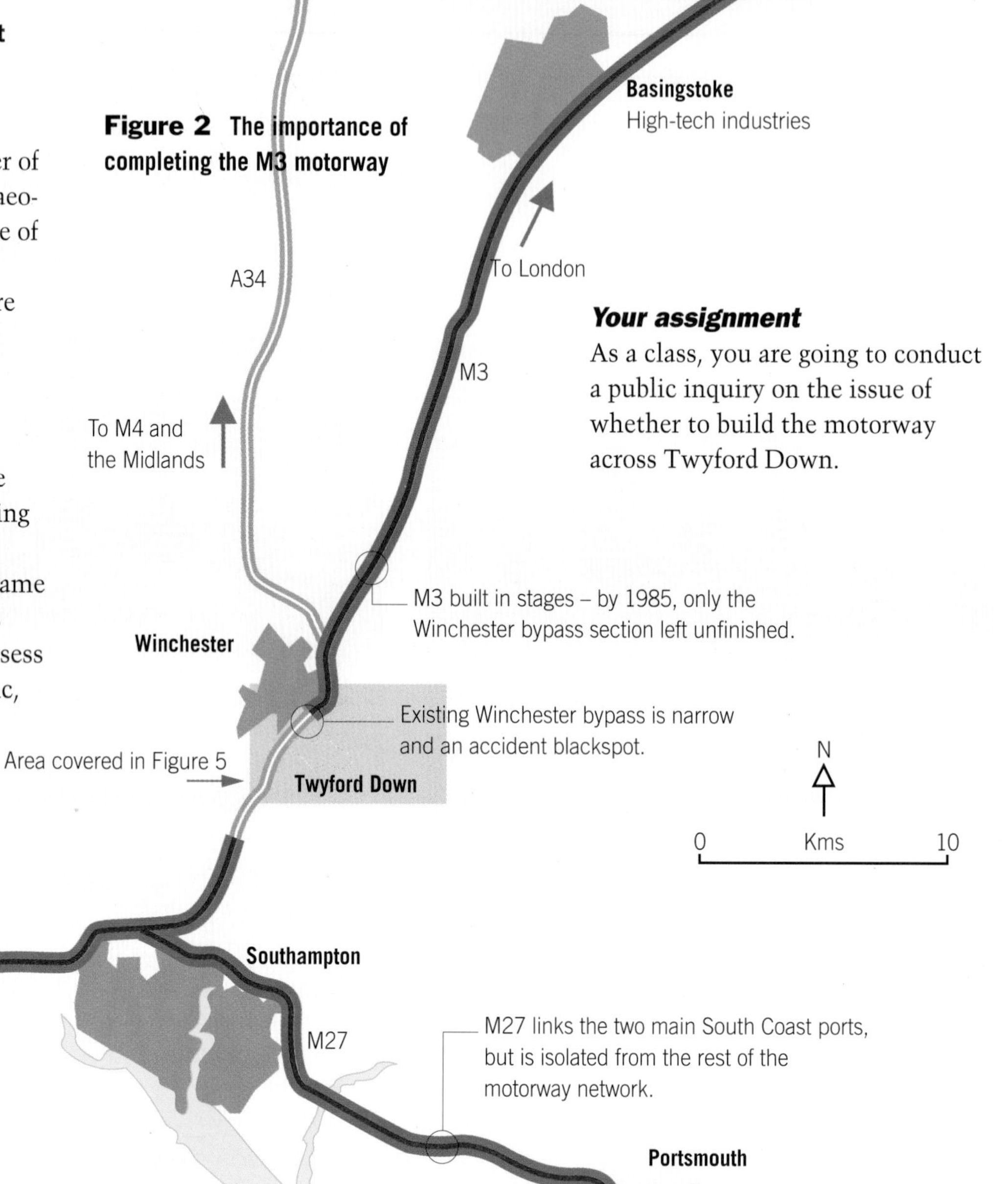

Your assignment

As a class, you are going to conduct a public inquiry on the issue of whether to build the motorway across Twyford Down.

Figure 1 Twyford Down

Figure 3 **What makes Twyford Down special?**

- Rich in flora and fauna
- Home to the rare Chalkhill Blue butterfly
- Two Sites of Special Scientific Interest (SSSIs)
- Popular for recreation
- 'Backcloth' for historic city of Winchester
- Celtic field systems
- Bronze Age burial grounds
- Site of Iron Age village
- Legendary resting place of King Arthur

Figure 4 Traffic congestion and road construction, Twyford Down

Figure 5 Which route for the missing link?

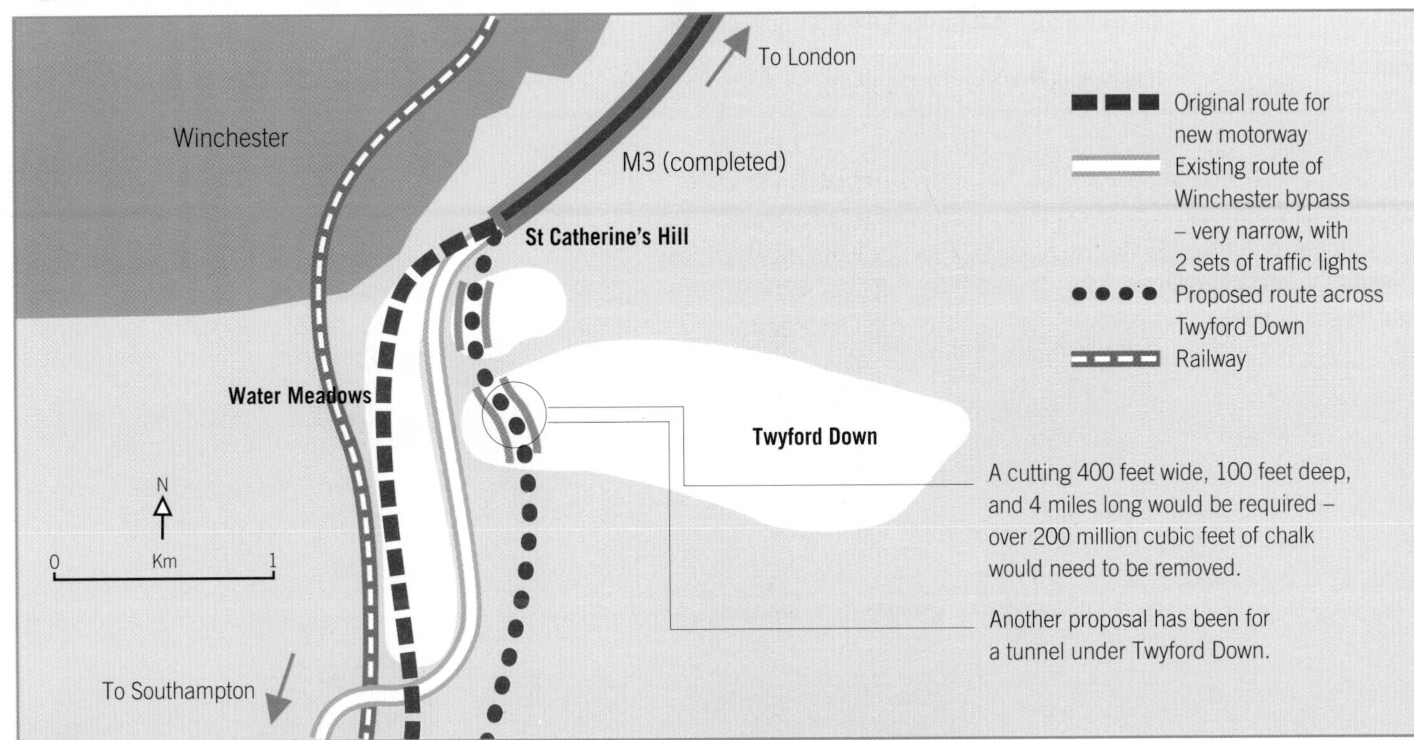

Figure 6 Views and opinions

Government minister

"This motorway is vital. It links the important south coast ports with the rest of the country. Obviously some sacrifices have to be made. After all, you can't make an omelette without breaking the eggs!"

Environmentalist

"What has this motorway brought us? I'll tell you ... bulldozers instead of butterflies, razor wire instead of orchids, and tarmac instead of trees. And that's called progress!"

Building contractor

"If this motorway isn't built there are 300 people working on this site who'll be on the dole! I've got a job to do and these protestors don't make it any easier."

Businesswoman

"My time is money! I regularly spend an hour a day in traffic jams. The motorway cannot be completed too soon! Of course I'm sorry about the butterflies, but there are other chalkland downs."

Teacher at Winchester College

"The college owned Twyford Down, but the DoT compulsory purchased it from us. We protested, but you can't win!"

Local resident

"What do planners know? Will their lives be affected by this motorway? It's us who'll have to put up with the construction traffic, the dirt, the noise, and the pollution."

Work Programme

- *Stage 1 Considering the arguments.*
  The class should divide into two groups, one in favour of the new motorway across Twyford Down, and the other opposed to it. As a group, discuss the reasons why you hold this view. After the discussion, individually produce an A4 leaflet or poster to be given out before the public inquiry setting out the reasons for your views.
- *Stage 2 Putting forward your case.*
  Each half of the class should decide on four 'witnesses' that they will call to give 'evidence' at the public inquiry. In smaller groups, carefully prepare what each witness will say, making sure that they can back up their case with facts and figures.
- *Stage 3 Holding the inquiry.*
  You will need a chairperson to ensure fair play and that everybody's arguments are heard. Each 'side' should take it in turns to present a witness, who may be questioned once all the witnesses have given their evidence.
- *Stage 4 Reaching a decision.*
  At the close of the inquiry, take a vote on whether or not the new road should be allowed - voting for yourself, not the role that you have been taking. In reality, the public inquiry would make a recommendation to the Secretary of State for the Environment, who then makes the final decision. Write a letter to the Secretary of State with your own recommendation, supporting it with as many reasons as possible.

Land of contrasts

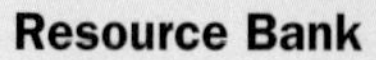

Resource Bank

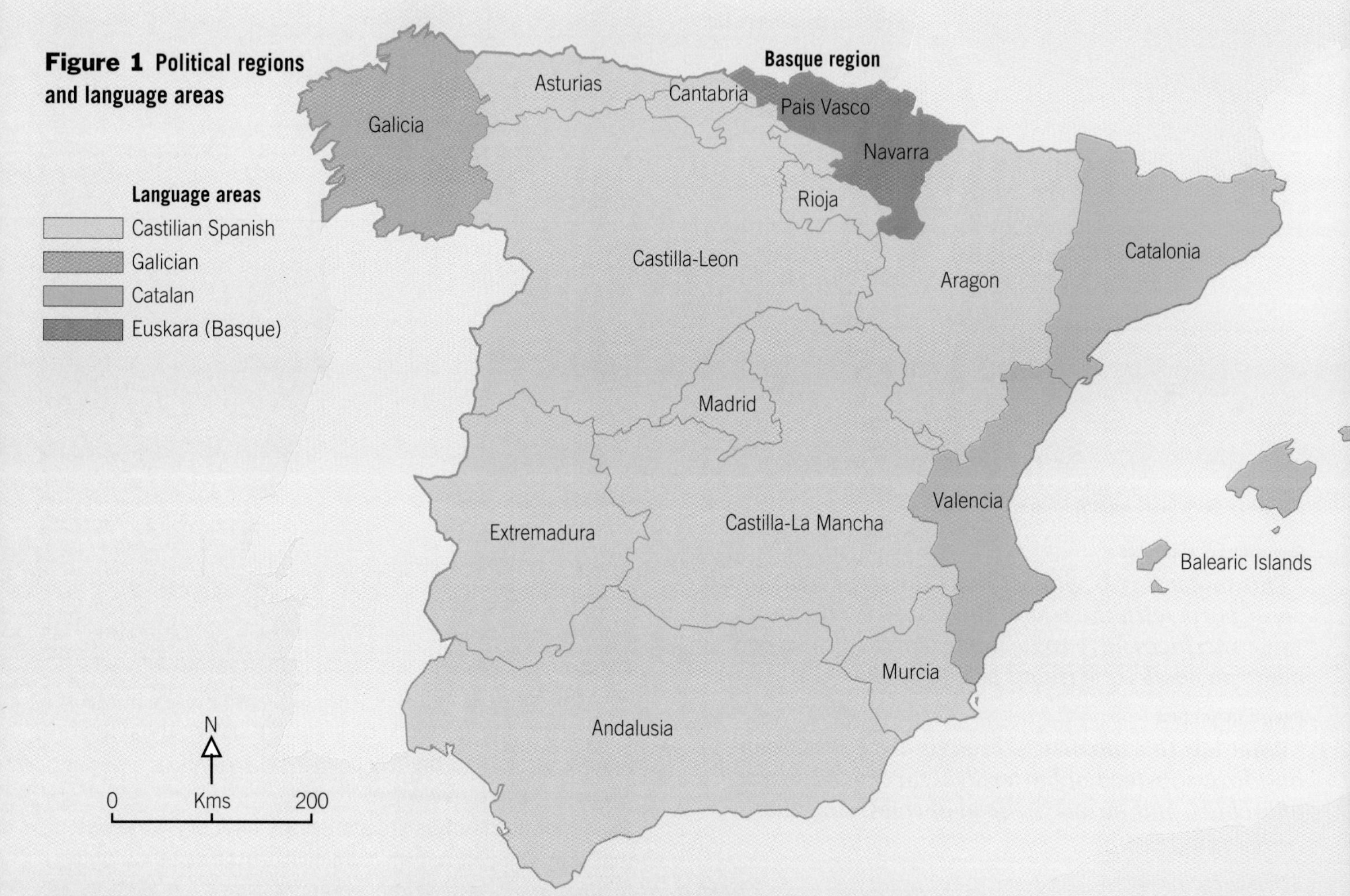

Figure 1 Political regions and language areas

Figure 2

- Spain is the second-largest country in Western Europe, occupying 85 per cent of the Iberian peninsula. Spain also includes the Balearic Islands and the Canary Islands.
- Its size and history mean that there is no one 'typical' Spain - it is a land of contrasts. The terrain, climate, language, and way of life of the people vary greatly throughout the peninsula.
- Until the late 1950s, Spain was largely a poor farming country. Now it is mainly an industrial and urban country. The tourist industry is the mainstay of the economy. Modern, large cities have developed, leaving many country areas almost empty. The central Meseta area is thinly populated, with the coastal regions containing most of the people.

Figure 3 Spain factfile

Area	504 780 sq km
Population	
1990	39.2 million
2000	40.7 million (estimate)
Capital city	Madrid
Major Religion	Roman Catholic
Major Language	Spanish (Castilian)
Currency	Peseta
Head of State	King (Juan Carlos I)
GNP	(1989) $358 352 million per year (5% agriculture, 9% industry, 86% services)
GNP per head	(1989) $9150
Land use	41% arable, 20% pasture, 31% forest, 8% other
Major Exports	Machinery and transport equipment, electrical goods, fruit and vegetables, iron and steel
Major Imports	Machinery and transport equipment, petroleum products

Figure 4 Spain time-line

- 600 BC Greeks settle in the north-east.
- 200 BC Romans settle.
- 300 Visigothic tribes and the foundation of the Christian Kingdom of Spain.
- 711 Moors (Muslim Arabs) invade.
- 1492 Last Moors expelled from Granada. Christopher Columbus sets out to discover the 'New World'.
- 1500 Exploration of the New World and growth of the Spanish Empire.
- 1588 Defeat of Armada. Period of Spanish decline.
- 1701 War of Spanish Succession.
- 1808-14 Peninsular War against Napoleon.
- 1898 War with USA - loss of remaining Spanish colonies in New World.
- 1936-39 Spanish Civil War.
- 1939-75 General Francisco Franco. Dictatorship, opposed to change.
- 1975 King Juan Carlos (grandson of Alfonso XIII) restores democracy.
- 1980 King becomes Head of State, Spain's 17 regions run their own affairs by regional parliaments.
- 1986 Spain joins EC.

Figure 5 Population statistics for Spain

	Birth rate *(per 1000 people)*	Death rate *(per 1000 people)*	Life expectancy *(years)* Male	Life expectancy *(years)* Female	Infant mortality *(per cent of babies dead before first birthday)*	Population density *(per sq km)*	Urban population *(per cent of total population)*
1950	20	10	62	66	6.0	55	52
1970	22	9	70	76	2.1	67	66
1990	13	9	74	80	0.9	78	78
2000 *(estimate)*	-	-	-	-	-	81	83

Figure 6 Climate graphs. Santander is on the north coast, Madrid is in central Spain, and Malaga is on the Costa del Sol in the south

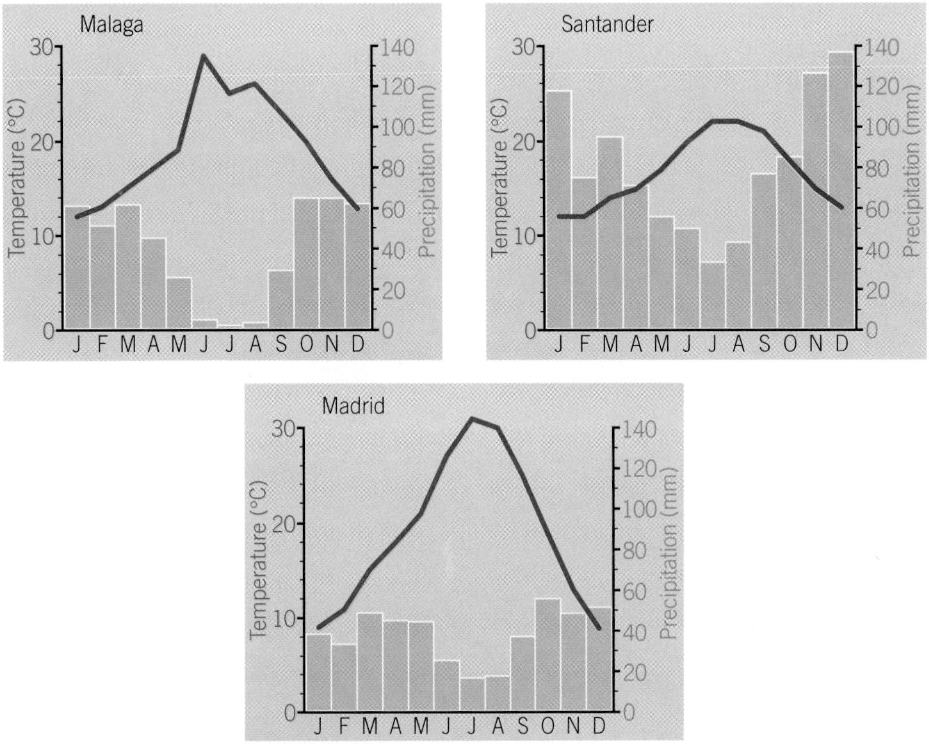

Figure 7 Spain's ten largest cities

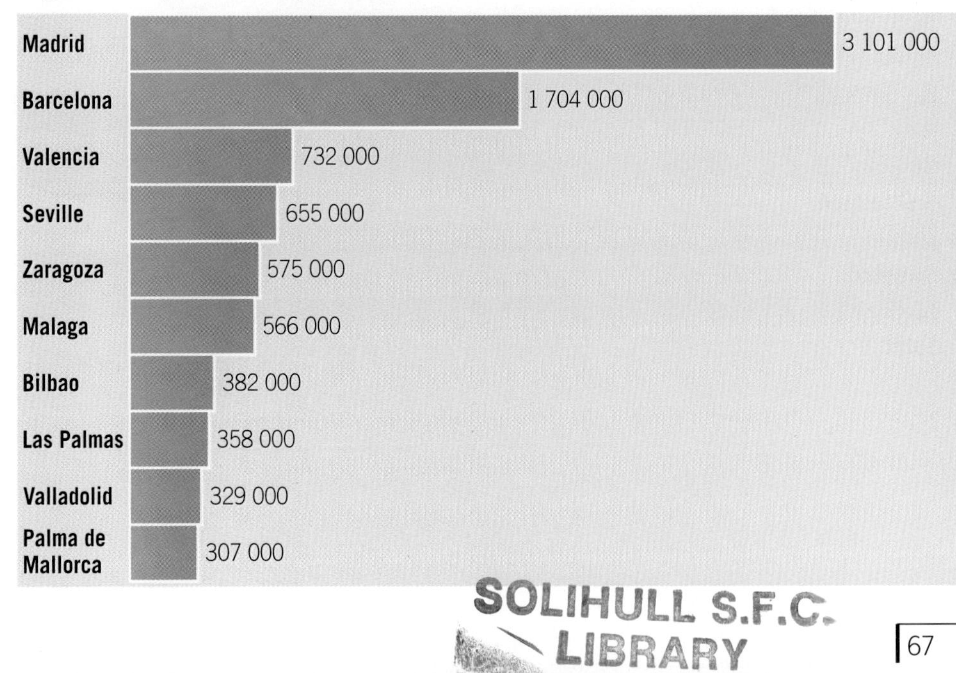

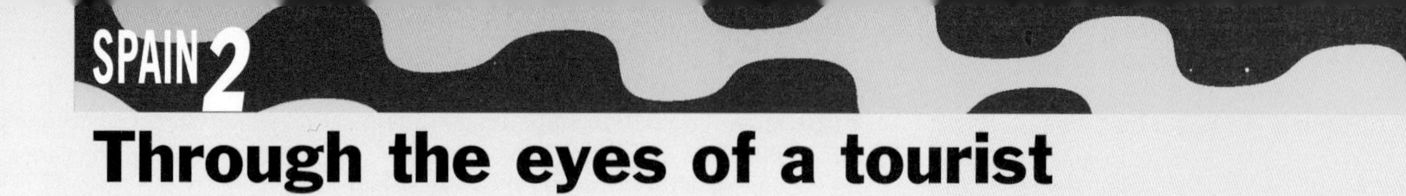

Through the eyes of a tourist

Figure 1
The importance of tourism varies considerably across Spain

Importance of tourism index
Spain = 100

- >150
- 125-150
- 100-124
- 75-99
- 50-74
- <50

N

0 Kms 200

Canary Islands

0 Kms 100

Figure 2 Origin of tourists arriving in Spain, 1989

	By air	By road	Total
France	675 695	10 780 401	11 994 421
Portugal	53 632	9 281 173	10 044 244
UK	6 462 071	617 325	7 345 831
Germany	3 600 707	2 913 255	6 783 753
Netherlands	674 435	1 271 272	2 034 717
Italy	478 507	19 780	1 511 618
Belgium	443 498	849 642	1 374 776
Switzerland	444 876	606 294	1 138 923
USA	411 464	195 408	953 782
Sweden	685 781	126 236	857 997
EC (EUR 12)	13 650 518	28 948 581	45 160 427
Total	17 007 087	32 603 437	54 057 562

Figure 3 A postcard from Spain

Spain, Tuesday 7th
Dear Gran,
I'm having a really exciting holiday, I loved going on the plane. The weather's really hot and the sun hasn't stopped shining since we got here. I'm already going very brown! We were met at the airport by the rep from the holiday company and he organised everything for us. I haven't had to use the Spanish that I learnt at school at all yet. Our hotel is great and has a beautiful pool, nicer than the beach which is very crowded. I was a bit worried that I wouldn't like the food, but its OK - we had steak and kidney pie and chips last night. Dad says that the drinks are really cheap! Tomorrow we're going on a coach trip up into the mountains to see a pretty hill village and to visit a craft centre.
Hope you are well. See you soon.

Love Jane xxx

Mrs V. Johnson
14 Mulberry Court
Wincanton
Somerset
UNITED KINGDOM

Jane's postcard in Figure 3 is typical of many millions sent from Spain every year. Different people go to Spain for their holidays for many different reasons. These include the weather, the beaches, the nightlife, and the local customs and culture. However, many tourists do not see the 'real Spain'. Instead, they see only a small part of the country that has been adapted to their needs. For example, very few Spanish people drink British beer and eat British food, but they are both available in many Spanish holiday resorts.

Tourism in Spain grew rapidly in the late 1960s and 1970s, much as it did in other countries of Southern Europe. This was because people had more money to spare and longer paid holidays from work, and because there was an increase in the availability of package holidays.

Tourism is now a vital part of the Spanish economy. Eighty-six per cent of its GNP is earned by services, of which tourism is a major part. In 1991, Spain earned 12 852 million ECU from tourism, which is more than any other country in the European Community. By contrast, the UK earned 8886 million ECU, and this was less than Britons spent on holidays abroad. Over 50 million people visit Spain every year and in 1991 this accounted for over 138 million nights spent in hotels. As well as providing employment in hotels, tourism creates a wide range of other jobs.

Figure 4 Growth of tourism, 1980-90

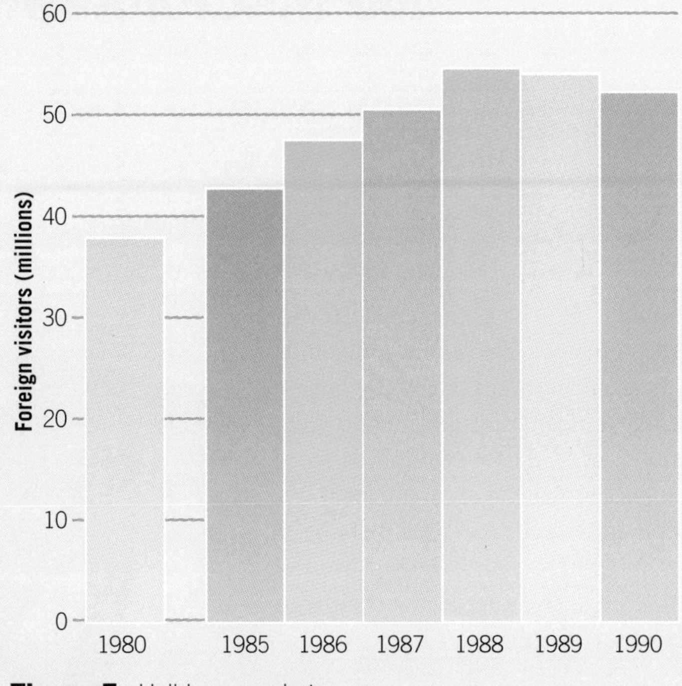

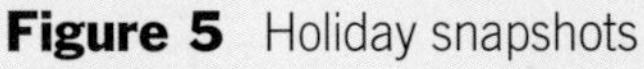

Figure 5 Holiday snapshots

Activities

1 a) How many tourists now visit Spain each year? How much money does that bring to Spain?
b) Make a list of a dozen different jobs that depend on tourism.

2 Make a detailed list of all the reasons why people go on holiday to Spain. For example, do not just put 'climate', explain what it is about the climate that attracts tourists.

3 Look closely at Figure 2.
a) Draw an outline map of Europe showing the national boundaries.
b) Use either located bar graphs or flow lines to show the origin of visitors to Spain on your outline map of Europe.

4 Study the map in Figure 1. Use the map in the Resource Bank on page 66 to identify the parts of Spain where tourism is more important than average (index >100). Make a list of these regions, giving the names of some important places in each one.

No place like home

The Costa del Sol, in common with many other parts of coastal Spain, has become home to many people from Northern Europe. For various reasons they have chosen a place in the sun away from their homeland. These 'expatriates' generally have a good standard of living and provide a much needed boost to Spain's economy. However, many local Spaniards feel that the increasing number of foreign nationals means that large areas are losing their true Spanish identity.

Figure 2 **Expatriates in Nerja**

"We retired to Spain six years ago. Our flat has beautiful views and is easy to look after, leaving us plenty of time to socialise with our friends from the large expatriate community here. We now have a phone, satellite TV, English newspapers, and lots of English goods - what more could we want? My husband is the English representative on the urbanizacion's residents committee as his Spanish is so good. He may even stand in the local elections next year - nearly half Nerja's electorate is foreign. Most of my time is taken up with the Anglican Church in Nerja. It is very active and a good way to meet people - we have lots of fun. Our doctor is Spanish, but speaks both English and German; she's in great demand. Earlier this year she was wonderful when my husband had to go into hospital. We miss our grandchildren of course, but we've got the phone now and we do get to see them when they come for their holidays!"

Figure 1 **Developments in Nerja**

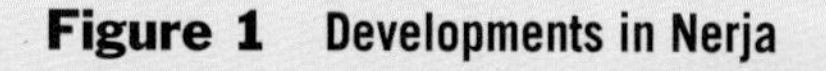

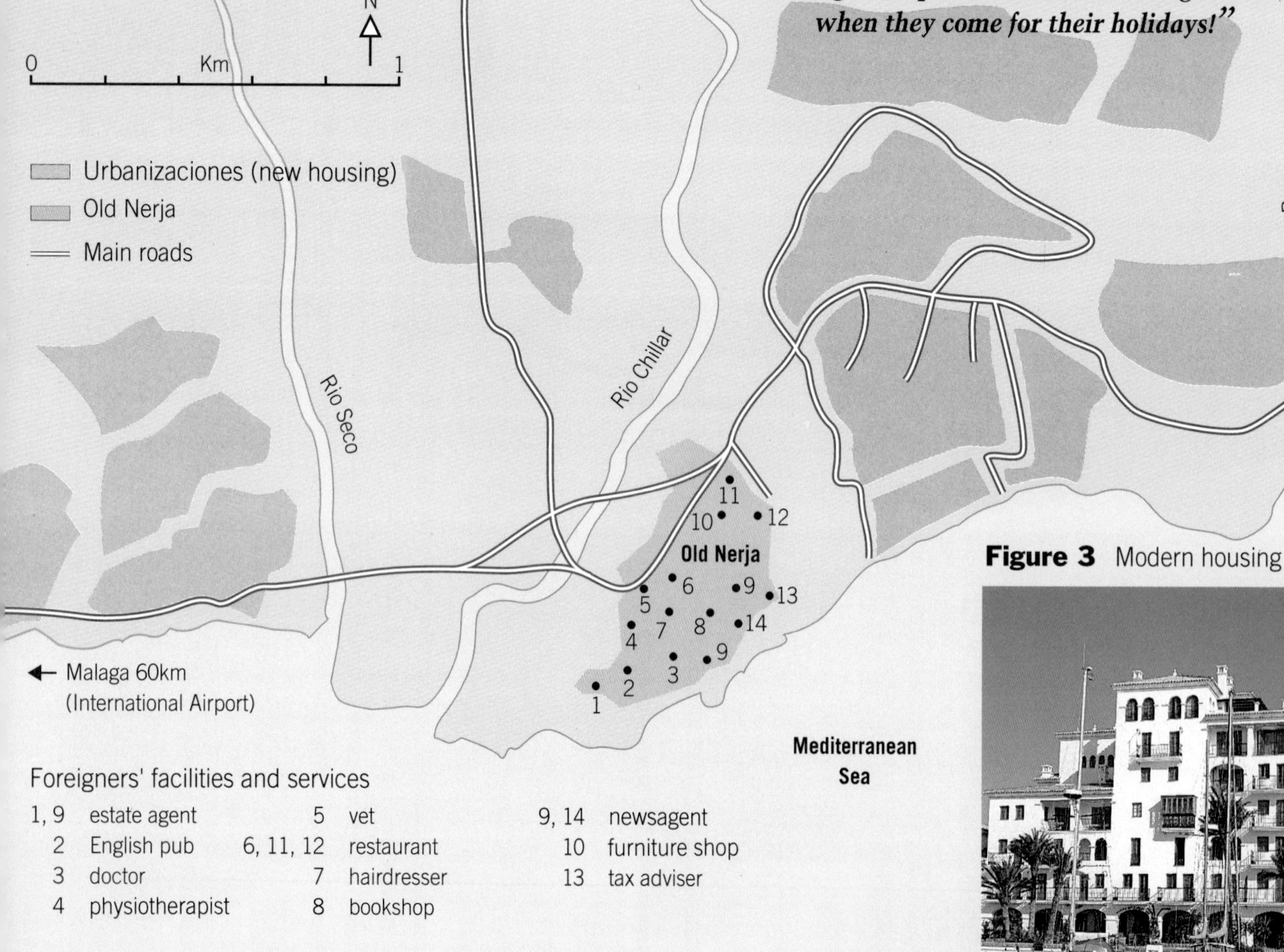

Foreigners' facilities and services

1, 9	estate agent	5	vet	9, 14	newsagent
2	English pub	6, 11, 12	restaurant	10	furniture shop
3	doctor	7	hairdresser	13	tax adviser
4	physiotherapist	8	bookshop		

Figure 3 Modern housing

Wolfgang and Elsa von Papen

"My wife and I have been coming to Nerja for over fifteen years. Our villa is in Torrox, within walking distance of the sea. Over the years we've extended it and built our own swimming pool. We now spend nearly six months of each year here. Consequently, we've applied for our residencia as we hope to move here permanently when I retire in the next year or so. I certainly won't miss the cold winters in Berlin! We have made some very good friends among the strong German community in Torrox, as well as Spaniards and other nationalities."

"We moved to Nerja in 1987 when I was made redundant back in Scotland. After working in an English-owned bar for a while, we opened our own book shop. We sell English books, newspapers, greetings cards, and anything else that the expats want. We've done very well, even if the hours are long - most shops in Spain stay open until at least nine in the evening, but with a siesta at lunchtime. We have a flat close to the shop, but would like to move out of town so that our sons can have a garden to play in. They go to the local school where they are very happy. Their Spanish is excellent! In the winter months the shop is relatively quiet as there are fewer British people around. So to make a little bit of extra money I take a minibus full of people up to ski in the Sierra Nevada once or twice a week."

Bill and Judy Smith

Figure 4 Nerja town centre

Activities

1 Read the different 'stories' in Figure 2. Use them to help you make a list of all the reasons why people from Northern Europe might go to live on the Costa del Sol.

2 What problems would a new foreign resident face when first arriving in a town like Nerja?

3 Make a list of the advantages and disadvantages of foreign residents to Nerja.

4 Imagine that you are working for a property development company in Nerja. A recently-completed estate of houses is still half empty. You must design an advertisement to be placed in *The Times* newspaper aimed at attracting people to go and live in Nerja. In your advertisement you should mention all the attractions that Nerja has to offer foreign residents. Your boss has given you the map in Figure 1 to start you off.

Madrid

Madrid is the capital city of Spain. It lies in the centre of the Iberian peninsula on a plateau 655 metres above the sea. It lies a long way from the coast and, as a result, its climate is very extreme. In winter, the temperature can drop as low as -14°C, whilst in summer it can rise to 42°C. Some people describe the climate as '9 months of winter and 3 months of hell'!

The city owes its name to the original Moorish settlement which was named after a small, insignificant stream; the Majrit. It was only in 1561, when King Philip II moved the court there from Toledo, that Madrid became the political capital of Spain. It did not grow quickly because of its isolated geographical position and a lack of mineral deposits. It was not until the road and railway improvements of the nineteenth century that Madrid became an industrial centre as well as an administrative one. The inhabitants of Madrid, the Madrilenos, now number over 3 million. Unlike other large European cities, Madrid is not surrounded by large suburbs. This means that the city ends and the countryside begins very quickly.

Figure 1
The Plaza de Espana. Madrid has an extensive underground railway or Metro system. It was built largely in the 1970s and has gone some way to overcoming the problems of traffic congestion brought about by increasing car ownership and an overcrowded road network

Figure 2
The Sunday flea market (El Rastro) in Old Madrid. Most Madrilenos live in apartments, usually in tall buildings. Nearly 70 per cent of people have bought or are buying their own homes. Urban living standards have risen rapidly in recent years

Figure 3
The Plaza de la Cibeles. Madrid has many sites for tourists to visit. These include the Royal Palace, the Cortes (parliament), the Plaza Major (a seventeenth century square where heretics were once burned at the stake), and the Prado (Spain's foremost museum and art gallery)

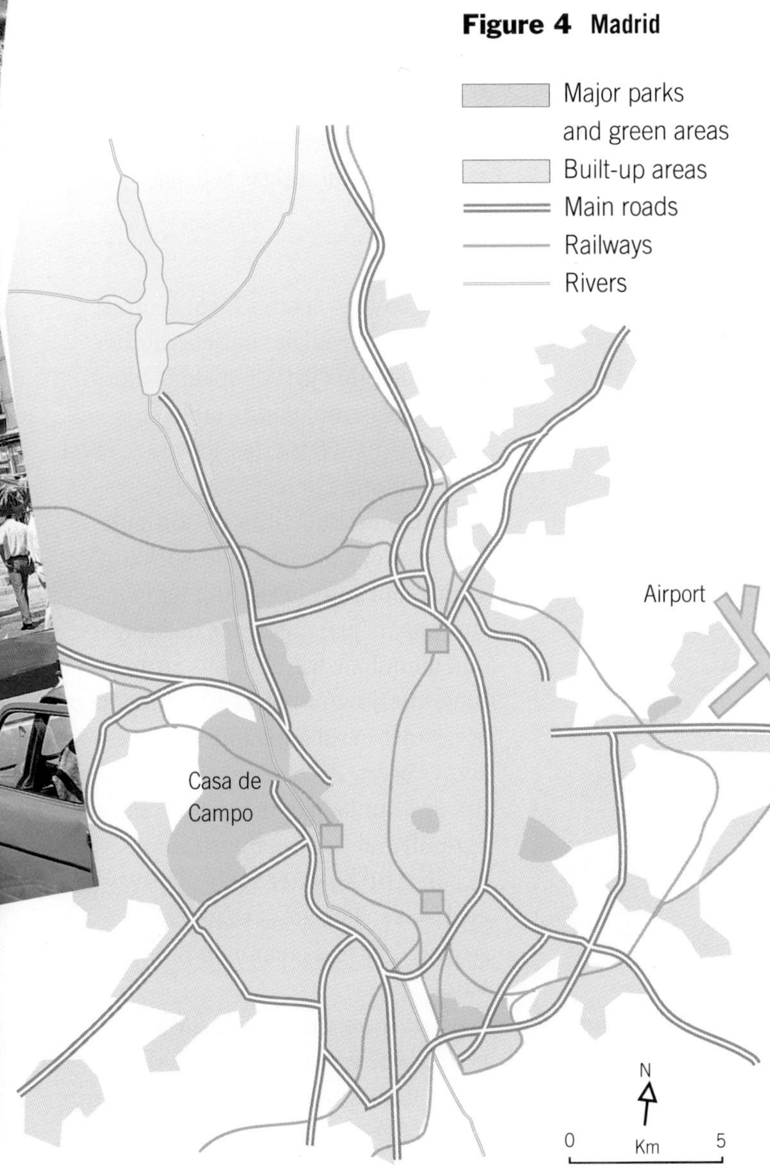

Figure 4 Madrid

Visitors to Madrid have the impression that there are several Madrids. In fact, the city does consist of different centres that are clearly separate and have a personality and function of their own.

Old Madrid can be divided into different architectural districts. Some of the famous buildings include the Plaza Mayor, a seventeenth century square of houses over shops or restaurants. In the past it has been the scene of bull-fights, executions, fairs, and popular markets. Other buildings include the Plaza de la Villa (Town Hall), the Mayor's Palace, and the Royal Palace, which replaced an older fortress destroyed by fire in 1734. Madrid has many parks and gardens, but the most famous and most popular with the Madrilenos is the Parque del Buen Retiro. It is Madrid's largest and most beautiful park.

The nineteenth century was a time of considerable urban development with the construction of civil buildings, squares, and boulevards. Madrid is a focus of communications because of its central position, as well as being Spain's chief administrative and financial centre, with the Royal Court and the national parliament. Today, the city is the base for Spain's national newspapers and television and the offices of many international companies. Since the 1950s, Madrid's population has more than doubled, many living in thousands of blocks of modern flats. Many industries have sprung up in and around the city. Their products include motor vehicles, chemicals, textiles, and leather goods.

Activities

1 Write a paragraph about Madrid, to include something about its location, climate, population, and history.

2 a) Madrid has grown considerably in the last 150 years. Give some reasons for the city's growth.
b) How has the rapid increase in population since 1950 changed the urban landscape?

3 After studying these pages about Madrid, decide whether or not you would like to live there. Why did you choose the way that you did?

4 Using an atlas to help you, work out the distance from Madrid to the other principal cities of Spain (see Figure 7 in the Resource Bank on pages 66-67). Present your findings in the form of a table like you might find in a road atlas.

Rural Spain

Figure 1 The Meseta

Figure 2 The main physical regions of Spain

Figure 3 Population figures for Madrid

Age group	Per cent of population	
	Males	Females
85+	0.1	0.5
80-84	0.2	0.8
75-79	0.4	1.1
70-74	1.5	1.7
65-69	1.7	1.9
60-64	1.9	2.1
55-59	2.6	2.7
50-54	3.2	3.1
45-49	3.1	3.1
40-44	2.9	3.0
35-39	3.3	3.3
30-34	3.5	3.4
25-29	3.4	3.4
20-24	3.9	3.7
15-19	4.0	4.0
10-14	4.4	4.4
5-9	4.7	4.5
0-4	4.3	4.1

Figure 4 Population pyramid for Guadalajara, a town on the Meseta

Males Age Females

85+ 80-84 75-79 70-74 65-69 60-64 55-59 50-54 45-49 40-44 35-39 30-34 25-29 20-24 15-19 10-14 5-9 0-4

5 4 3 2 1 0 % 0 1 2 3 4 5

The Meseta is Spain's high, central plateau. In Spanish, 'meseta' means 'table' and this part of Spain is like a high, gently undulating table. It is largely over 500 metres above sea-level.

The climate of the Meseta is extreme, making life very difficult. The winters are very cold with high winds, but in summer the temperatures soar. The area once had forests and abundant wildlife, but farmers have cut down the trees, turning large areas into scrubland and, in places, semi-desert. As most of the Meseta is dry and sunbaked, it has little or no agricultural use except for things needing little water such as olives or cork oaks. The areas that can be irrigated have a greater agricultural value.

Apart from the crowded Madrid region, the central Meseta is thinly populated. Life is hard, and agriculture is really the only economic activity.

Spain has many mountainous areas. In fact, 5 per cent of the land is over 1500 metres above sea-level (Britain's highest mountain, Ben Nevis, is only 1347m high). Like on the Meseta, life in the mountains is hard. Most people struggle to make a living. In the north are the Cantabrian Mountains. This is 'Green Spain', with ample rainfall and lush forests. These mountains, together with the Pyrenees, are the centre of Spain's forestry industry.

Spain's highest mainland peak, Mulhacen (3478m), is in the Sierra Nevada. These mountains in the south are much drier than the mountains in the north. Much of the precipitation falls during the winter as snow, and the trees have adapted to withstand long periods of drought. The mountain towns and villages are found on hill-top sites, originally for safety. Here the houses are huddled together along narrow streets and are painted white to reflect the sun in an effort to keep them cool.

The Sierra Nevada's closeness to the Costa del Sol makes it possible for tourists to combine a few days skiing with a beach holiday during the winter months.

Figure 5 A scene from Cantabria

Figure 6 Causes and effects of migration from rural Spain

	1950	1970	1990	2000
Urban population *(% of total)*	52%	66%	78%	est. 83%

Causes
- Better standard of living
- Technical improvements mean less workers required
- Perception of a better life
- Few or poor services
- Paid employment
- Economy dependent on climate

Effects
- Unsightly high-rise apartment blocks
- Declining villages
- Ageing populations
- Overcrowding
- Urban unemployment
- Crime rate increases
- Problems of pollution
- Farmland abandoned

Activities

1 a) Study Figure 4 and then describe the population structure of Guadalajara.

b) Using Figure 3, draw a similar population pyramid for Madrid.

c) Describe and explain the differences between the two pyramids.

2 Write an account describing life in rural Spain. It should include sections on life-styles and economic activity, as well as how these are affected by the climate and the physical terrain.

3 Make a large copy of Figure 6. Study the labels showing causes and effects of migration. Annotate your diagram, putting the labels in their correct places. Can you think of two more causes and effects?

Agricultural change

Assignment

Background information

As in other Western European countries, major changes have taken place in farming in Spain over the last thirty years.

Your assignment

You will investigate some of the reasons for these changes, and the impact that they have had on farmers and on Spanish society as a whole.

Figure 2 The Vigon farm at the present time

0 Metres 200

Farm

← Malaga

Nerj

Mediterranean Sea

- Main road
- Track to farm buildings
- Contours at 50m intervals
- Seasonal watercourse
- Well, source of domestic and irrigation water
- Farm boundary
- Market gardening (beans, tomatoes)
- Rough grazing
- Orange grove
- Almond grove
- Olive grove

Note: The soils get deeper towards the sea. At the top of the farm they are very thin and stony.

Figure 1 The Vigon family

Senor Carlos Vigon died a year ago, leaving the family farm to his two sons, Alberto and Francisco. In an attempt to ensure the continuity of the farm, he said in his will that neither of them could sell their share of the farm for five years.

Name Alberto Vigon
Age 25 years
Present occupation Farm labourer
Background
Left school at 16. Married with two children. Worked on family farm with father since leaving school. Sees no reason to change farm as it was good enough for father and grandfather.

Name Francisco Vigon
Age 29 years
Present occupation Banking
Background
Went to university in Madrid. Unmarried. Keen to go back into farming and develop the family farm as a business.

Figure 3 Newspaper article by Spain's Minister of Agriculture

Calling all Spanish farme..

Since joining the EC in 1986, our agriculture has had to face intense competition from other EC nations such as France and Italy. The Ministry of Agriculture urges you to think of farming as an industry which must be modern and efficient. Only then will we be able to feed the nation and earn sufficient money from exports to finance the building of more schools, hospitals, and the like. It will also mean greater individual prosperity for you, the farmer!

There is a great deal of help available to you to achieve this transition. It comes from both your own government and from the EC. These are just some of the schemes open to you:

a) Grants are available to assist with the cost of:
- clearing and improving your land;
- improving the accessibility of your farm;
- installing irrigation systems;
- planting export orientated crops such as oranges and avocados;
- fencing and other security measures.

b) Low interest loans are available which can be paid back over ten years or more.

c) There are technical and financial departments to advise you.

d) The government supports cooperatives and self- help schemes set up by farmers.

Act today! The country needs your support. Get more details from your local Ministry office.

and I hope that she'll be out of hospital soon.

As you are thinking about the future of your farm, I thought that I'd tell you about the changes that I made to my farm and the effects that they have had. Financially, I'm sure that I will be better off in the long run, but at the moment I'm out of pocket. I had to hire someone to help me fill in all the forms for the grants and so on! What's more, the trees that I planted won't fruit for several years and so aren't earning me anything!

I had to get rid of old Rafael, even though he'd worked for me for 15 years. The farm is now more mechanised so I don't need any labourers.

The local conservation group have been on to me as well. They say that I've destroyed the habitat of wild animals by clearing the land. They also claim that I'll suffer from increased erosion as there are less trees to protect the soil. I must admit that the soil doesn't seem as fertile as it once did, and the intensive cropping means that I have to use lots of expensive fertilisers.

Figure 4 Letter from an uncle to Alberto and Francisco

Figure 5 New developments in farming

- Huge areas of southern Spain have been covered with greenhouses, leading many people to dub it the 'Costa del Plastic'. They provide warmth and shelter from the wind, meaning that this semi-desert region can produce intensive crops such as strawberries and peppers.
- Irrigation has helped to transform the arid south of Spain. Dams in the Sierra Nevada regulate the supply which is then transferred to areas of need by large canals.
- The advent of refrigerated transport and a better road network have made it possible for Spanish farm produce to arrive in the supermarkets of Europe looking as fresh as when it was harvested.

Work Programme A

- Working with a partner, study the information about farming in Spain and how it has been changing.
- Design an information sheet which would give people a good idea about farming in Spain today.

Work Programme B

- Working with a partner, imagine that you are the brothers who have just inherited the farm. One of you wants to develop the farm, the other does not.
- You should each prepare a case in support of your viewpoint, stating what you want to do and why.
- Take it in turns to put your case to the other brother.
- Try to agree on a compromise course of action. Write a joint plan outlining the future of your farm.

Figure 6 Farming facts

Land use (per cent of total area)	
Arable	31.2
Permanent crops	9.6
Grassland	20.4
Forest	31.4
Other	7.4

Per cent of workforce in agriculture	
1944	52
1964	35
1970	26
1980	17
1990	11

Tractors in use (thousands)	
1950	15
1970	261
1980	524
1990	720

Fertiliser consumption (Kg/ha)	
1970	37.9
1980	53.2
1990	65.2

Agricultural production (thousand tonnes)	1950	1970	1990
Barley	1909	3922	9325
Peaches	94	233	751
	(8.7% of world total)		
Butter	6	7	26
Strawberries	3	10	227
	(9.6% of world total)		
Oranges	975	1884	2457
	(4.8% of world total)		
Horses *(000 head)*	686	287	241

(Spain is the largest producer of olives in the world, with 33 per cent of the world total. It also produces 35 per cent of the world's olive oil.)

Industrial change

Resource Bank

Figure 1 Spanish industry

The Cornisa Cantabria

The traditional Atlantic coast industrial region made up of Pais Basque, Cantabria, and Asturias provinces. However, this area is now often termed 'the Spain in crisis'. The reasons for this include:

1. Original strength based on physical resources and nineteenth century links with industrial Europe.
2. Crisis in 'traditional' industries.
3. Huge job losses due to industrial change and de-industrialisation.
4. Pais Basque unemployment 2.4 per cent in 1975, 25.1 per cent in 1987.
5. Traditional livestock raising under pressure from EC competition.
6. Infrastructure too run-down or inappropriate for new activities.
7. Buildings old and environment can be unpleasant.
8. Labour organisations resistant to change.
9. Area marginalised by European communications network.

— New rail link
═ Motorway
Major fishing grounds

In the mid-1980s, a third of Spain's 1700 fishing boats were considered ill-equipped for modern needs. The EC has called for big cuts in the Spanish fishing fleet.

La Coruna
El Ferrol
Gijon
Santander
Bilbao
Leon
Zn
Fe
Burgos
Pamplona
Zaragoza
Madrid
Barcelona
Valencia
Palma de Mallorca
Cu
Pb
Seville
Pb
Murcia
Cadiz
Fe

Shipbuilding

The major centres of shipbuilding in Spain are El Ferrol in Galicia and Cadiz in Andalusia. The shipyards were nationalised in the 1980s in an attempt to cope with a slump in world demand and soaring financial losses. The workforce has now been cut by over 50 per cent, but the losses are still huge.

Main mineral deposits

Fe Iron
Zn Zinc
Pb Lead
Cu Copper

South-North divide

Spain's economic and industrial development has come to be characterised by a South-North divide, the greatest development being in the North. Many of Spain's industries are still small scale (with fewer than 50 employees). This is likely to change if Spain is to remain competitive.

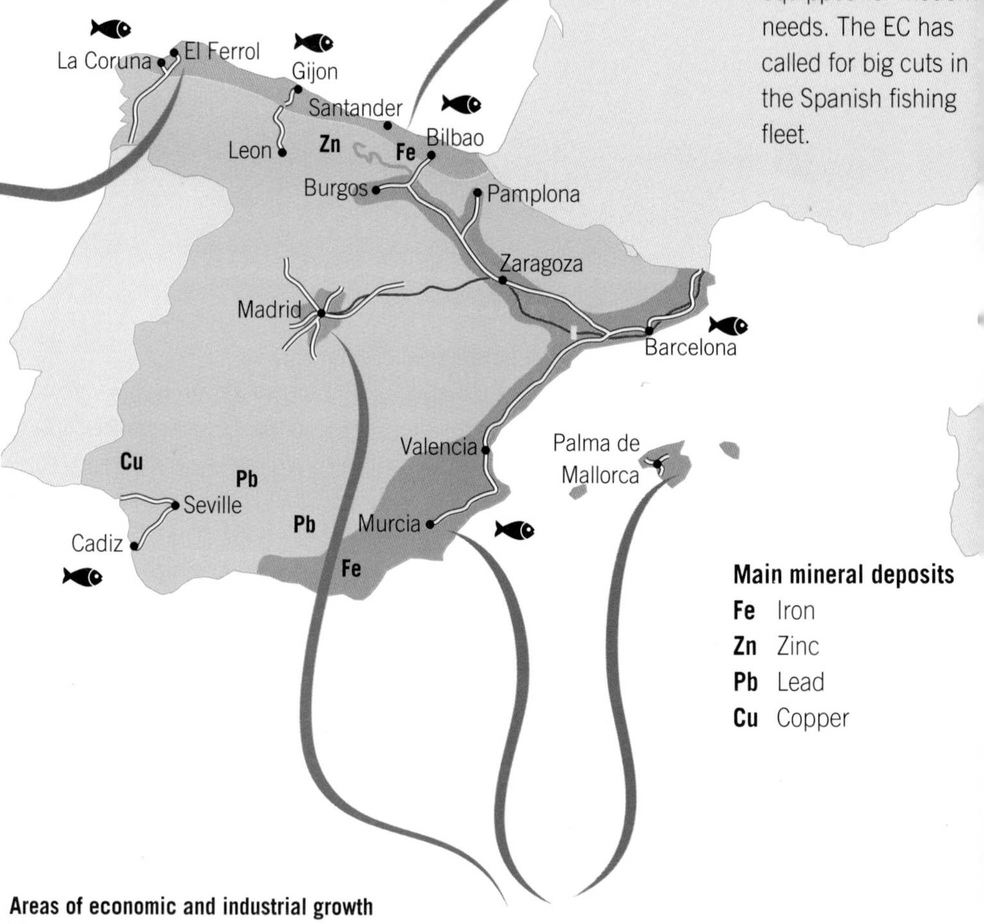

Areas of economic and industrial growth

These areas are:

- The Ebro valley;
- The Balearic Islands;
- The Canary Islands (not shown on this map);
- The Mediterranean Axis, stretching from the French border to Murcia province. In this region, 28 per cent of the Spanish population live on only 13 per cent of the land and yet produce 44 per cent of the country's exports.

These areas are all characterised by:

1. record increases in wealth;
2. a strong tertiary sector;
3. specialised agriculture;
4. a flexible industrial base;
5. a diverse economy which allows rapid response to change;
6. large amounts of foreign investment (45 per cent of national total);
7. a pleasant, attractive environment;
8. a young and energetic workforce that is receptive to new ideas.

Figure 2 Industrial production, 1948-1990

	TV sets (thousands per year)	Cement (thousand tonnes per year)	Shipbuilding (thousand tonnes launched per year)	Lignite (million tonnes per year)	Aluminium (thousand tonnes per year)
1948	39	1803	22	1.4	1
1970	618	16702	926	2.8	147
1980	763	28752	509	15.4	325
1990	1233	28092	275	21.3	431

Figure 3 Ford in Spain

- Ford started making cars in the USA in 1903. The first European branch opened in 1908.
- Ford is now one of Europe's leading industrial organisations. It provides employment for 115 000 people in fifteen European countries. European plants make nearly two million units a year, with a value of over $21 billion.
- Ford vehicles have been sold in Spain since 1907.
- The assembly of Ford vehicles in Spain began in 1920, but was interrupted by the Spanish Civil War, 1936-39.
- Ford Espana SA was opened in 1973.
- Ford had record car sales in Spain in 1990 with 157 700 units (a 14.7 per cent share of the market). Truck sales were 9300 (4.1 per cent of the market).
- Ford has 9500 employees in Spain, as well as a network of 900 dealers.

Madrid Ford Espana sales company headquarters.
Almusafes, near Valencia Manufacturing complex. Produces vehicles (Fiestas, Escorts, Orions), and engines and body panels for use in other Ford plants (particularly Cologne in Germany and Dagenham in the UK).
Puerto de Santa Maria, near Cadiz A new $68 million plant to produce electronic control models is under construction.

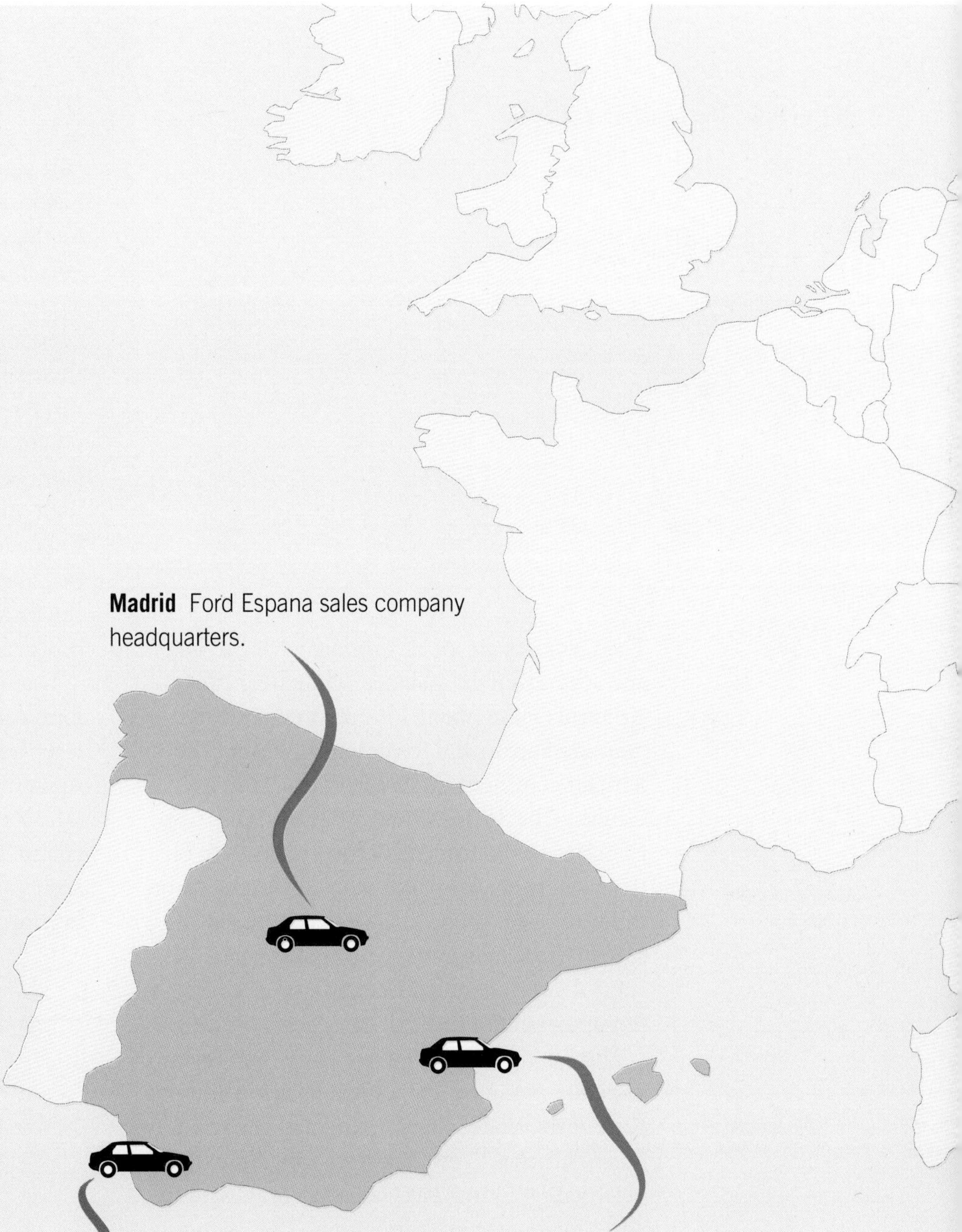

The Canaries - the impact of tourism

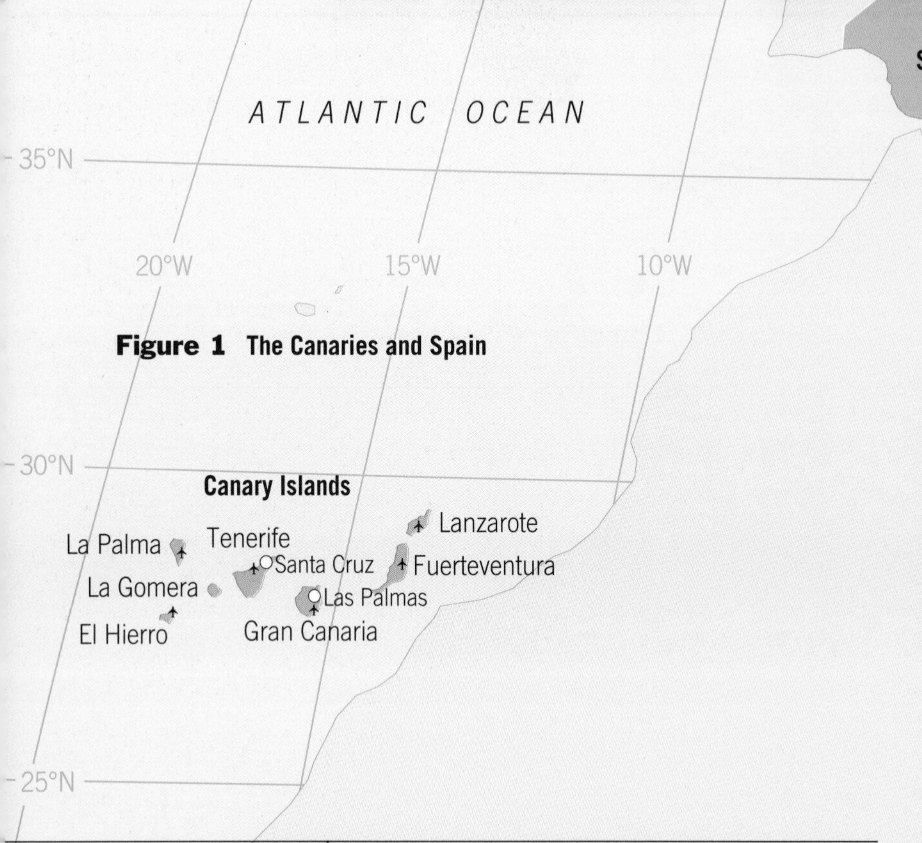

SPAIN

ATLANTIC OCEAN

35°N
30°N
25°N
20°N
20°W
15°W
10°W

Canary Islands
La Palma
Tenerife
Santa Cruz
La Gomera
El Hierro
Gran Canaria
Las Palmas
Lanzarote
Fuerteventura

AFRICA

Figure 1 **The Canaries and Spain**

The Canaries are an archipelago of seven large and several smaller islands. They lie in the Atlantic Ocean about 1500 kilometres from mainland Spain and to the north-west of the African continent, 4° North of the Tropic of Cancer. The Spanish first conquered the Canaries in the fifteenth century. Because of their position the islands were a useful stop on the way to southern Africa or Asia for sailing ships. The Canaries have been under Spanish central control since 1492 and they are likely to remain so in the future.

The Canary Islands have a climate of their own due to their geographical position and the path of the trade winds, with local variations due to altitude. Temperatures vary annually between 18°C and 24°C and the sun is said to shine every day, even in winter. The sea breezes make the islands less hot than their desert climate would imply. As a result, the Canaries are popular for holidays throughout the year.

All the Canaries were formed by volcanic eruptions of the sea-bed. Some of the islands are still active - a big eruption took place on La Palma in 1971. Each island has its own unique scenery, ranging from high peaks, valleys, and sandy deserts to sheer rock faces and forests. Not surprisingly the beaches of the Canaries are black sand, which results from lava broken up by the sea. The highest mountain in Spain is the volcano Mount Teide on Tenerife (3718m).

The Canaries play a significant part in Spain's economy. Where water is available to irrigate the rich volcanic soil the constant climate means that crops such as bananas, tomatoes, potatoes, and peppers ripen earlier than in other parts of Europe. These are exported and sold at high prices. The islands have long been important ports-of-call and trading points for international shipping, a situation promoted by the establishment of free ports. Tourism, however, continues to grow in importance.

The island of La Palma is just 47 kilometres long and 29 kilometres wide. It is dominated by a central volcanic mountain range, reaching up to its highest peak, Roque de los Muchachos, which is 2426m high. Many tourists visit the island, attracted by its magnificent natural scenery as well as its cultural and architectural heritage.

Figure 2 **Extract from tourist brochure**

The photo shows Santa Cruz de la Palma, the capital of the island. Situated on the island's east coast, it is a working port as well as the centre of the island's tourist industry

Connections

The island of La Palma can be reached by air as well as by sea. The port of Santa Cruz de la Palma has a direct ferry service with the ports of Santa Cruz de Tenerife and Las Palmas de Gran Canaria. Ship's traffic to the mainland of Spain is carried out by fruit carriers.

Daily regular flights with modern jets from Iberia airlines, connect La Palma with the other Canary Islands and Madrid.

An extensive bus service, taxis and rental cars provide transport on the island

Accommodation & other services

Santa Cruz and Los Llanos have comfortable hotels and guest houses in several categories. The restaurants offer international cuisine as well as local dishes, accompanied by the typical wines of the island. On La Palma there are a few discotheques and night clubs.

Population: 76,000

Surface area: 726 square km. (280 square miles).

Average temperature: 19°-20°C (66°-68°F)

Figure 3 **Advantages and disadvantages of tourism to La Palma**

Advantages

- Increased local employment.
- Market for local produce.
- Improved local services like electricity and water.
- Higher standard of living.
- Better communications.
- Preservation of local craft industries.
- Economic prosperity.

Disadvantages

- Loss of traditional way of life.
- Modern developments spoil landscape.
- Increased congestion and pollution.
- Many hotels owned by 'outsiders'.
- Loss of valuable farmland.
- Employment in tourism can be temporary.

Activities

1 You are the travel writer for a small local newspaper. Write a short article (maximum 500 words), with a map, outlining the advantages of the Canary Islands as a tourist destination.

2 Study the photo of Santa Cruz in Figure 2. Draw a sketch diagram of the resort showing these features: the marina, the coastline, apartment blocks and hotels, low-rise residential areas.

3 Should there be more tourist development in the Canaries? Argue for or against as if you were:
a) a local taxi driver;
b) a person who had retired to the islands.

The Gibraltar issue

Spain has changed a great deal in the last twenty years. It has changed from a Fascist dictatorship under General Franco into a modern democracy. It has developed from a relatively backward agricultural society into an advanced industrial nation. Spain's previous isolation has disappeared since it became a member of both NATO and the EC.

However, Spain still has challenges to face - challenges which involve politics and economics, and other aspects of geography. One challenge for Spain is the question of the future of Gibraltar.

Figure 1 **The location of Gibraltar**

1 Car ferry to Tangiers.
2 Shipping to and from the Suez Canal passes Gibraltar. Gibraltar is used for refueling.
3 Gibraltar 'controls' shipping in the Straits of Gibraltar, which are just 15 km wide.
4 British naval and air force base in Gibraltar until 1985.
5 Britain, about 2000 km. Gibraltar was of vital strategic importance during both World Wars.
6 Ceuta and Melilla are Spanish colonies on the African coast.

Figure 2 Gibraltar from the south, with Spain in the background

Figure 3 The site of Gibraltar

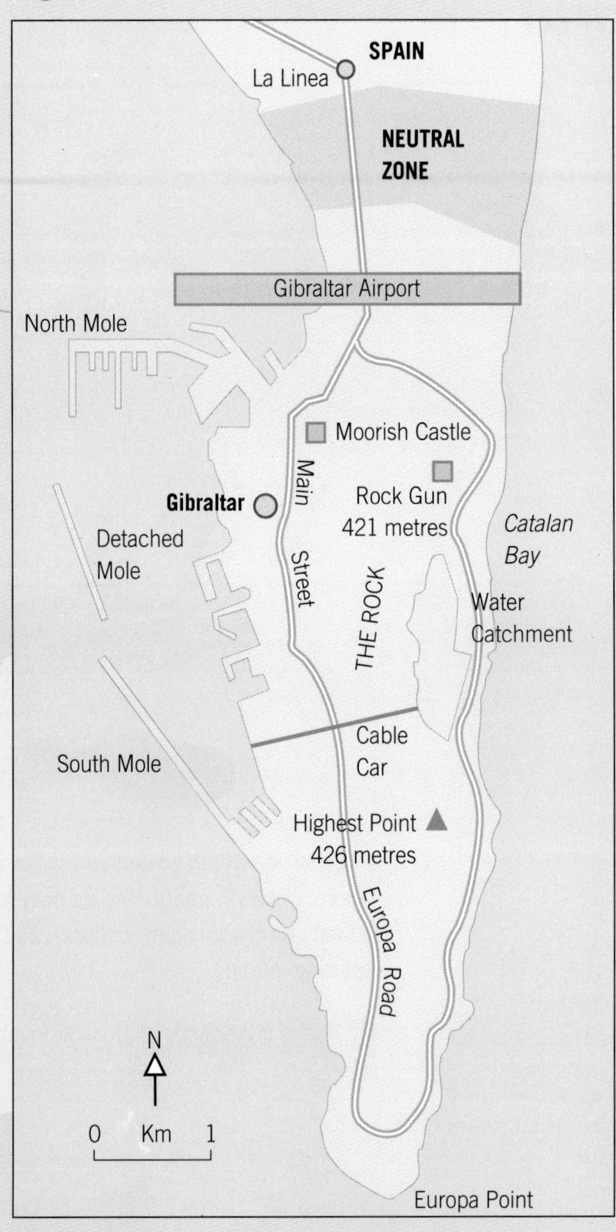

History
Settled by Moors in 711. Taken by Spain in 1462. Ceded to Britain in 1713. British Crown Colony since 1830.

Geology
The Rock is a limestone massif linked to Spain by a sandy plain. The Rock has many caves - used in the past for storing ammunition.

Size
6.5 sq km.

Wildlife
The Rock is home to the Barbary apes, the only native monkeys in Europe.

Figure 4

What is the issue?
'A little bit of Britain with added sunshine, tax-free shopping, and an intriguing history.' This is how one British holiday brochure describes Gibraltar. But ask any Spaniard and you will get a different view. They see it as part of Spain, occupied by the British for nearly 300 years. The 'Rock', as it is known locally, is a Crown Colony of the United Kingdom (in much the same way as Hong Kong is until 1997), self-governing in all respects except defence. Most of its population of around 30 000 are full British citizens, electing a seventeen-seat House of Assembly. Because of lack of space, there is no agriculture on the Rock and all food has to be imported. There is some light industry, but the main sources of income are refuelling and provisioning ships, as well as tourism. The British government also gives considerable amounts of development aid to the colony.

How and why has the issue arisen?
From a military point of view, Britain has always recognised the strategic importance of Gibraltar. It was captured from the Spanish in 1704 and was formally ceded to Britain in 1713. Spain tried to recapture the Rock several times, but the British turned it into a military fortress. Gibraltar was a vital repair and assembly point for convoys during both World Wars, and later became an important base for NATO.

What has it meant for the people?
General Franco made the last real attempt to regain Gibraltar, starting in 1965 when Spain began a blockade which lasted until 1985. During the blockade, people had great difficulties with their work, travel, and getting consumer goods. A referendum was held in Gibraltar over its future in 1967: 12 138 voted for remaining British with just 44 against. When the blockade was lifted, Spain agreed to no longer demand the Rock back, so long as Britain supported Spanish membership of the EC and NATO. The border was closed by Spain in 1969; it was reopened in 1985.

What are the possible solutions?
There are four possible futures for Gibraltar:
a) remain a British Colony;
b) become a part of Spain;
c) become an independent state;
d) become a colony of the EC.

Activity

1 Study the information about Gibraltar. For each of the possible futures, consider what are its advantages and disadvantages. Record your findings in the form of a table. Which future would you support, and why?

Spain and the world

Resource Bank

Figure 1
The Spanish-speaking world

Areas where Spanish is the main language

Areas where Spanish is spoken by a large minority

Figure 2 The Spanish language

- Twenty countries in Central and South America have Spanish as their official language.
- Most of these countries were part of the Spanish Empire until the 1820s. They are now independent, but most maintain close links with Spain.
- Brazil is the only country in South America not to have Spanish as its official language.
- Mexico has more than twice the number of Spanish-speakers as Spain itself.
- Christopher Columbus landed first in the Caribbean. Today, the Dominican Republic, Haiti, Cuba, and Puerto Rico still speak Spanish.
- In western USA, many places have Spanish names given by Spanish explorers - examples include Los Angeles (the angels) and San Francisco (St Francis).
- In the USA, the main Spanish-speaking areas are New Mexico and California. Most large cities, such as New York, have 'Spanish Quarters'.

Figure 3 Spain's alliances

Spain has been a member of the European Community (EC) since 1st January 1986.

Spain belongs to the Organisation for Economic Cooperation and Development (OECD).

Spain is a member of the United Nations (UN).

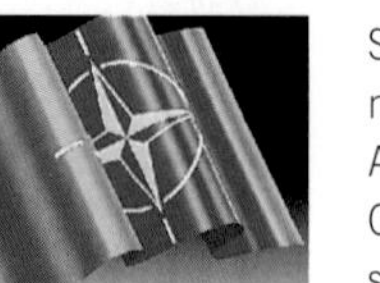

Spain has been a member of the North Atlantic Treaty Organisation (NATO) since 1982.

Spain is also a member of the Council of Europe and the Western European Union (WEU).

Figure 4 Spain hosted two major world events in 1992, confirming its position as an important economic, cultural, and sporting nation

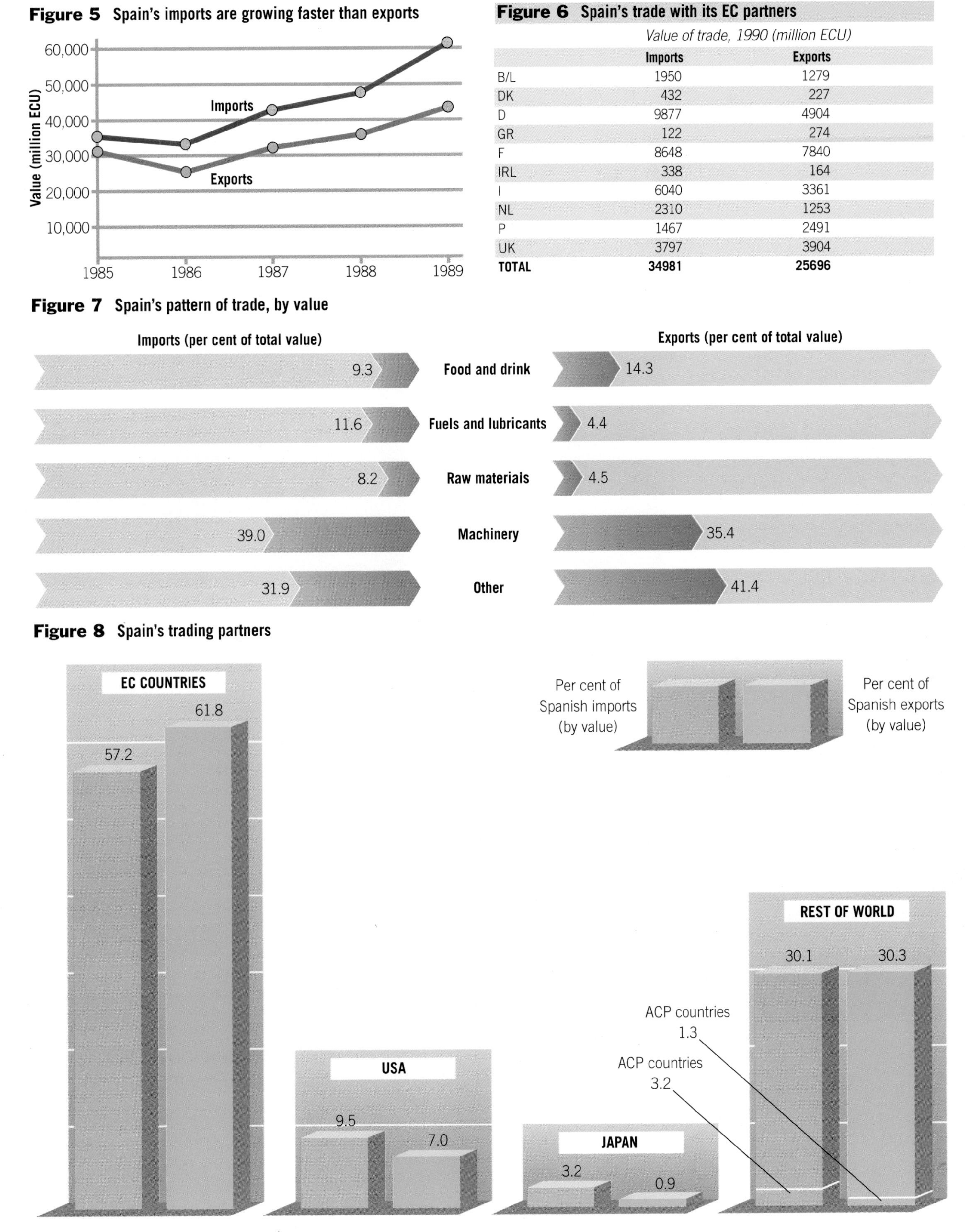

Figure 5 Spain's imports are growing faster than exports

Figure 6 Spain's trade with its EC partners

Value of trade, 1990 (million ECU)

	Imports	Exports
B/L	1950	1279
DK	432	227
D	9877	4904
GR	122	274
F	8648	7840
IRL	338	164
I	6040	3361
NL	2310	1253
P	1467	2491
UK	3797	3904
TOTAL	**34981**	**25696**

Figure 7 Spain's pattern of trade, by value

Figure 8 Spain's trading partners

African giant

Resource Bank

Figure 1 A street scene, Lagos

Figure 2
It is very difficult to carry out an accurate census of the population in a country like Nigeria. The latest one put the total population at 108 542 000 people, although it is thought that this could be inaccurate by as much as 10 million either way!

Population growth

	millions	*per cent growth*
1950	32.9	-
1960	42.3	28.4%
1970	56.6	33.7%
1980	78.4	38.6%
1990	108.5	38.4%
2000	149.6 *(estimated)*	37.8%

Urban population

	per cent of total population
1950	10%
1970	20%
1990	35%
2000	43% *(estimated)*

Age structure

years: 60+, 55-60, 45-54, 35-44, 25-34, 15-24, 5-14, 0-4

4 8 12 16 20 24 28

per cent of total population

Median age
16 years

Population density

	people per sq km
1950	36
1960	46
1970	61
1980	85
1990	119
2000	162 *(estimated)*

Birth and death rates

	Birth rate	Death rate
	number per 1000 per year	
1950	51	27
1970	49	20
1990	47	14

Infant mortality rate

percentage of babies who die before their first birthday

1950	20.7%
1970	13.5%
1990	9.6%

Life expectancy

	men *years*	women *years*
1950	35	38
1990	51	54

Figure 3 Nigeria

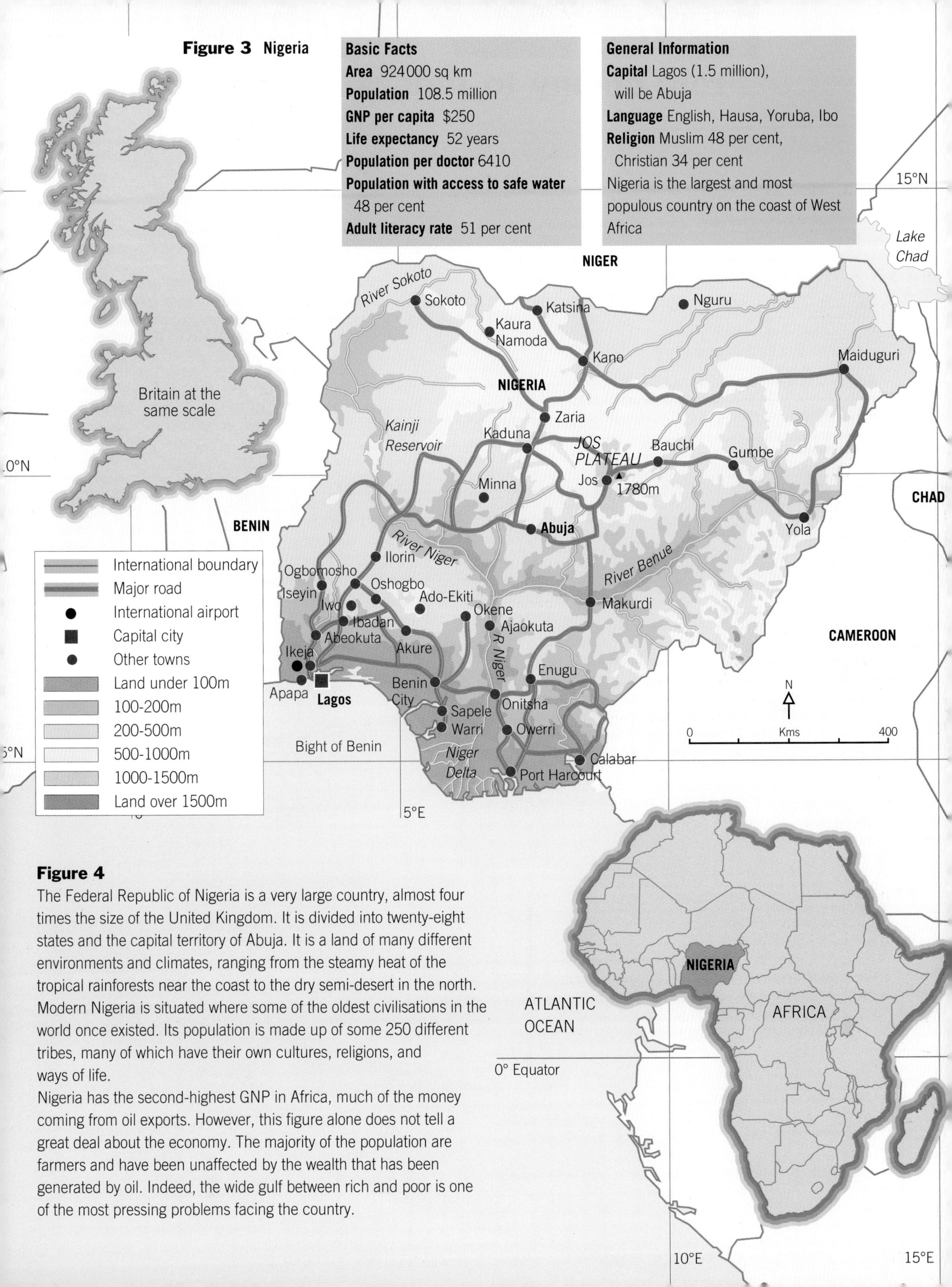

Basic Facts

Area 924 000 sq km

Population 108.5 million

GNP per capita $250

Life expectancy 52 years

Population per doctor 6410

Population with access to safe water 48 per cent

Adult literacy rate 51 per cent

General Information

Capital Lagos (1.5 million), will be Abuja

Language English, Hausa, Yoruba, Ibo

Religion Muslim 48 per cent, Christian 34 per cent

Nigeria is the largest and most populous country on the coast of West Africa

Figure 4

The Federal Republic of Nigeria is a very large country, almost four times the size of the United Kingdom. It is divided into twenty-eight states and the capital territory of Abuja. It is a land of many different environments and climates, ranging from the steamy heat of the tropical rainforests near the coast to the dry semi-desert in the north. Modern Nigeria is situated where some of the oldest civilisations in the world once existed. Its population is made up of some 250 different tribes, many of which have their own cultures, religions, and ways of life.

Nigeria has the second-highest GNP in Africa, much of the money coming from oil exports. However, this figure alone does not tell a great deal about the economy. The majority of the population are farmers and have been unaffected by the wealth that has been generated by oil. Indeed, the wide gulf between rich and poor is one of the most pressing problems facing the country.

From colony to federation

Figure 1 A time-line of Nigeria's history

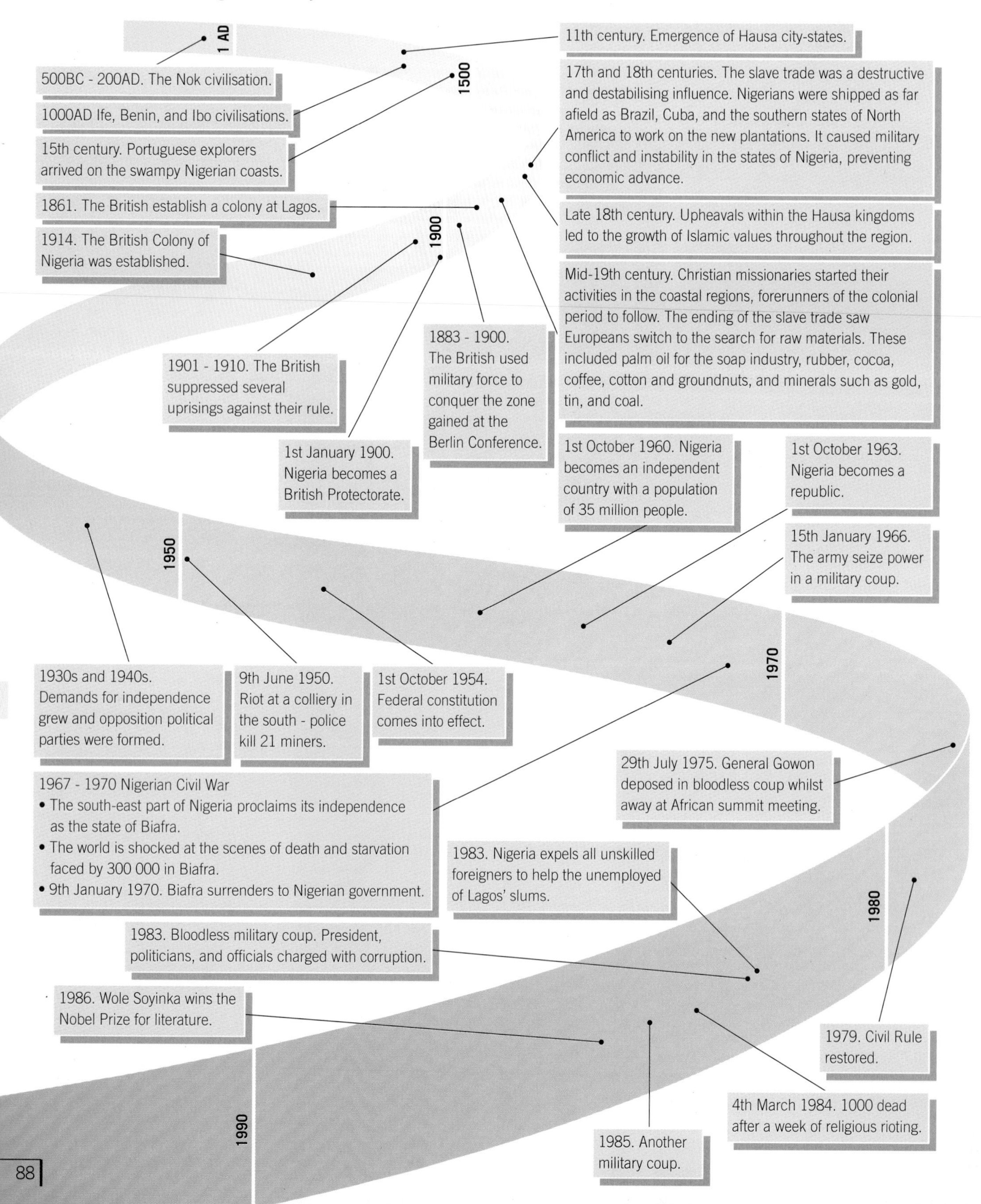

1 AD
1500
1900
1950
1970
1980
1990
500BC - 200AD. The Nok civilisation.
1000AD Ife, Benin, and Ibo civilisations.
15th century. Portuguese explorers arrived on the swampy Nigerian coasts.
1861. The British establish a colony at Lagos.
1914. The British Colony of Nigeria was established.
11th century. Emergence of Hausa city-states.
17th and 18th centuries. The slave trade was a destructive and destabilising influence. Nigerians were shipped as far afield as Brazil, Cuba, and the southern states of North America to work on the new plantations. It caused military conflict and instability in the states of Nigeria, preventing economic advance.
Late 18th century. Upheavals within the Hausa kingdoms led to the growth of Islamic values throughout the region.
Mid-19th century. Christian missionaries started their activities in the coastal regions, forerunners of the colonial period to follow. The ending of the slave trade saw Europeans switch to the search for raw materials. These included palm oil for the soap industry, rubber, cocoa, coffee, cotton and groundnuts, and minerals such as gold, tin, and coal.
1901 - 1910. The British suppressed several uprisings against their rule.
1883 - 1900. The British used military force to conquer the zone gained at the Berlin Conference.
1st January 1900. Nigeria becomes a British Protectorate.
1st October 1960. Nigeria becomes an independent country with a population of 35 million people.
1st October 1963. Nigeria becomes a republic.
15th January 1966. The army seize power in a military coup.
1930s and 1940s. Demands for independence grew and opposition political parties were formed.
9th June 1950. Riot at a colliery in the south - police kill 21 miners.
1st October 1954. Federal constitution comes into effect.
29th July 1975. General Gowon deposed in bloodless coup whilst away at African summit meeting.
1967 - 1970 Nigerian Civil War
• The south-east part of Nigeria proclaims its independence as the state of Biafra.
• The world is shocked at the scenes of death and starvation faced by 300 000 in Biafra.
• 9th January 1970. Biafra surrenders to Nigerian government.
1983. Nigeria expels all unskilled foreigners to help the unemployed of Lagos' slums.
1983. Bloodless military coup. President, politicians, and officials charged with corruption.
1986. Wole Soyinka wins the Nobel Prize for literature.
1979. Civil Rule restored.
4th March 1984. 1000 dead after a week of religious rioting.
1985. Another military coup.

Nigeria contains around 250 tribal groups, the largest being the Hausa and Fulani in the north and the Yoruba and Ibo in the south.

There is a simple explanation why this great variety of people, with different religions and ways of life, should be part of just one country, and that is the European colonisation of West Africa. The Europeans first came looking for gold and slaves, then minerals and plantation crops became more important. At the Berlin Conference in 1883, West Africa was shared out between the powerful nations of Europe. In 1914, the British created the colony of Nigeria. Nigeria became independent in 1960. The country has faced many problems, including conflict between the different groups. There has been a succession of military and civil governments. The government still needs to weld the people together, and be seen not to favour any particular tribe, religion, or region.

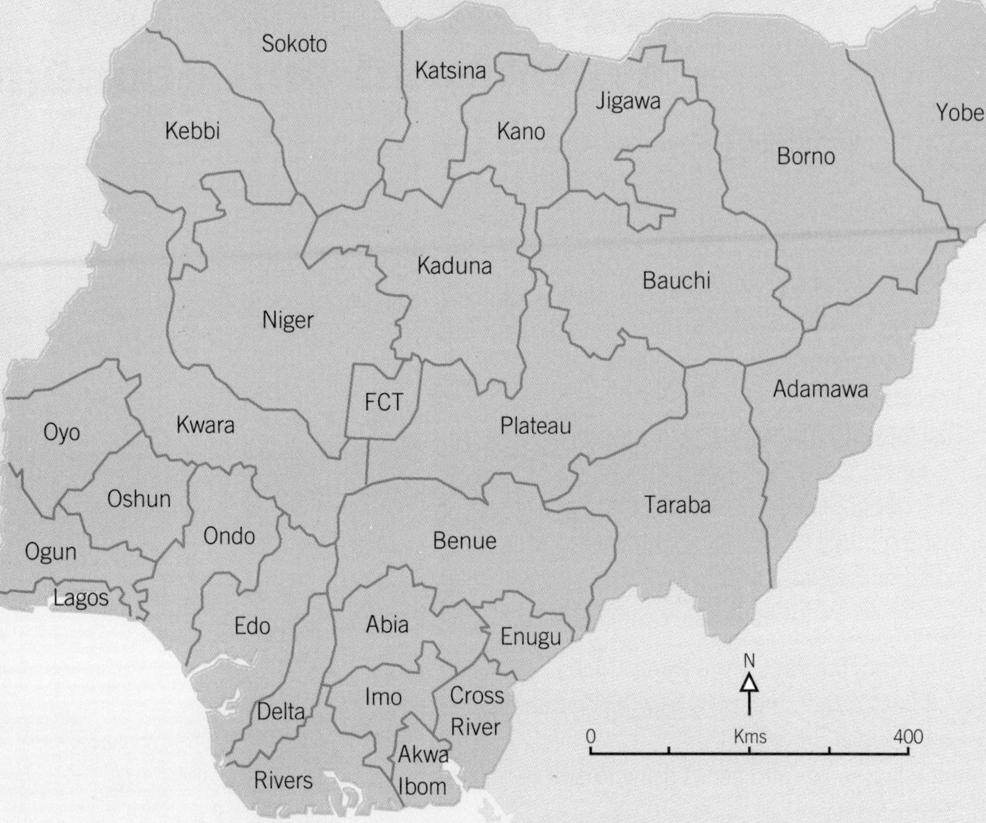

Figure 2 **The states of Nigeria**
The government has gradually increased the number of states - just twelve were created in 1967

Figure 3 **Nigeria's system of government**
Nigeria has a three-tier system of government:

FEDERAL GOVERNMENT
This is in the process of moving to Abuja. It is responsible for such things as defence and foreign affairs.

STATE GOVERNMENTS
Each state has its own government, responsible for things like police, education, and health care.

LOCAL GOVERNMENT COUNCILS
There are now over 500 of these. They provide services such as water supply and deal with the day-to-day running of their area.

ELECTIONS
The military took power in 1983. In 1989, General Babangida announced a new constitution and a return to civilian government by 1993. Two political parties have been recognised, although they have very similar manifestos, drawn up by government officials. Voting is by an open ballot system - voters line up to be counted in front of a poster of their favoured candidate.

Activities

1 a) How many states are there in Nigeria today?
b) Suggest one reason why there are so many states.

2 a) Nigeria has a federal system of government. What does this mean?
b) How does it differ from the system that we have in Britain? What similarities are there?

3 a) For how long was Nigeria a British colony? What does this mean?
b) In what ways do you think this link between the two countries is still reflected in modern Nigeria?

4 *Research idea:*
Nigeria's history has been very different to Britain's. Find out what was happening in this country at the times mentioned on the time-line of Nigerian history. Produce a large time-line of your own to display what you have found out.

Environment and economy

Figure 1 Nigerian environments

Rainforest region

Vegetation

Rainforest forms an east-west zone. Towards the north, the vegetation changes gradually from dense rainforest to the more open woodland of the savanna grassland region.

Relief

Away from the flat coastal area the land becomes higher and more hilly. Along the border with Cameroon there is a mountain range with peaks rising to over 2000 metres.

Climate

Hot and humid with over 3000 millimetres of rainfall in places. Rain falls throughout the year, although it is heaviest in the wet season between March and October.

N

0 Kms 400

Vegetation regions in Nigeria

- Sahel Savanna (poor savanna)
- Sudan Savanna (true savanna)
- Guinea Savanna (rich savanna)
- Rainforest
- Freshwater swamp forest
- Mangrove swamp forest
- Plateau grasslands
- Mountain grasslands

Climate statistics for Lagos

	Jan	Feb	Mar	Apr	May	Jun	Jul	Aug	Sep	Oct	Nov	Dec	**Year**
Rain *(mm)*	28	46	102	150	269	460	279	64	140	206	69	25	**1836**
Temp *(°C)*	27	28	29	28	28	26	26	25	26	26	28	28	**27**

Nigerian rainforest

River Niger

The great River Niger rises in Guinea and then flows through Mali and Niger before entering the north-west of Nigeria. It is the third-longest river in Africa, with a total length of 4100km. It is dammed at several locations, including Lake Kainji in western Nigeria. The river is joined by its major tributary, the River Benue, which drains the north-east of Nigeria. The combined rivers flow into the Gulf of Guinea across its delta, which is 320km wide. In common with most African rivers, the Niger is only navigable in sections because of rapids or because of lack of water at certain times of the year. The first European to explore the river was Mungo Park in 1795-6.

Nigerian savanna

Mangrove swamps

Along the coastline are long stretches of sandy beaches and lagoons. Mangroves are a type of rainforest that grows in the wet areas behind the lagoons and along the mouths of rivers. The River Niger Delta has one of the largest areas of mangroves. This ecosystem is very delicate and is particularly vulnerable to water pollution - a major problem in the oilfields of the Niger Delta.
The climate of the mangrove region is very similar to that of the rainforest. mangroves are characterised by 'stilt-roots' which keep the tree out of the tidal water. They also help to trap silt and nutrients from the water. The protection afforded by the roots makes an excellent breeding ground for many species of fish, reptiles, and even mammals.

Savanna region

Vegetation

The typical savanna vegetation consists of scattered trees, bushes, and tall grasses. However, it varies considerably from open woodland in the south to increasingly dry grassland in the north. In the far north the vegetation is little more than desert scrub, especially in the dry season or when the rains fail.

Relief

This region is one of large, level surfaces broken by a variety of sandstone ridges, inselbergs, and volcanic hills. The Jos Plateau is a good example of lava flows having created a large upland area.

Climate

It is the amount of rainfall which mainly determines the type and thickness of vegetation in the savanna region. Some areas in the south receive 1000mm a year, whilst in the north it may be as low as 250mm or even less. The rain falls almost entirely during the March to October wet season. The dry season brings drought, the length of which increases towards the north. In recent years, the unreliability of the rainfall has been an increasing problem for farmers - the rains have 'failed' to arrive.

Climate statistics for Kano

	Jan	Feb	Mar	Apr	May	Jun	Jul	Aug	Sep	Oct	Nov	Dec	**Year**
Rain *(mm)*	-	-	3	10	69	117	206	310	142	13	-	-	**869**
Temp *(°C)*	21	24	28	31	31	28	26	25	26	27	24	22	**26**

Figure 2 **The Nigerian economy**

Gross National Product
$28.3 billion (1989);
Agriculture 31%, Industry 44% (Manufacturing 10%), Services 25%

UK comparison: $834.2 billion (1989);
Agriculture 2%, Industry 36% (Manufacturing 20%), Services 62%

Industrial production

Cement	1970	664 000 tonnes
	1980	1 714 000 tonnes
	1990	3 000 000 tonnes
Oil	1970	53.9 million tonnes
	1980	102.0 million tonnes
	1990	86.5 million tonnes
Natural gas	1970	4 300 terrajoules
	1980	51 700 terrajoules
	1990	164 000 terrajoules

Agricultural production

	Thousand tonnes 1970	Thousand tonnes 1990	Per cent of total world production
Cassava	9 473	15 000	11.1
Cocoa beans	261	170	7.0
Cotton	62	42	-
Groundnuts	1 660	680	3.0
Maize	1 215	1 832	-
Millet	2 792	4 594	13.2
Plantains	1 635	1 800	7.2
Rubber	63	80	1.6

Agricultural change

Proportion of active population employed in agriculture	
1970	71%
1980	68%
1990	65%

Tractors in use	
1970	2 900
1980	8 600
1990	11 000

Use of fertiliser	
1970	0.2 kg per ha
1980	3.4 kg per ha
1990	6.0 kg per ha

Capitals old and new

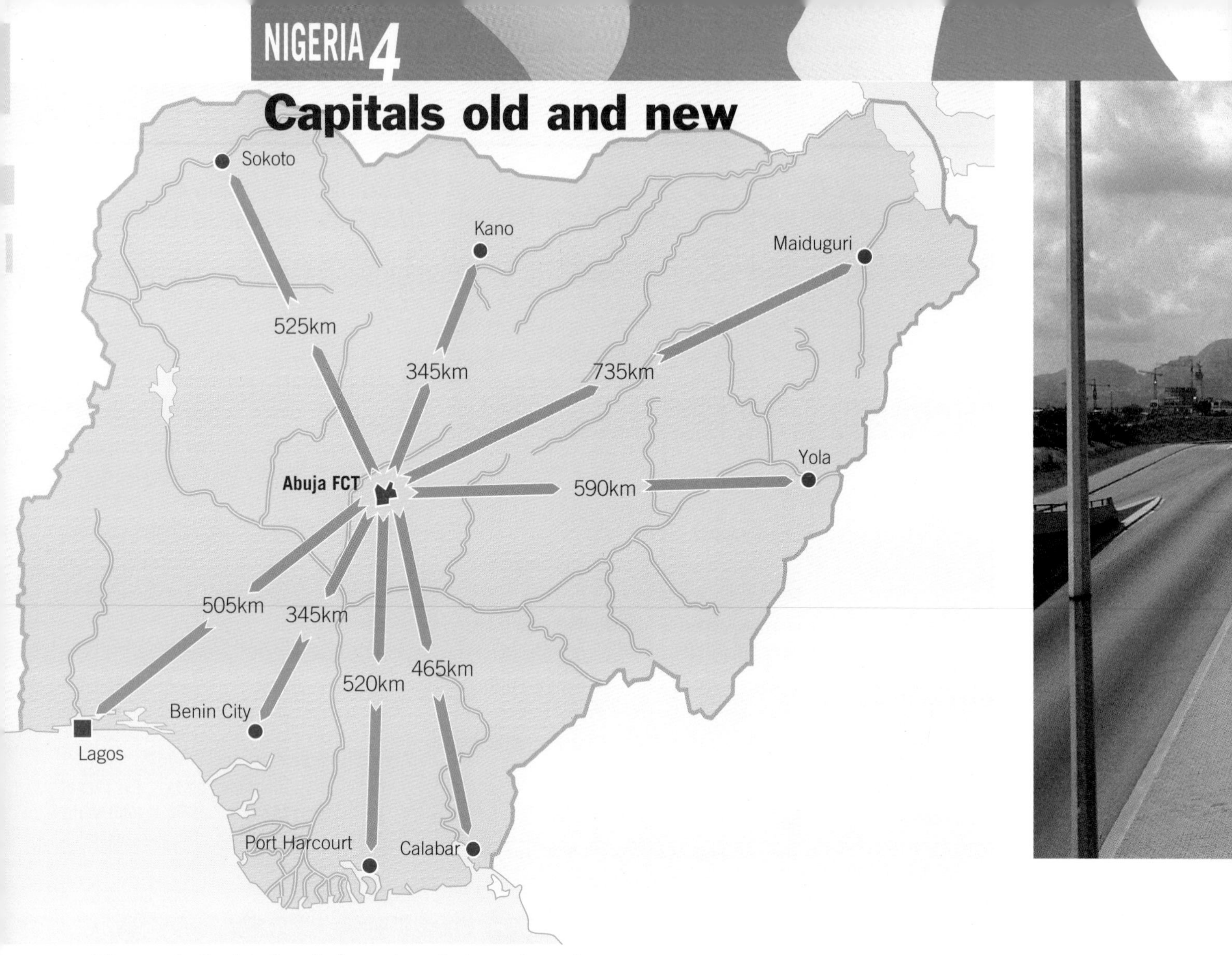

Figure 1 **Straight-line distances from Abuja to other major cities**

Figure 2 Lagos is a modern city, but parts are like this

There has been a settlement on Lagos Island, the heart of Lagos, since the fifteenth century. It was a good site because of its defence potential and its position at a natural break in the coastal dunes, allowing ships to enter the sheltered Lagos lagoon. It became a trading post between the Benin Kingdom and the Portuguese until the arrival of British traders in the nineteenth century who started the colonisation of the interior. Large ships had to anchor outside the port until 1912, when a channel was dredged through the sand bar at the entrance to the lagoon and quay facilities were built on the mainland at Apapa.

Lagos is divided into several parts, each with its own distinctive character. Lagos Island contains most of Nigeria's commercial and administrative headquarters, with large shops and offices. It is linked to the mainland by two road bridges, and also to Ikoyi Island and Victoria Island by road. These islands are mainly residential areas, with large houses, expansive gardens, and smart hotels.

Lagos has a population of nearly 5.5 million. It is one of

Figure 3 Part of Abuja

the most congested cities in Africa and has a reputation for crime. It is the country's main port and commercial centre, but the great shortage of land and resulting congestion has resulted in a completely new Federal capital being built in the centre of Nigeria at Abuja.

Lagos has many of the social and economic problems associated with 'millionaire' cities in the developing world. But it continues to attract many people from the country-side, resulting in the development of shanty 'box' towns. Sanitation is less than adequate and in some areas non-existent as the islands are low-lying and often flooded. Demand for fresh water greatly exceeds supply, while supplies of food, fuel, and building materials have to be transported in from all over the country. Even though the country now has a new Federal capital, Lagos will remain the nation's major business centre and one of the largest cities in Africa.

On 12th December 1991, President Babangida took up residence in the Presidential Palace, Abuja, fulfilling a sixteen-year dream cherished successively by six governments and four presidents. His move marked the inauguration of Abuja as the new administrative capital of Nigeria.

The Federal Capital Territory (FCT) was created on 3rd February1976, to ease pressure on Lagos. The territory covers about 8000 square kilometres. It is more than twice the size of Lagos state, and is located at virtually the geographical centre of Nigeria.

The Federal Capital City (FCC) of Abuja, in the north-eastern part of the FCT, covers 250 square kilometres. It was previously an area of sparse population.

Abuja's designation as capital is still relatively recent. A shortage of housing and office space may hold back the pace at which Abuja transforms itself into a fully fledged capital. Evidence of Nigeria's commitment to its new capital includes an international airport, conference centre, national mosque, and several large hotels. Water supply to Abuja is from the Jabi and Lower Usuma dams and 600 kilometres of road have been built to connect the various districts of the territory to the rest of the country. Many foreign embassies remain in Lagos for the time being, but all have plans to move. Abuja will increasingly become the place that foreign businessmen have to visit to see officials.

Activities

1 Using the information on these pages, draw an annotated sketch map to show the positions of Lagos and Abuja within Nigeria.

2 Why has the Nigerian government built a new capital at Abuja?

3 Make two lists - one of the advantages and one of the disadvantages of moving the capital city from Lagos to Abjua.

4 In which of the two places do you think you would prefer to live? Why?

Grassroots agriculture

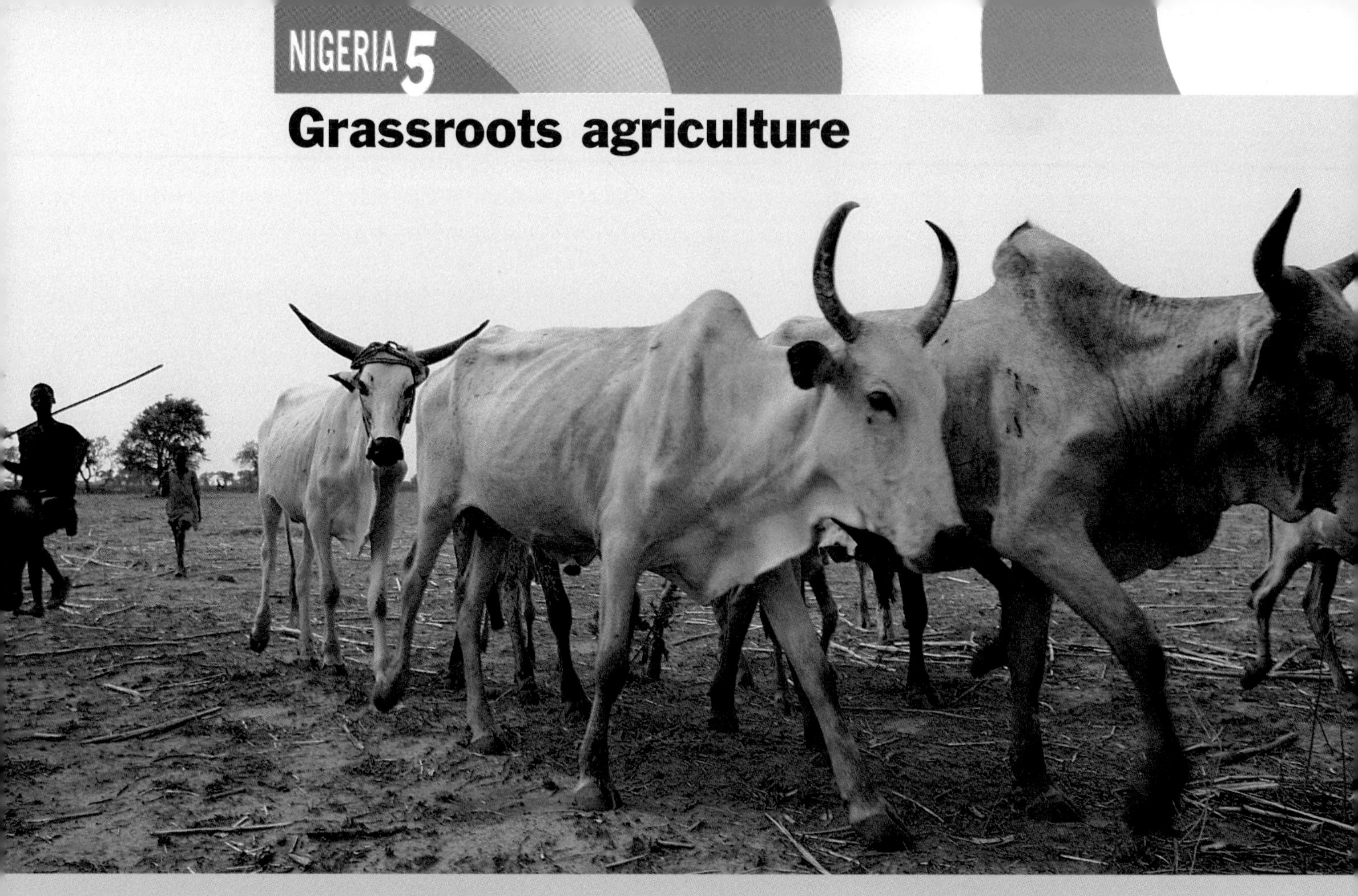

Figure 1 Cattle farming is found mainly in northern Nigeria. Overgrazing is a problem in many areas

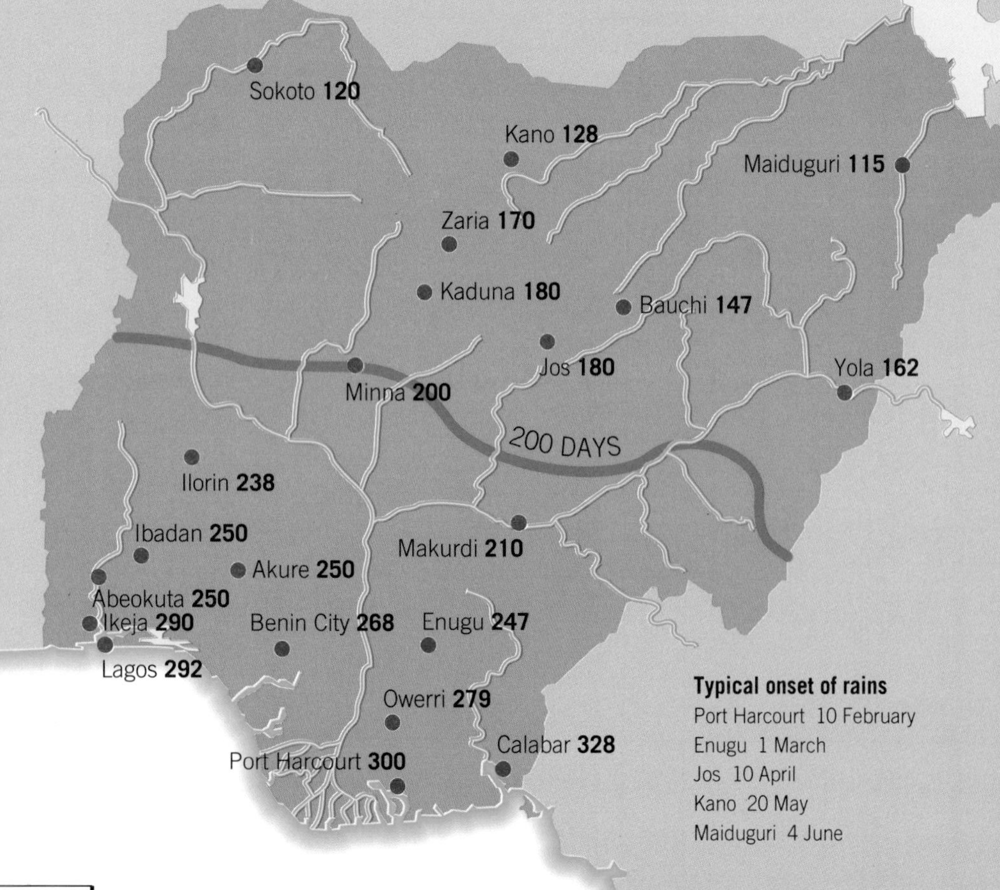

Figure 2 The duration of the wet season (in days)
The amount of rainfall, and the length of the rainy 'wet' season, has an important effect on the types of farming that can be carried out

Nigeria is more fortunate than some African countries in that it has great potential for agricultural development. It is estimated that about three-quarters of the country could be cultivated. However, at the moment, only about a third of the land is actually used for growing crops. About 70 per cent of Nigerians win their livelihood from agriculture in one form or another.

Most farms are small, as shown by Figure 4, and are used predominantly for growing food for the farmers and their families. There is little production of cash crops. Most farmers are subsistence cultivators. The majority of farmers are very skilled at their work, but they are also poor and understandably cautious about new ideas. Consequently, it is all too easy for agricultural 'experts' to interpret this caution as 'peasant stupidity'.

Nigerian farms are very different to those found in Europe. It is unusual for a Nigerian farmer to grow just one crop in a field. Instead, several are grown together in the same field, having been planted at different times. This practice is known as intercropping. As one crop is harvested, the next is given room to spread and to ripen. This has several advantages:

- the soil is never left bare and exposed to erosion;
- it gives the farmer several chances of success - one of the crops should do well whatever the weather;
- it ensures that none of the short growing season is wasted.

Figure 3 Harvesting cassava

Figure 4 Farm size in Nigeria

Farm size	Per cent of farms					
	Western states		Eastern states		Northern states	
<0.1 ha	6	94	21	95	1	69
0.1-0.2 ha	14		21		3	
0.2-0.4 ha	24		21		9	
0.4-1.0 ha	33		24		28	
1.0-2.0 ha	17		8		28	
2.0-4.0 ha	5		4		22	
>4.0 ha	<1		<1		9	

Figure 5 Problems facing small-scale farmers in Nigeria

- Almost totally at the mercy of the climate. A series of poor harvests can quickly force a farmer into debt. Crops in store are liable to damage by insects.
- No capital to spend on new agricultural inputs like improved seed varieties and fertiliser, let alone a new plough.
- Banks will not lend money to farmers who are already in debt.
- Cattle in the humid south are affected by tsetse-fly.
- Increasing population puts great pressure on the land, with the danger of soil exhaustion and erosion.
- Traditional patterns of land ownership give rise to an inefficient system of small farms with small and scattered fields.
- Young people move to the cities in search of a better life. They leave behind them a severe farm labour shortage.

Activities

1 a) Why is the wet season so important to Nigerian farmers?

b) Make a large copy of the map in Figure 2 which shows the length of the wet season. Draw on a series of isolines to show the changing length of the wet season from south to north across Nigeria. One isoline has been drawn in to help you.

c) Using all of the information available to you, explain the variation in the date of the start of the wet season.

2 a) Decide on the different ways in which you could display the data in Figure 4 and then draw it up by using the most appropriate technique.

b) Use the Nigeria Resource Banks to suggest reasons why farm sizes vary so much across the country.

3 Work in a small group. Discuss each of the problems facing small farmers given in Figure 5. Think of ways in which they could be tackled. What obstacles do you think you would come up against?

Improving Nigerian farming

Nigeria's oil boom of the 1970s led to a dramatic decline in the country's agricultural output as the oil wealth was used to pay for importing food. However, since the 1980s, the government has been using a range of ways to improve farming. At first, these were large, expensive projects like the Bakolori Project (Figure 4), but more recently the government has favoured small-scale schemes that aim to help individual farmers. Laws have also been passed to simplify the complex patterns of land ownership.

In an attempt to boost the output and efficiency of the majority of farmers, the government now gives subsidies for crops actually produced. The government has also started to encourage the use of hand tools and animal power instead of complicated, foreign technology and expertise. In addition, the import of many agricultural products such as wheat and rice has been banned to help boost the country's self-sufficiency.

A new class of farmers is emerging in this country. This class comprises civil servants, military men, businessmen and landowners who see agriculture as the new frontier for becoming wealthy or for storing their windfall wealth. This class of absentee landlords and farmers are capable of using their position of power in national policy making institutions to frustrate meaningful efforts at establishing self-reliance and agricultural changes in rural areas.

Figure 1
Extract from the *New Nigerian*

Figure 2
Modern machinery like this tractor is used mainly on the larger farms. It increases the efficiency of the production of major cash crops. In 1970, there were 2.9 million tractors in use in Nigeria, now there are over 11 million. However, machinery is largely out of the reach of small farmers who cannot raise the capital to buy it, nor can they afford to run or maintain it

Figure 3
Crop breeding at the International Institute of Tropical Agriculture, Ibadan, Nigeria. Increased agricultural production has been possible through the use of high yield crop varieties, together with the heavy use of fertilisers and pesticides. This has not necessarily been good for small farmers who often get into debt trying to buy them. It has been the larger scale farmers who are already quite wealthy who have benefited

Figure 4 The Bakolori Agricultural Development Scheme

- Low rainfall, 3-4 months only.
- Traditionally, all cultivation done during the short wet season.
- River discharge great during rains, but virtually nil for the rest of the year.
- Initial survey to choose site consisted of soil sampling, aerial photographs, and geological analysis.
- Project involves a dam on Sokoto River, a 120 sq km reservoir, 30 km of concrete-lined irrigation canal to irrigation site of 30 000 ha of flood plain and terraced land.
- Total cost over 300 million naira.
- Old farm boundaries and most trees destroyed.
- Initial plan was to take the land at the start of the dry season and do all the work in time to return the land, irrigated, to the farmers in time for the growing season. In practice, delays meant that some farmers were without land for several years.
- Several thousand people previously lived in the area covered by the reservoir. They all had to be rehoused.
- Plans were made to build proper resettlement villages. But time ran out and people were moved to three hastily built settlements that had no proper services and poor farmland.
- The maintenance and running costs of the scheme are very high. Farmers are told to grow high profit crops like tomatoes to cover these costs, but they grow their traditional crops instead.

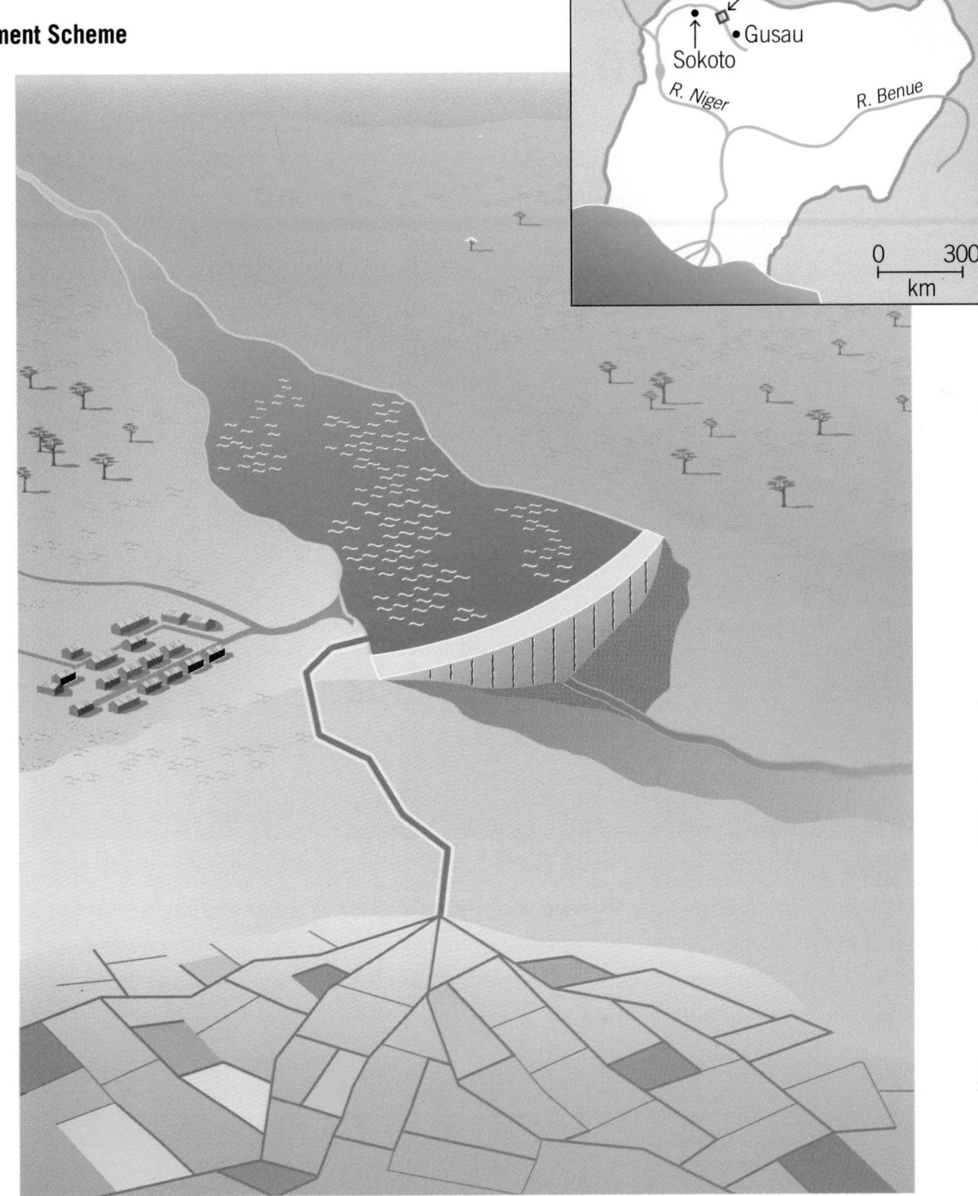

Figure 5 Integrated Agricultural Development Projects (IADPs)

What are they?
They are projects aimed at the small farmer. They attempt to raise production by overcoming some of the problems met by small farmers, instead of by imposing a totally new farming system.

Who pays for them?
They are jointly funded by the World Bank and the federal and state governments. To date, the World Bank has contributed nearly $2 billion.

How do they work?
They provide services to farmers. These include advice, marketing facilities, agricultural credit, new seeds and fertilisers, and new facilities such as better roads and water supplies.

They are one of the notable successes of Nigerian agriculture, why?
The farmers did not have to join the project, the projects had to appeal to the farmers. The priorities for development were worked out with the farmers themselves. The projects had a lot of help from very committed people from abroad, many of them volunteers. The sites chosen were all on good, fertile land.

Activities

1 a) What problems has Nigerian farming had to face since the 1970s?
b) Why have these problems occurred?

2 a) Look closely at Figure 4, which shows some of the effects that the Bakolori Scheme had on the surrounding area. Discuss them with a partner.
b) Decide whether the effects were social, economic, or environmental.
c) Make a table to show your findings.

3 Imagine that you work for the Nigerian Ministry of Agriculture. You have been asked to produce a leaflet for farmers telling them about the benefits of IADPs. Remember that some of the farmers will not be able to read well, so your leaflet will need to be visually informative.

Oil - boom or bust?

Figure 1
An oil rig in a mangrove swamp. Nigeria has some of the easiest environments from which to extract oil. Even the off-shore wells are close to the coast, in shallow water, and not exposed to high winds. However, many wells are below international standards for safety and environmental protection

Figure 2
An oil refinery - most of Nigeria's oil is refined close to the wells. Most of the international oil companies have invested in Nigerian oilfields. In return they receive part of the profits from oil sales

Before the 1960s, Nigeria relied heavily on farming for its income, but then came the oil boom. Many changes took place. A lot of the new wealth went into the building of ports and airports, bridges and roads, and new education and health facilities. A reduction in oil revenues has meant that many have closed or remain unfinished.

- Commercial production of oil in Nigeria began in 1957, but it was between 1970 and 1975 that it transformed the economy.
- OPEC raised the price of oil sharply in 1973. As a result Nigeria's production increased four-fold. The income from oil trebled.
- By 1975, oil provided over 90 per cent of Nigeria's export earnings, which had also increased considerably. Nigeria had become a rich country.
- The government could afford to pay higher salaries, service industries sprang up, and manufacturing grew. Lots of people moved to the towns and cities to get a share of Nigeria's new-found wealth.
- People developed a taste for imported foods such as breakfast cereals and tinned food. As a result imports grew, whilst local agricultural production fell. In some places farmers stopped growing crops altogether.
- The value of the Naira went up. This meant that Nigeria's exports became more expensive and so other countries stopped buying them. As a result, the production of exports like groundnuts, palm-oil and cotton fell dramatically.
- In the late 1970s the dangers of

relying on just one export began to be realised in Nigeria.

- World trade and economic activity were declining, and there was a fall in the demand for oil. This was partly due to the over-pricing of a few years earlier.
- The world price of oil dropped, and it has continued to fall. In 1990, Nigerian oil fetched $23 a barrel. By 1992, it had fallen to $18.8 a barrel.
- The fall in both the production and the price of oil has resulted in a huge reduction in Nigeria's income.
- At first the country used its savings to pay for the building projects and its imports. When these were used up, the government was forced to borrow money from the World Bank and other institutions - but they require interest to be paid.
- Many projects have been cancelled or postponed. Unemployment and other social problems have increased.
- In an attempt to reduce these difficulties, the government has agreed to exchange oil for help with projects from several European countries.

Figure 3 **Oil data**

OPEC quota levels, 1992

Figures in million barrels per day

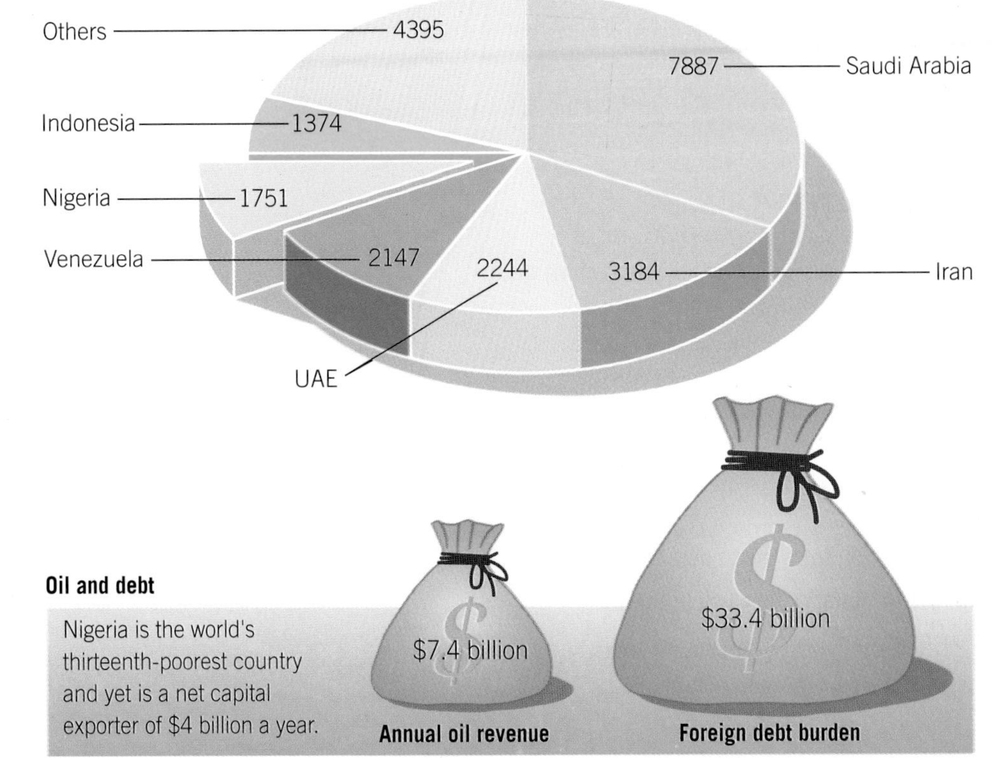

Government targets

Present figures in brackets

Oil production: 2.5 million barrels per day (1.95 million)

Proven oil reserves: 20 billion barrels (18 billion)

Activities

1 Work in pairs to produce two Nigerian newspaper front pages. One should date from the mid-1970s and depict a booming economy based on oil wealth. The other should date from about ten years later when things have started to go wrong. The articles must do the following:

- explain why the economy is like it is;
- describe what this means for the country as a whole;
- describe what it means for individual Nigerians.

Remember to use eye-catching headlines. You may also find it appropriate to include relevant maps and illustrations.

2 Consider the role of foreign oil companies in Nigeria.

a) Why does Nigeria need them?

b) What sort of measures could they take to help Nigeria out of its present economic difficulties?

3 *Essay:*
To what extent does the Nigerian economy reflect the saying 'Don't put all your eggs in one basket'?

Development projects

Assignment

Background information

Development projects can vary in their approach, scale, and impact.

Your assignment

- To examine the implications of possible options for developing an area in central Nigeria.
- To consider the views that different people have about the development projects.
- To decide whose views are given the most consideration, and why.

Figure 1 Map showing area of proposed development

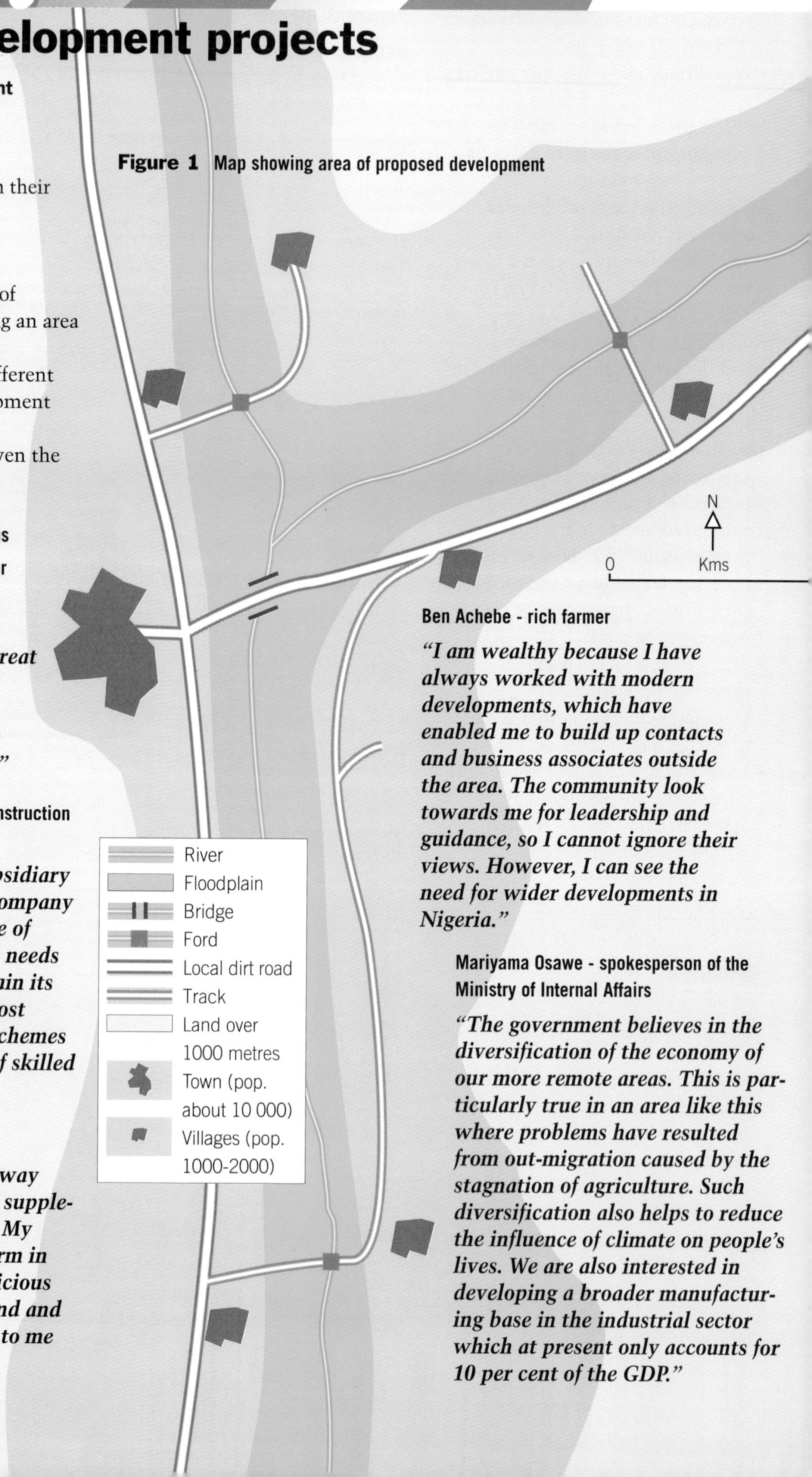

Figure 2 Some views and opinions

Marie Hellstrom - Swedish aid worker

"I believe in appropriate and sustainable development. Traditional methods have a great deal to offer in developing a Nigeria for the Nigerians. Development should build on existing skills and traditions."

Robin Bristowe - executive of construction company

"I work for a Nigerian subsidiary of a British construction company that has a lot of experience of dam construction. Nigeria needs prestige projects to maintain its profile as one of the foremost African economies. Such schemes help to increase the pool of skilled Nigerian workers."

Ibrahim Onabolu - traditional farmer

"I have been forced to work away from home for long periods to supplement my living from farming. My wives and children run the farm in my absence. I am deeply suspicious of change, especially as my land and skills have been passed down to me over many generations."

Ben Achebe - rich farmer

"I am wealthy because I have always worked with modern developments, which have enabled me to build up contacts and business associates outside the area. The community look towards me for leadership and guidance, so I cannot ignore their views. However, I can see the need for wider developments in Nigeria."

Mariyama Osawe - spokesperson of the Ministry of Internal Affairs

"The government believes in the diversification of the economy of our more remote areas. This is particularly true in an area like this where problems have resulted from out-migration caused by the stagnation of agriculture. Such diversification also helps to reduce the influence of climate on people's lives. We are also interested in developing a broader manufacturing base in the industrial sector which at present only accounts for 10 per cent of the GDP."

Figure 3 **Development Area factfile**

- Proposed Development Area covers approximately 100 sq km.
- It is located on the Plains of Hausaland in south-west Katsina, Northern Nigeria.
- The vegetation is savanna grassland.
- Soils are light, sandy, and water-holding - suitable for crops like cotton, groundnuts, and tobacco.
- The rainy season lasts for four months - May to September.
- Temperatures can reach 45°C during March, April, and May.
- It is an area of impervious rock; water is rarely more than 10m down.
- The area has very poor communications - fords are impassable in the rainy season, except by boat, making access to some villages difficult.
- Most of the local population are from the Hausa tribe and make a living from small farms.
- The only school and hospital in the area are in the town.

Figure 4 **The development options**

Project A

- Large-scale irrigation project, consisting of a large dam and a network of irrigation canals.
- A new all-weather road to be built to give access to the HEP station at the dam.
- Existing population will be moved to new settlements. The land will be re-distributed and given to farmers on merit.
- The area will produce cash crops for the home market and for export.
- Many unskilled jobs will be available during the construction phase.
- The scheme will cost $100 million and will be financed by a consortium of Arab businessmen.

Project B

- Small-scale water projects, consisting of boreholes and wells.
- Small-scale irrigation scheme, using hand tools and animal power.
- Education programme for farmers, as well as small grants made available to them.
- New bridges to be built to improve communications within the area.
- Cooperatives to be established to help with the marketing of surplus produce.
- The scheme will cost $20 million and will be financed mainly by Nigerian banks.

Project C

- Small dam and irrigation network.
- The land to be used mainly to grow cotton.
- Cotton mill and textile factory to be built, manufacturing garments for the home market - thus reducing imports.
- Farmers will be compensated for their lost land, but few of them will be required on the cotton farms due to high level of mechanisation.
- Jobs will be created in the mill and the factory for both men and women.
- New roads will be built, as well as housing for the workforce.
- The scheme will cost $80 million, the money coming from a variety of sources, including the World Bank, IMF, and EC.

Work Programme A

The three projects

- Working in groups of three, make three large copies of the map of the area where the developments are planned.
- Use annotations and a key to show details of the three development projects on these maps.

Work Programme B

What do people think of the projects?

- Divide into groups of five. Each member of the group is to represent one of the interested parties in Figure 2. Decide which project your person would want and why.
- Spend some time preparing your case for your chosen project. This needs to be done well so that you can put your views effectively. For example, think how each of the projects would affect the lives of your family and friends.
- The group should then discuss each of the projects in turn. Everyone must be allowed the chance to express their opinions. They may suggest modifications to the projects if they wish.
- Try to reach a decision about which of the projects should be allowed.

Work Programme C

Who is listened to?

- Imagine that you were an independent witness at the discussion about the projects. Write a report of what you saw and heard.
- What did each of the people think of the projects?
- Who (if anyone) changed their mind? Why?
- How effective were the farmers in influencing other people?
- If each of the projects were sent to the government in Abuja, which do you think would be approved?
- In reality, who would have the biggest say in a decision like this? How could the views of farmers such as Ibrahim Onabolu be taken into account?

Links with the world

Resource Bank

Figure 1 Exports and imports

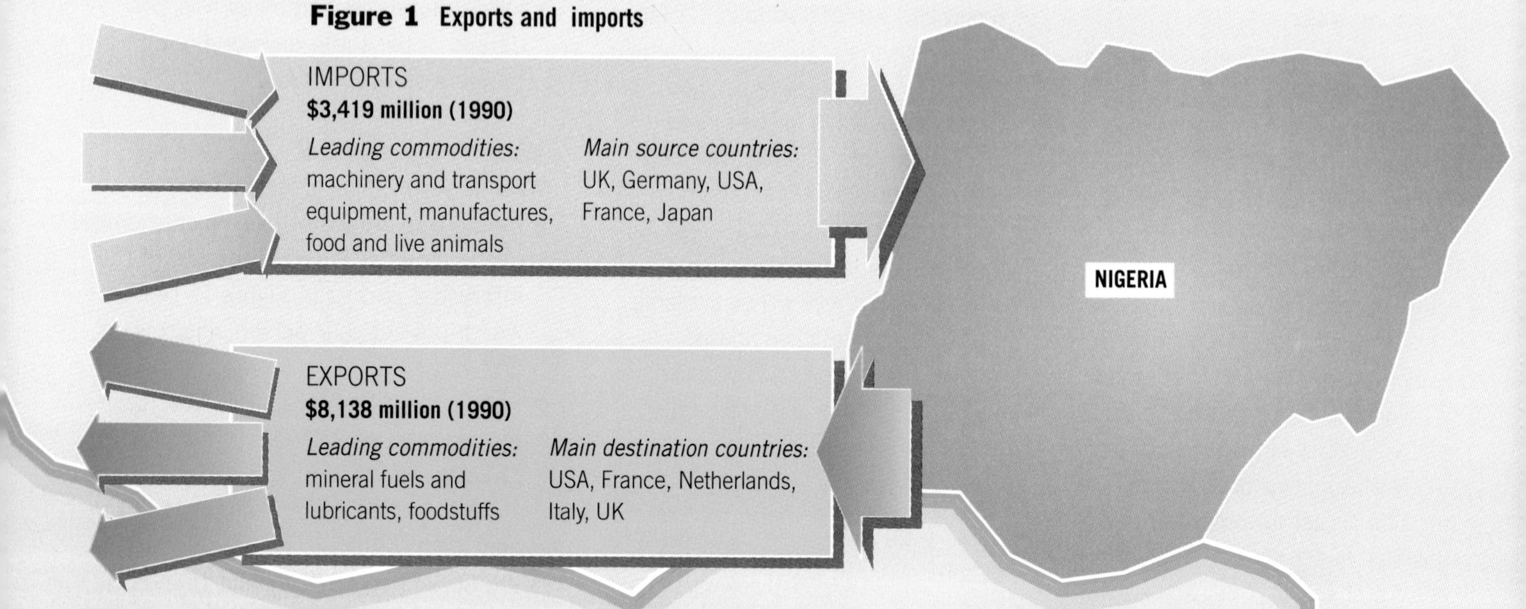

IMPORTS
$3,419 million (1990)

Leading commodities: machinery and transport equipment, manufactures, food and live animals

Main source countries: UK, Germany, USA, France, Japan

EXPORTS
$8,138 million (1990)

Leading commodities: mineral fuels and lubricants, foodstuffs

Main destination countries: USA, France, Netherlands, Italy, UK

NIGERIA

Figure 2 Nigeria's exports

Per cent of exports by value

	Cocoa	Palm-oil	Groundnuts	Oil
1962	20	15	24	10
1967	23	4	24	30
1971	11	2	19	73
1975	4	<1	3	93
1978	7	<1	0	89
1990	2	<1	1	96

Figure 3 Aid figures for selected African countries

	Total aid received, 1990 *millions of dollars*	Aid received per capita, 1990 *dollars*
Nigeria	234	2.0
Ethiopia	888	17.4
Uganda	557	34.1
Burkina Faso	315	34.9
Niger	358	46.7
Mauritania	211	107.0

Figure 4 Nigeria's international relations

Nigeria is a member of the following:

The United Nations (UN)
An international organisation of countries set up in 1945 to promote international peace, security, and cooperation. Its headquarters are in New York. Now has 160 members.

The Commonwealth
An international association consisting of the UK and countries that were previously part of the British Empire. Provides for joint consultation and cooperation in many things, like agriculture, education, and science. Membership stands at 50.

Organisation of African Unity (OAU)
An association of African countries founded in 1963. Its main aims are African unity, mutual cooperation, and the elimination of colonialism in Africa. Based in Addis Ababa, it now has 51 members.

Organisation of the Petroleum Exporting Countries (OPEC)
An association of the 13 major oil-producing countries. Founded in 1960, it coordinates the petroleum policies of members, especially prices and production levels. Its headquarters are in Vienna.

Nigeria is a member of ECOWAS (see Figure 5), and is also one of the 69 African, Caribbean and Pacific (ACP) countries which, through the Lomé Convention, receive development cooperation from the European Community.

Figure 5 The Economic Community of West African States (ECOWAS)

ECOWAS member states	Population *millions, 1990*	Main exports
Nigeria	108.5	Oil, foodstuffs
Cape Verde Islands	0.4	Fish, salt
Mauritania	2.0	Iron, fish
Mali	9.2	Cotton, live animals
Niger	7.7	Uranium, livestock
Benin	4.6	Fuels, cotton
Togo	3.4	Phosphates, cocoa
Ghana	15.0	Cocoa, gold
Burkina Faso	9.0	Cotton, livestock
Côte d'Ivoire	12.0	Coffee, cocoa
Liberia	2.4	Iron ore, rubber
Sierra Leone	4.2	Diamonds, coffee
Guinea	5.8	Bauxite, iron ore
Guinea-Bissau	1.0	Fish, salt
Gambia	0.9	Groundnuts, oil palm
Senegal	7.3	Groundnuts, phosphates

- Founded in 1975 by the Treaty of Lagos.
- Nigeria is the dominant member, with almost 60 per cent of the combined population and 70 per cent of the combined GNP.
- Administrative centre is in Nigeria — now Abuja, previously Lagos.
- Aims include free trade, development of common agricultural and economic policies, sharing of research and marketing, freedom of movement of labour.
- Problems arise due to huge variations in the wealth, size, and political systems of member countries.

The economic puzzle

Nigeria's hopes of becoming an engine for growth in Africa rest on two main assets. One is its energy riches. As well as enough proven reserves to keep pumping out oil at the current rate for 27 years, Nigeria has huge natural-gas reserves, which are flared off wastefully by the oil companies. The outlook for the upstream oil industry is healthy. BP is returning to Nigeria after 14 years, in a joint venture with Statoil; Exxon has turned up for the first time; Shell has just launched a multi-billion-dollar investment programme.

The companies are coming because the government is allowing them more freedom. Chief Ernest Shonekan, Nigeria's transitional head of government since January (an unelected post answerable to General Babangida), and a respected businessman, has pushed through new production-sharing contracts that let foreign firms invest in exploration, so long as the proceeds are shared with the government. Oil companies, handcuffed for years to the state-owned NNPC in joint ventures the politicians rarely allowed it to finance, are delighted.

Nigeria's other alluring feature is its plentiful, cheap labour: according to the World Bank, textile workers, for example, cost 3% of American ones – as little as Indonesians. Nigeria is Africa's biggest labour market and one of its fastest growing. Nigerians also seem to be natural capitalists. They are tremendous traders. Go to the vast market in Kano, Nigeria's second-biggest city, and the evidence is piled up on the market-women's stalls: soap made in France, baby clothes made in Indonesia, shirts made in Thailand, batteries made in China. Even the daily crawl through the Lagos traffic jam is an instant opportunity for a quick sale, as hawkers dangle all manner of goods through the car and bus windows – potted plants, acrylic socks, lemon drops, live chickens, plastic toy trucks, cartons of eggs, birdcages, white wonderbread in plastic bags.

Figure 6 Magazine extract

the Uncertain

Nigeria faces an uncertain future. It is a country with great potential, but it also has many problems. Working in groups of four or five, discuss the issues outlined below. Use the earlier pages on Nigeria to provide you with information - you may also be able to find out more from other sources, such as the library.

1 *The Environment*

This newspaper article considers the future of Nigeria's rainforests. Read the article and then discuss these questions.....

- What problems are facing the rainforests?
- Why have these problems occurred?
- What needs to be done to solve them?
- Are there any other environmental problems that are likely to occur in Nigeria in the future?

Reread Nigeria 3.

Not yet out of the woods

The Okumu rain forest is one of the last protected areas of primeval rain forest in Nigeria's southern equatorial belt.

Amid huge mahoganies, irokos, and other tropical hardwoods, baboons and monkeys scatter quickly at the sound of human approach.

Six years ago, logging was banned within 112 square kilometres of the forest, and the government and the Nigerian Conservation Foundation established a sanctuary in the Okumu forest, in Edo state. The sanctuary policy may be one of the last hopes for preserving an invaluable gene pool of flora and fauna in the face of the ravages of timber merchants, farmers and hunters.

Nigeria's southern states were once covered by rain forest. Fifty years of uncontrolled exploitation, rapid population growth and land pressure have taken a devastating toll on thousands of square kilometres of primary forest. According to estimates, only 5 per cent of the original rain forest cover is left today. The last 15 per cent disappeared in the past 15 years. Many species of flora and fauna, perhaps vital to medical research, were destroyed before they could be discovered.

A problem is that government concessions are granted on a maximum period of between five and ten years - too short to encourage the operators to have a sustainable logging strategy which would allow the forest to recover.

Reports suggest that, in spite of a gove[rn]ment ban on timber exports, logs and sa[wn] timber continue to leave the country i[lle]gally.

Plans to start regeneration projects a[re] costly and unlikely to come into effect wit[h]out significant funds from foreign donors.

'The real problem is the massive, seeming[ly] unstoppable population explosion and th[e] complete inability of the government to po[]lice the controls it has established,' says on[e] environmentalist. 'It's a very bleak pictur[e] for the future of the environment'.

Philip Hall of the Nigerian Conservatio[n] Foundation believes the remedy lies in con[]servation efforts which compensate farmers in the surrounding areas, in return for denying them the exploitation of the rain forest.

The NCF is pioneering agricultural projects such as bee-keeping and fish-farming for the local residents, as alternatives to logging and hunting.

Destruction of the rain forests is one of the many severe environmental problems facing Nigeria.

A recent World Bank report said Nigeria was losing $5bn a year as a result of environmental degradation caused by soil damage, water contamination, deforestation, desertification, flooding, gully and coast[al] erosion, inefficient sewerage, water hyacint[h] and fishery and wildlife destruction.

Elephants in the Yankari Game Reserve, Bauchi State, Nigeria

2 *Tourism*

Tourism is still relatively undeveloped in Nigeria, but it is believed to have great potential.....

- What attractions can Nigeria offer tourists?
- What benefits would tourism bring to the country? What problems?
- How do you think the Nigerian government should manage tourism so that the country gets the maximum benefit?

Reread Nigeria 3, 4, and 9.

3 *Trade with the rest of the world*

International trade is vital to Nigeria, but.....

- What does this cartoon suggest is the relationship between Nigeria and the rest of the world in terms of trade? Do you agree with its sentiments?
- What are Nigeria's main imports and exports? How and why have they changed?
- How are richer countries like the UK involved with Nigeria's development? Is this a good or a bad thing?

Reread Nigeria 7, 8, and 9.

future....

4 *The Economy*

These tables give a brief summary of Nigeria's economy.....

- What reasons can you think of for Nigeria going further and further into debt since 1980?
- What has this increasing debt burden meant to Nigerians?
- In what ways has Nigeria's economy got stronger?
- Do you think that the change to civilian rule will affect the country? If so, how?

Reread Nigeria 3, 6, and 7.

Economic change in the 1980s

	1981-86	1987-91
GDP growth *(per cent per year)*	0.2	5.7
Investment *(per cent of GDP)*	12.6	6.0
Inflation *(per cent per year)*	17.0	24.0
Exports *(per cent of GDP)*	14.3	18.0
Imports *(per cent of GDP)*	11.8	3.8

Domestic public debt

	billion naira
1980	26
1985	40
1987	50
1988	66
1989	81
1990	107
1991	120

Note: In 1991, 9.96 naira = US$1

5 Imagine that you work for one of these Nigerian government ministries:

- Ministry of the Environment
- Ministry of Finance
- Ministry of Trade
- Ministry of Tourism

Use the expertise that you have gained during your discussions to write a report for the government about what the future holds for Nigeria.

An overview

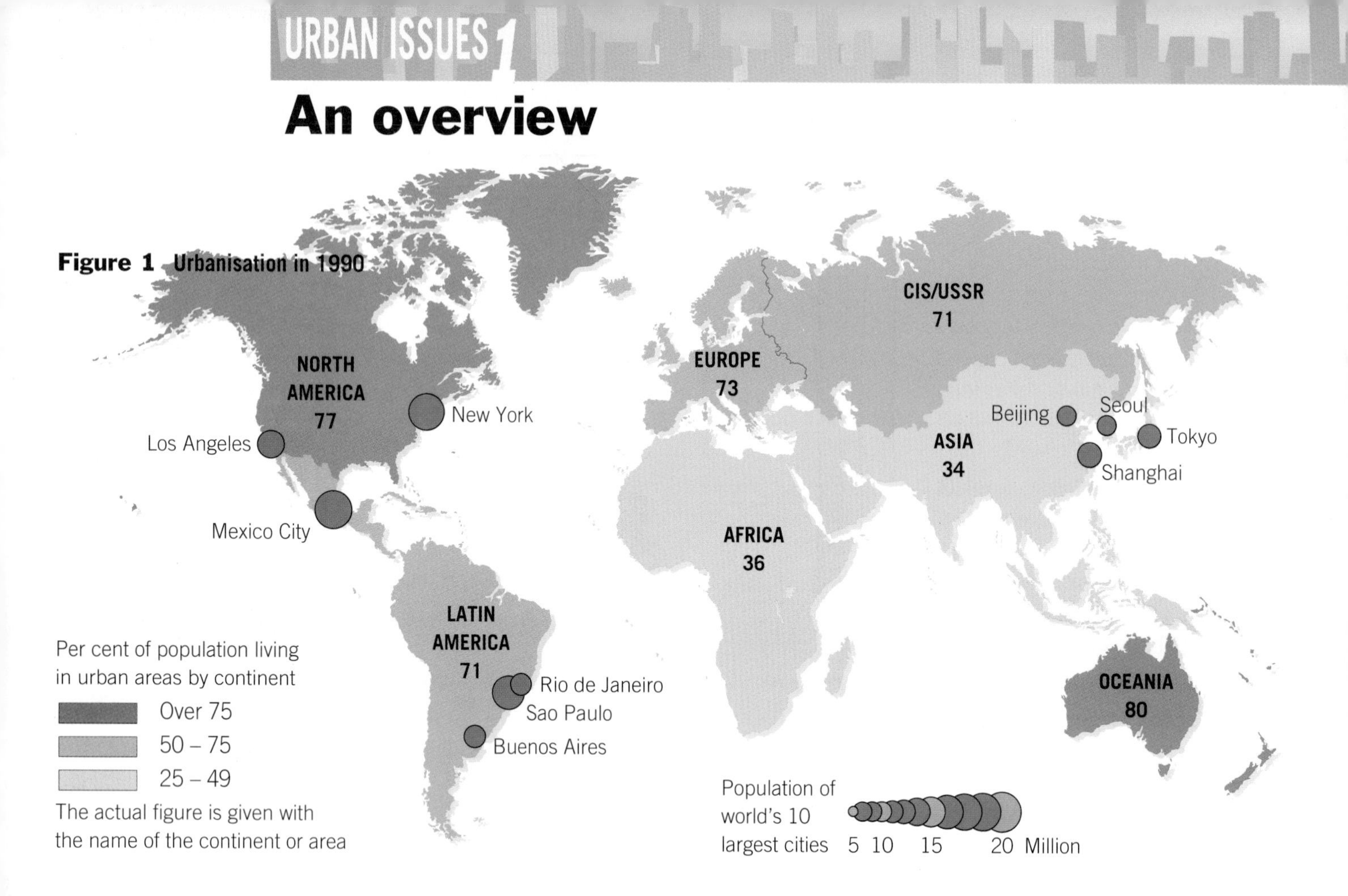

Figure 1 Urbanisation in 1990

The world is rapidly becoming a more urban place. Over half of the world's people now live in urban areas. Fifty years ago there were 40 cities with over a million inhabitants. Today there are more than 200 such cities. There are two main reasons for this. The world's population is growing, especially in urban areas; and more and more people are moving to cities in the hope of a better life, something they feel a city can provide.

Rapid growth creates many problems and difficulties for cities, some of which are illustrated by the photos in Figure 4.

These problems are most pronounced in Third World cities, but even cities in the rich North have their difficulties. And effective solutions are proving hard to find.

Figure 2 Urbanisation in 1950

The top ten millionaire cities	*population in millions*
New York	12.3
London	8.7
Tokyo	6.7
Paris	5.4
Shanghai	5.3
Buenos Aires	5.0
Chicago	4.9
Moscow	4.8
Calcutta	4.4
Los Angeles	4.0

Per cent of population living in urban areas	
North America	64
Oceania	61
Europe	54
Latin America	41
USSR	39
Asia	17
Africa	15

Figure 3 Percentage growth rate, 1975-1990

Los Angeles	63
New York	15
Mexico City	113
Bogota	146
Lima	121
Sao Paulo	115
Rio de Janeiro	68
London	6
Moscow	13
Tehran	132
Lagos	186
Karachi	163
Bombay	109
Bangkok	137
Beijing	71
Seoul	124
Tokyo	69
Osaka	55

A modern housing development on a greenfield site, Kent, England

Traffic, Mexico City. Urbanisation is occurring most rapidly in the Third World

Figure 4 **Some urban issues**

Rural decay, France

Anti-crack campaign poster, New York, USA

Inner city street, Liverpool, UK

Activities

1 Using Figure 1, describe the world pattern of how many people live in urban areas.

2 a) Using the data in Figure 2, produce a similar map to show the situation in 1950.

b) What differences do you notice between the two maps? Can you explain them?

3 a) What does the expression 'percentage growth rate' mean in Figure 3?

b) If a city's population had been 10 million in 1975, what would it be in 1990 if the growth rate was 120 per cent?

c) What pattern do you notice in these figures?

4 Work in a group for this question. Discuss the photographs in Figure 4. Make a list of the urban issues for the 1990s that they depict.

New developments in the Don Valley

Figure 1 **Sheffield and the Lower Don Valley**

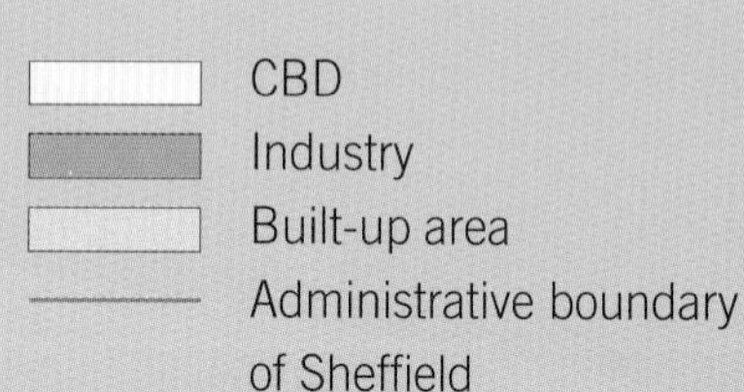

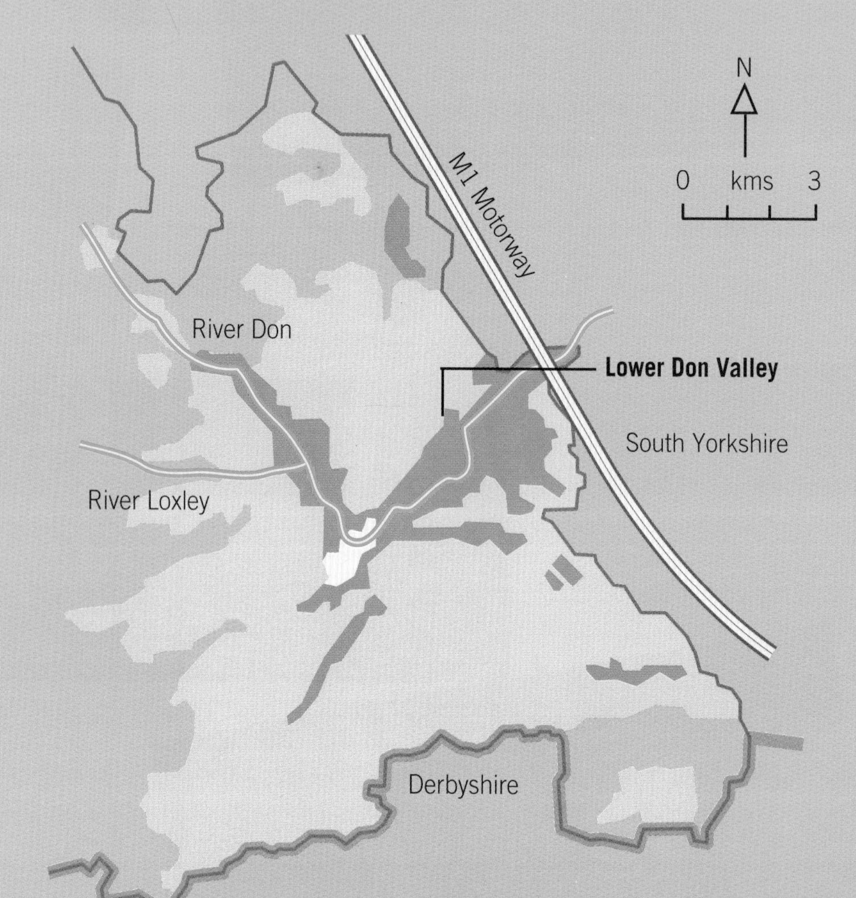

The Lower Don Valley was the centre of Sheffield's heavy industry, especially the iron and steel industry, until the late 1970s. However, rapid industrial decline in the early 1980s resulted in many factory closures and massive unemployment. Between 1976 and 1986, 25 000 jobs were lost. Over two decades, the demolition of the old terraced housing on the valley floor had resulted in the population being cut from 15 000 to just 300. By 1985, the combined effect of slum clearance and steel closures had resulted in over one-third of the valley floor being derelict and vacant. The scene was compared to the devastation caused by wartime bombing and the whole area was faced with a very bleak future.

In 1985, Sheffield City Council launched an Integrated Development Plan for the Lower Don Valley to include not only new factory sites but also sport and leisure complexes as well as environmental improvements. In 1988, the government established the Sheffield Development Corporation, which took over planning responsibilities from the city council. The new development corporation was given a budget of £50 million and wide powers, including the compulsory purchase of land, in order to implement the plan. The future looks bright for the Lower Don Valley.

Figure 2 The old face of the Don Valley

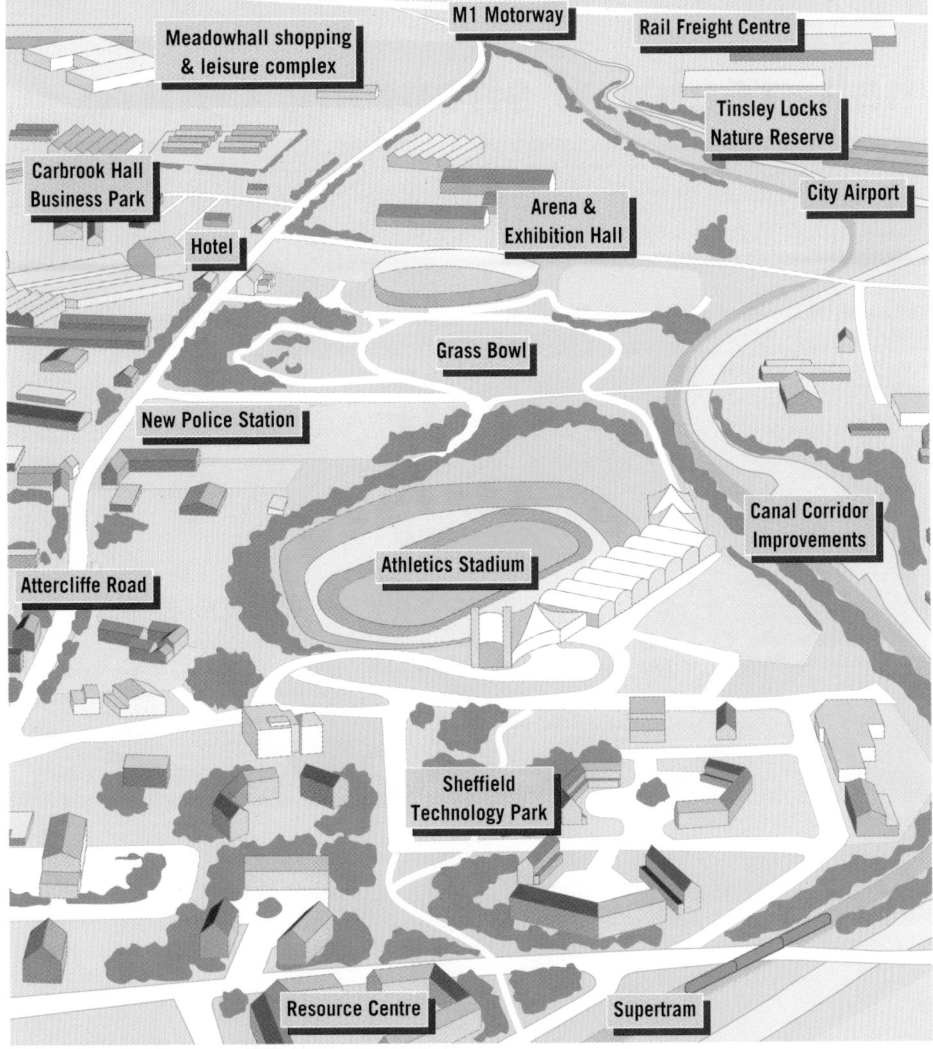

Figure 3 The new face of the Don Valley

Meadowhall
Opened in 1990, Meadowhall is one of the largest out-of-town shopping malls in Europe. It offers a vast choice from some 223 shops, with a retail area of 1.5 million square feet and free car parking for 12 000 cars. There is a multi-screen cinema and other leisure facilities are planned.

The Don Valley Stadium
When Sheffield hosted the World Student Games in 1991, the opening and closing ceremonies were staged in this 40 000 capacity all-seater stadium, together with the track and field events. The stadium provides world-class facilities for a wide range of sporting and other events.

Sheffield Arena
This 15 000-seat indoor arena has been built with a multi-purpose objective in mind. It can accommodate many sports, from ice hockey to indoor bowling, and has been the venue for other things ranging from rock concerts to political rallies.

Carbrook Business Park
Modern, purpose-built factory units to rent or buy. Firms locating here benefit from easy access to both suppliers and markets.

Technology Park
This comprises factory and office buildings on a pleasant, landscaped site, and aims to attract high-tech businesses to Sheffield.

City Airport
Plans have been approved for a city airport at Tinsley Park. This will be for short take-off and landing (STOL) aircraft, mainly for the business market.

Canal Corridor improvements
The Sheffield Canal is to be upgraded and redeveloped for leisure cruising. Warehouses along the canal have been refurbished to create shops, craft workshops, offices, pubs, restaurants, and houses - all with a waterfront theme.

Transport improvements
A new supertram system links Meadowhall and the city centre. Additions are planned to serve all the major developments in the valley.

Environmental improvements
A cleansing programme has been initiated along the length of the River Don. After years of industrial pollution, it can now be used for recreational purposes, such as fishing, canoeing, and walking.

Activities

1 Study all the new and planned developments in the Don Valley that are outlined on these pages. Make a table to show them according to whether they are improvements to transport, industry, or the environment.

2 How do you think each of the following people might react to the question 'Have the changes in the Don Valley been beneficial on the whole?'

- Unemployed ex-steelworker
- A local corner shop owner
- A foreign business person, interested in setting up a new factory in Sheffield
- A pensioner who has lived in the area all her life
- The manager of a city centre store
- A member of a local athletics club

Meadowhall, regional shopping centre

The Meadowhall shopping and leisure centre was opened on 4th September 1990, at a cost of £400 million. It was built to the east of Sheffield, adjacent to junction 34 of the M1 motorway in the Lower Don Valley.

The site had been home to the iron and steel industry since the twelfth century. The building of the motorway in 1968 came too late to save the already declining steel industry, but it made the area much more accessible and meant that re-development was possible.

Meadowhall is in the heart of Britain's most densely populated area. Nine million people live within an hour's drive of the centre - that is about one in six of the UK population (Figure 2). The complex provides 223 stores on two levels, creating 7000 jobs. The trading area of 1.5 million square feet is equal in size to twenty football pitches. It is divided into five shopping areas, each with its own theme and identity for different types of shopping:

- The Arcade - fashion and fashion accessories.
- The High Street - 100 shops of familiar household names like Boots, C&A, and W H Smith.
- Park Lane - upmarket and exclusive shopping.
- Market Street - day-to-day shopping from kiosks and carts, including a massive Savacentre.
- The Oasis - the largest food court in the world, created in the style of a Spanish square, offering a variety of fast food outlets.

Meadowhall also boasts an eleven-screen cinema, and there are plans to build other leisure facilities.

Figure 1 Meadowhall

Figure 2 Meadowhall - its location in relation to surrounding towns

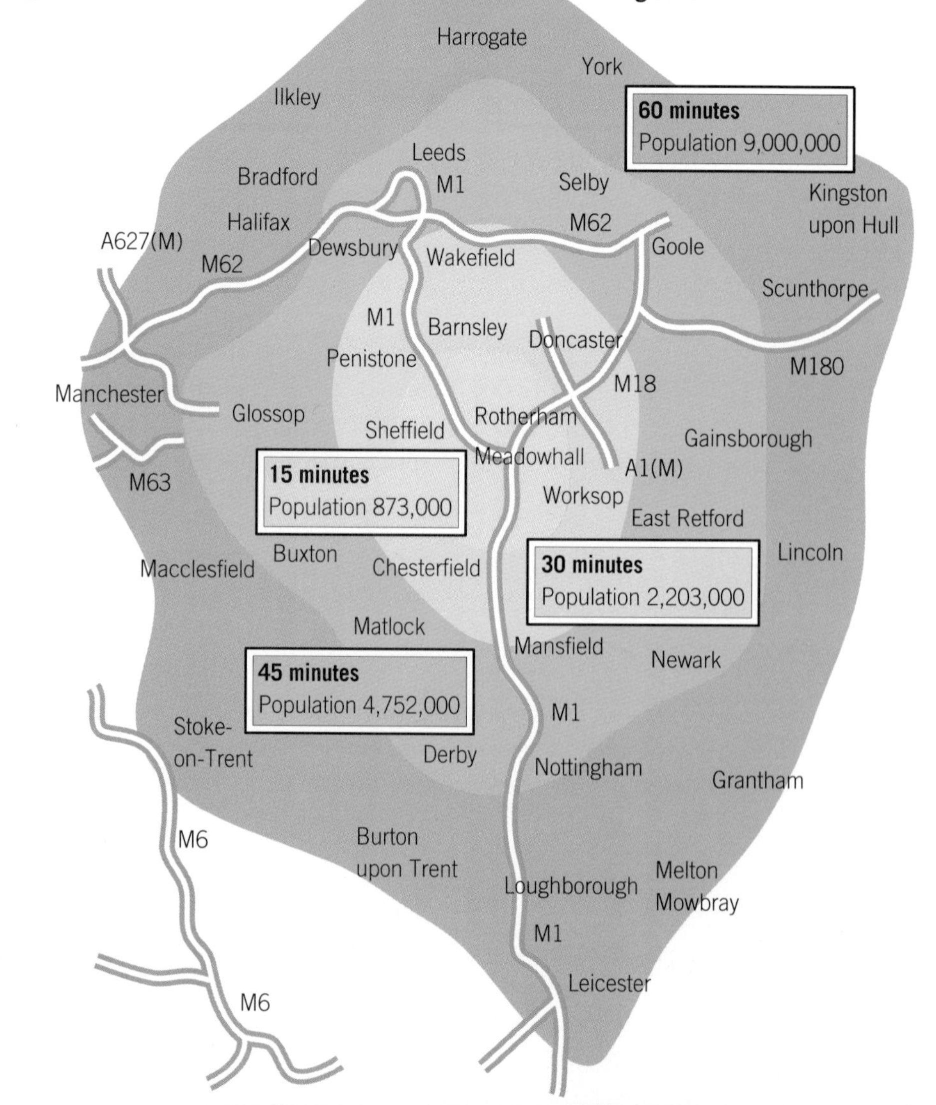

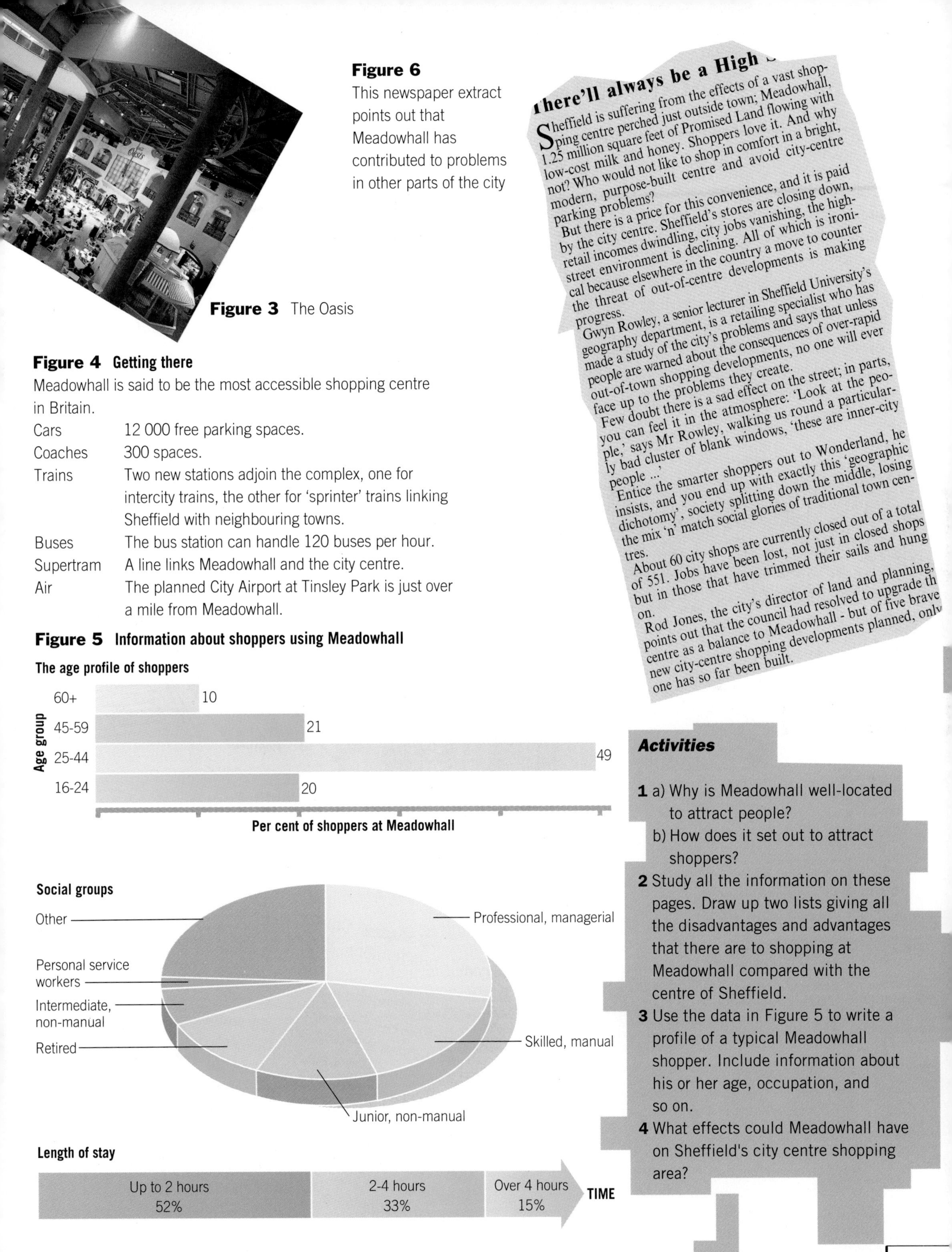

Figure 3 The Oasis

Figure 6
This newspaper extract points out that Meadowhall has contributed to problems in other parts of the city

There'll always be a High

Sheffield is suffering from the effects of a vast shopping centre perched just outside town; Meadowhall, 1.25 million square feet of Promised Land flowing with low-cost milk and honey. Shoppers love it. And why not? Who would not like to shop in comfort in a bright, modern, purpose-built centre and avoid city-centre parking problems?

But there is a price for this convenience, and it is paid by the city centre. Sheffield's stores are closing down, retail incomes dwindling, city jobs vanishing, the high-street environment is declining. All of which is ironical because elsewhere in the country a move to counter the threat of out-of-centre developments is making progress.

Gwyn Rowley, a senior lecturer in Sheffield University's geography department, is a retailing specialist who has made a study of the city's problems and says that unless people are warned about the consequences of over-rapid out-of-town shopping developments, no one will ever face up to the problems they create.

Few doubt there is a sad effect on the street; in parts, you can feel it in the atmosphere: 'Look at the people,' says Mr Rowley, walking us round a particularly bad cluster of blank windows, 'these are inner-city people ...'

Entice the smarter shoppers out to Wonderland, he insists, and you end up with exactly this 'geographic dichotomy', society splitting down the middle, losing the mix 'n' match social glories of traditional town centres.

About 60 city shops are currently closed out of a total of 551. Jobs have been lost, not just in closed shops but in those that have trimmed their sails and hung on.

Rod Jones, the city's director of land and planning, points out that the council had resolved to upgrade th centre as a balance to Meadowhall - but of five brave new city-centre shopping developments planned, onl one has so far been built.

Figure 4 Getting there

Meadowhall is said to be the most accessible shopping centre in Britain.

Cars	12 000 free parking spaces.
Coaches	300 spaces.
Trains	Two new stations adjoin the complex, one for intercity trains, the other for 'sprinter' trains linking Sheffield with neighbouring towns.
Buses	The bus station can handle 120 buses per hour.
Supertram	A line links Meadowhall and the city centre.
Air	The planned City Airport at Tinsley Park is just over a mile from Meadowhall.

Figure 5 Information about shoppers using Meadowhall

The age profile of shoppers

Age group	Per cent of shoppers at Meadowhall
60+	10
45-59	21
25-44	49
16-24	20

Social groups

Other
Professional, managerial
Personal service workers
Intermediate, non-manual
Retired
Skilled, manual
Junior, non-manual

Length of stay

Up to 2 hours	2-4 hours	Over 4 hours
52%	33%	15%

TIME

Activities

1 a) Why is Meadowhall well-located to attract people?
b) How does it set out to attract shoppers?

2 Study all the information on these pages. Draw up two lists giving all the disadvantages and advantages that there are to shopping at Meadowhall compared with the centre of Sheffield.

3 Use the data in Figure 5 to write a profile of a typical Meadowhall shopper. Include information about his or her age, occupation, and so on.

4 What effects could Meadowhall have on Sheffield's city centre shopping area?

Planning for the urban future

Assignment

Background information

Many urban redevelopment schemes have been more concerned with new building than preserving the old. This is particularly true of those schemes dating from the 1960s when thousands of traditional terraced homes were demolished and replaced by high-rise blocks of flats. It is such schemes that gave rise to the view illustrated in the cartoon in Figure 1. More recently, however, conservation has become a key word in British town planning, with an emphasis on the enhancement and re-use of existing buildings. Not only does this make economic sense, but it is also essential to preserving things such as 'our historic past' and 'a town's character'.

Your assignment

Your assignment is to plan the re-development of the derelict inner city area shown in Figure 4. It is important that you make use of the existing buildings and plan new ones to be in keeping with the traditional character of the area. You must also consider the needs of the new residents.

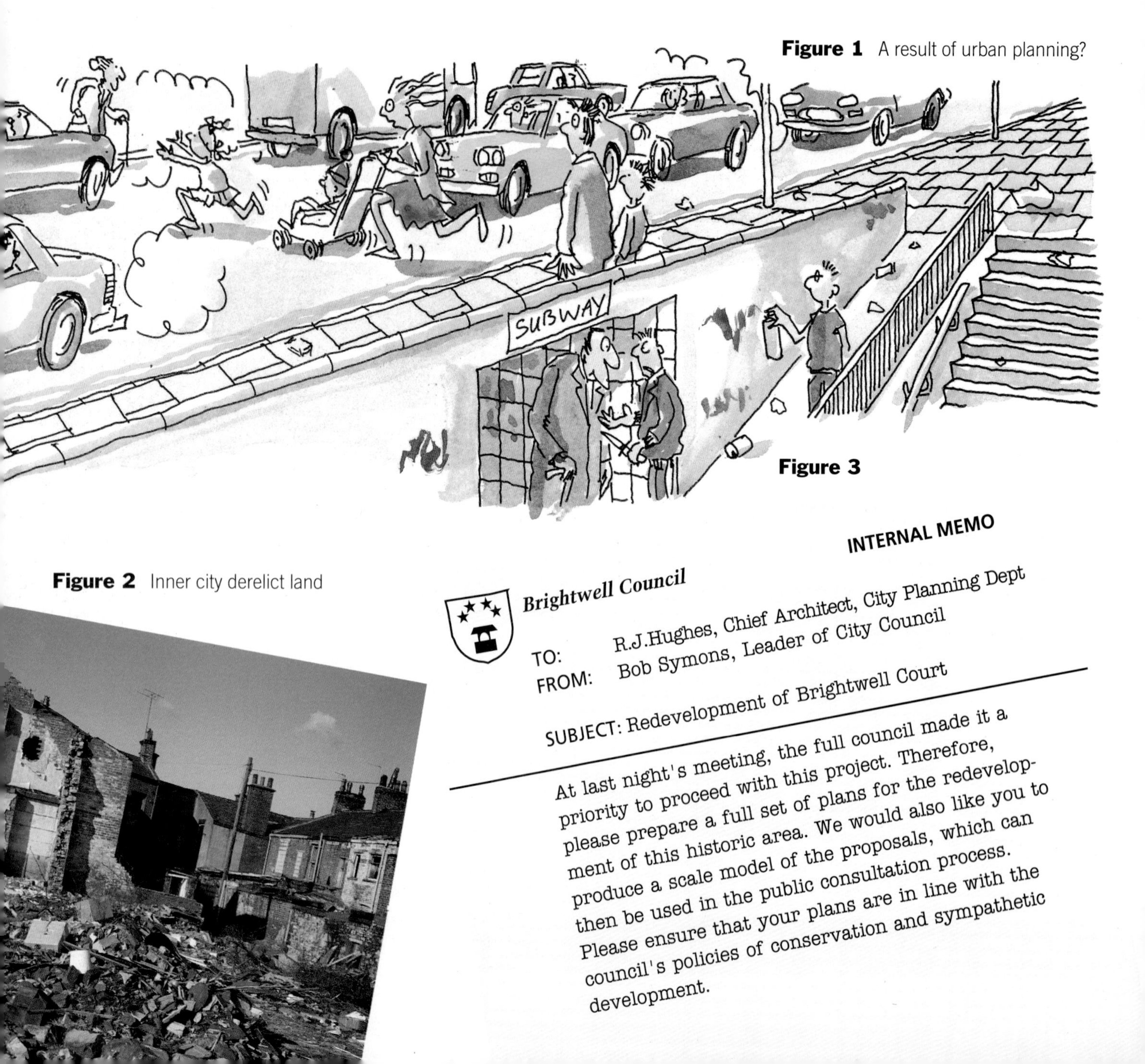

Figure 1 A result of urban planning?

Figure 3

Figure 2 Inner city derelict land

INTERNAL MEMO

Brightwell Council

TO: R.J.Hughes, Chief Architect, City Planning Dept

FROM: Bob Symons, Leader of City Council

SUBJECT: Redevelopment of Brightwell Court

At last night's meeting, the full council made it a priority to proceed with this project. Therefore, please prepare a full set of plans for the redevelopment of this historic area. We would also like you to produce a scale model of the proposals, which can then be used in the public consultation process. Please ensure that your plans are in line with the council's policies of conservation and sympathetic development.

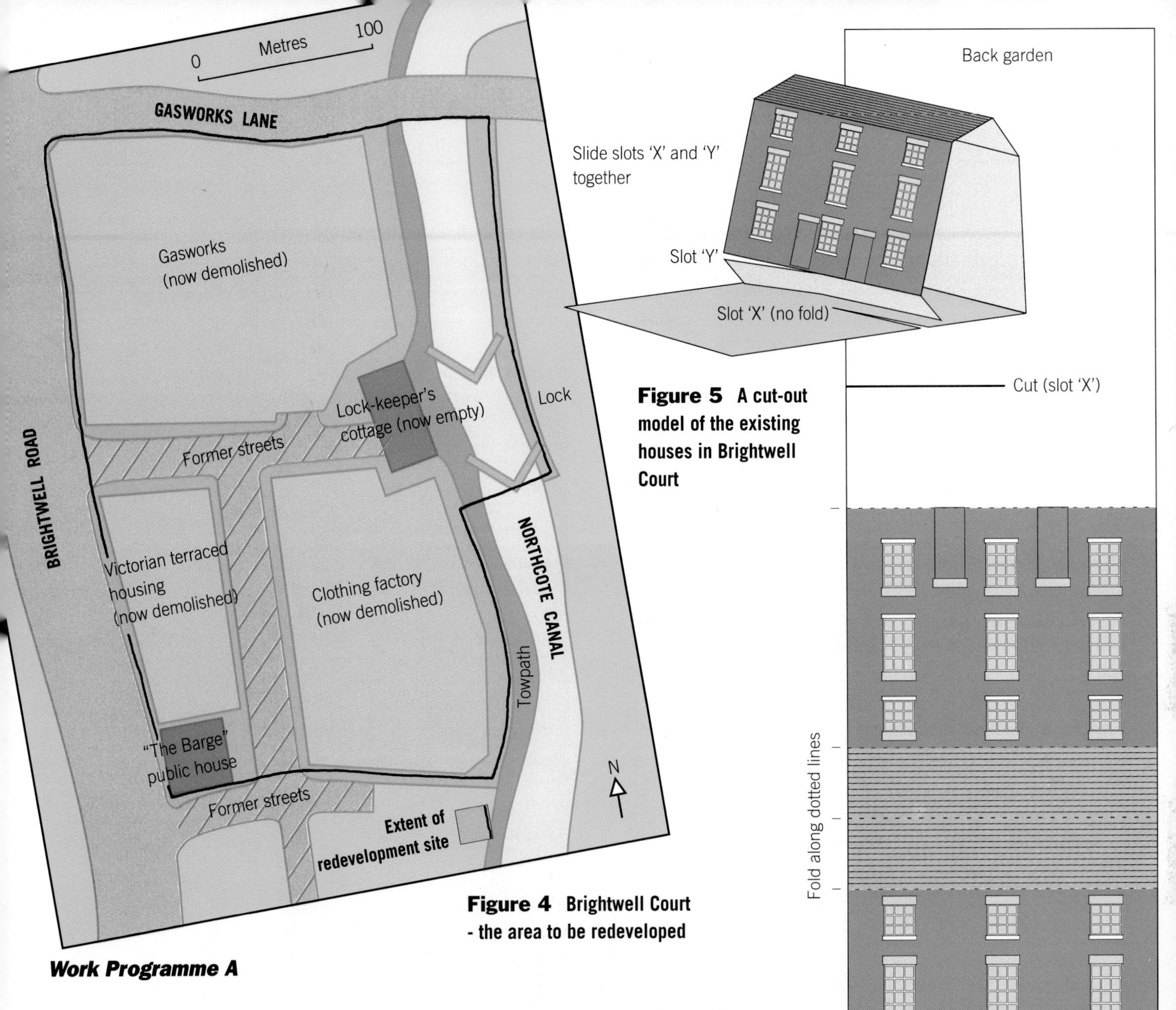

Figure 4 Brightwell Court - the area to be redeveloped

Figure 5 A cut-out model of the existing houses in Brightwell Court

Work Programme A

- Work in groups to prepare the plans called for in the memo in Figure 3.
- Prepare a large copy of the map of the area to be redeveloped (Figure 4).
- Decide how you can best use this area for:
  - housing
  - leisure facilities
  - shops/offices

  Think about who might use these and what their needs will be. Mark them on your map.
- You must also consider access to the site, open space, and street furniture (lamps, seats, litter bins, and so on). Some of these you can put on the map, others can be shown by sketches.
- Use the method shown in Figure 5 to make a scale model of your redevelopment proposals. Remember that the existing buildings shown in Figure 4 must be included in the plans.

Work Programme B

- Hold a class discussion about the future of Brightwell Court.
- Decide who would be interested in these proposals at a public planning hearing. Allocate these roles between members of your group. Remember that you will need a chairperson for the hearing.
- Agree to accept, reject, or modify your proposal.

Work Programme C

- Prepare a press release from the council following the public hearing, giving details of what is to happen to Brightwell Court.

Growing into the countryside

In the period between the two world wars, London and the major cities in the UK began to expand rapidly, especially along major transport routes. An attempt to check this growth by the government was the introduction of 'green belts' in 1947. A green belt is a zone of land which can be used only for farming, recreation, or open space. They were introduced to stop towns merging, to improve the urban environment, and to provide new recreation facilities.

However, green belts are under threat. Many people leaving London, for example, have gone beyond the green belt and settled in new towns such as Crawley and Stevenage. The government is under constant pressure to allow development of London's green belt. Many local authorities have relaxed policies aimed at encouraging and coordinating the maintenance of the urban fringe with respect to farming, forestry, and recreation.

Figure 1 **Britain's conurbations**

Conurbations
Merseyside
Greater Manchester
Clydeside
Tyneside
West Midlands
Greater London
West Yorkshire
South Yorkshire

Figure 2 **British cities with green belts**

Edinburgh, Glasgow, Grangemouth, Prestwick, Newcastle, Leeds, Sheffield, Liverpool, Manchester, Birmingham, Stoke-on-Trent, Nottingham, London, Cambridge, Oxford, Bournemouth, Bristol

Figure 3 Part of the green belt area around Newcastle

Figure 4 **Tyneside**

The Tyneside conurbation has a population of over 750 000 people. It consists of a number of settlements which have grown up along the River Tyne, several of them for industries like shipbuilding. These settlements include Newcastle, Gateshead, Jarrow, Wallsend, and North and South Shields. Following serious industrial decline, much of the area has been made a special development area. There are many pressures for the conurbation to expand into the surrounding countryside; it is this expansion that the green belt has been designed to limit.

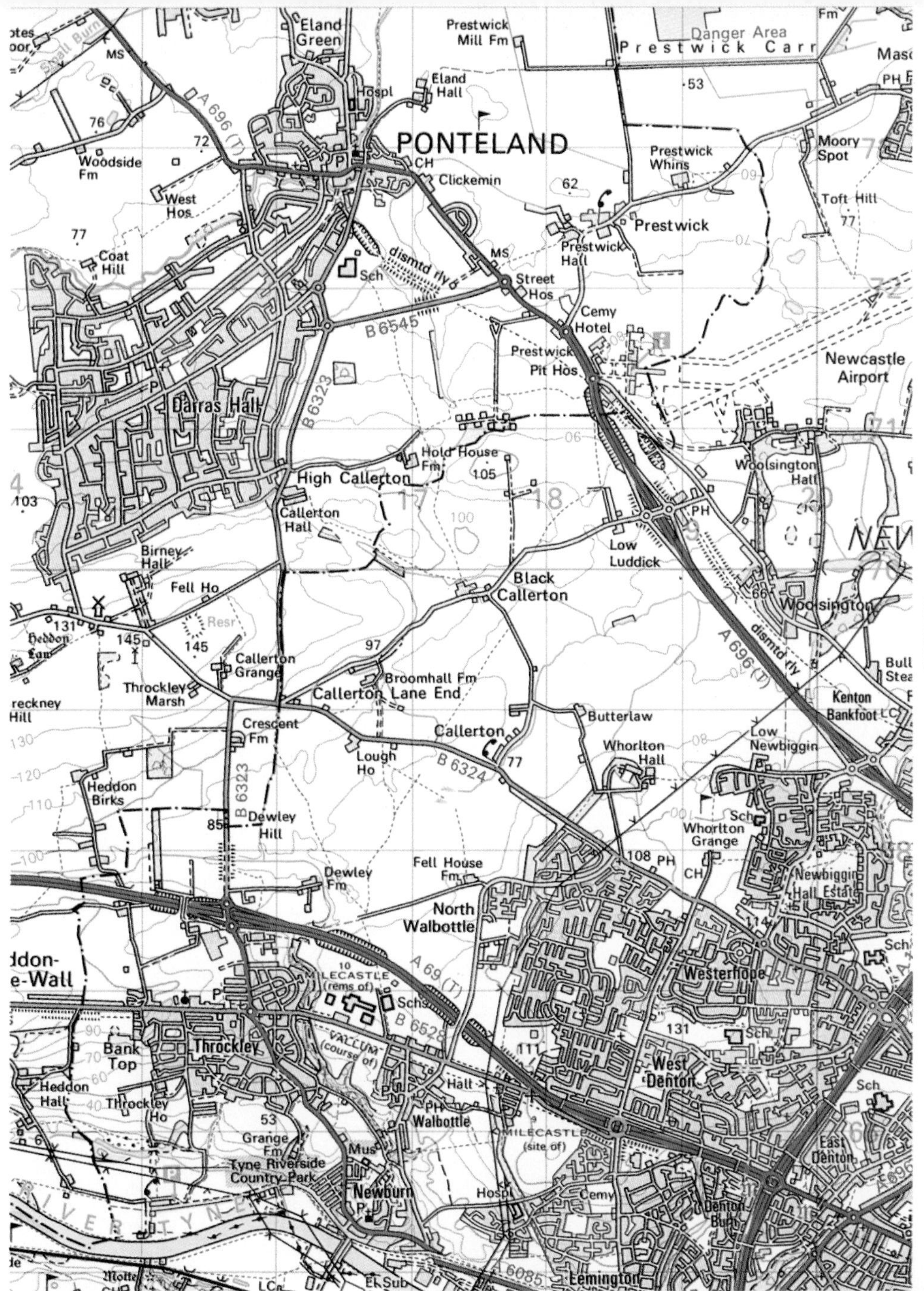

Figure 5 Part of Tyneside, from an Ordnance Survey 1:50 000 map

4 The residential area in the south of the map extract is part of the Tyneside conurbation. The area to the north is part of Newcastle's green belt.

a) Make a full-size copy of the map to show the main roads and the conurbation.

b) The A69(T) to the north of Throckley is a new bypass through the green belt. What map evidence is there to show that this is a new road? What impact will it have on the green belt?

c) Darras Hall is a new residential development in the green belt. Compare the layout of its streets with those in the older residential area in the south-east corner of the map.

d) What other examples of pressure on the green belt can you find? Group them under these headings:

- residential
- transport
- recreation
- industry
- others

e) Mark them onto your map using a colour key.

f) Does the green belt to the north of Newcastle seem to be serving its purpose?

Activities

1 Figure 1 shows the eight major conurbations in Britain. Make a copy of the map and, using an atlas to help you, label the conurbations.

2 a) On tracing paper, draw an outline map of Britain to the same scale as your map in Activity 1.

b) Use an atlas to locate the major railway lines onto your overlay map. Similarly, mark on the routes of the M1, M3, M4, M6, and A1(M) motorways.

c) How many of the conurbations lie along these routeways? Why is this?

d) Identify some cities that do not lie on these routeways. What factors have influenced their growth? Do they also apply to the conurbations?

3 a) Using the information in Figure 2, make another overlay map to show the conurbations and cities that have green belts.

b) Why do you think that only some urban areas have green belts?

Rural change

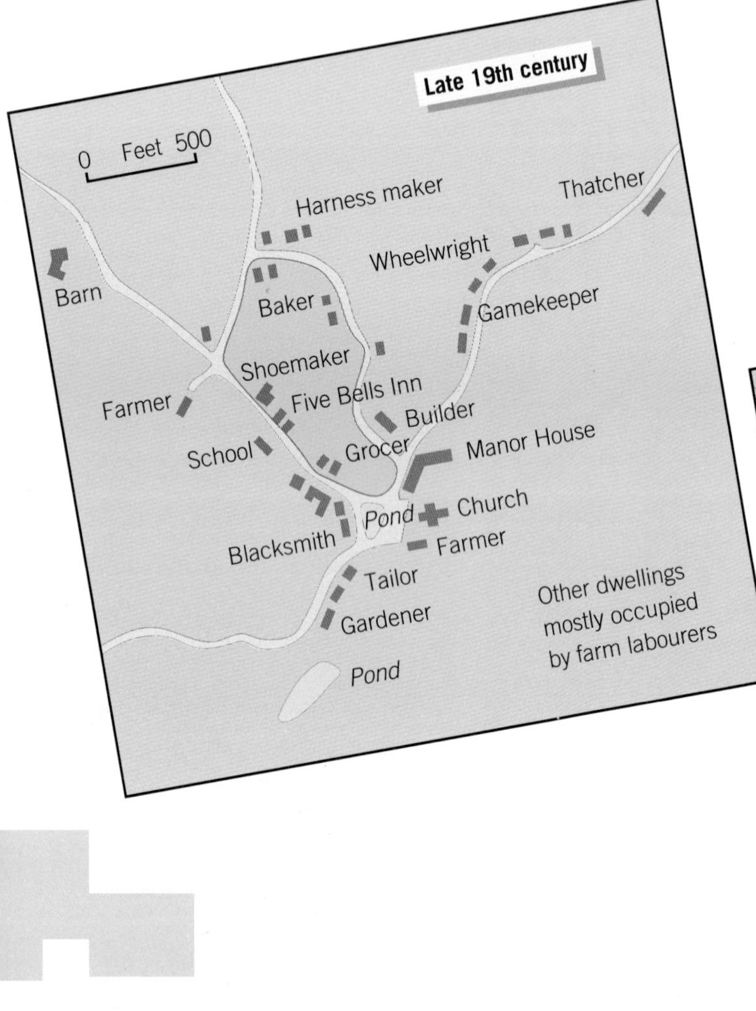

Figure 1 How a Hampshire village has changed

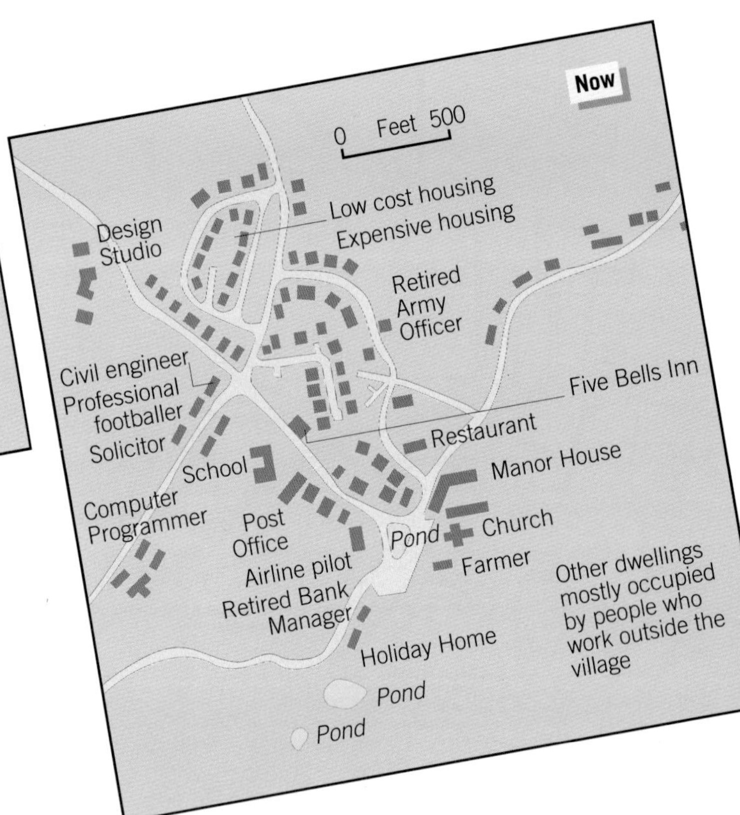

Major changes have taken place in Britain's villages. A hundred years ago, most people lived and worked in their local community. Today, this is no longer true, and the character of most villages has changed considerably. Many people like to live in villages, but their jobs are in towns and cities, so they have to travel each day.

A 'commuter' is a person who travels from their home in a rural area or small town to a larger town or city for work. The number of commuters has grown greatly with transport improvements, new road networks, and increasing car ownership. Most large towns have surrounding 'commuter belts'. People commute long distances, in both time and mileage, for various reasons. These include lower house prices or a desire to live in a quieter environment. However, in recent years, 'involuntary' reasons, like job availability and the development of out-of-town industrial estates, have meant that 'reverse commuting' takes place from urban areas and areas of low cost housing on the edge of the city centre to the urban fringe.

The main result of this growth in commuting is an increase in the volume of traffic, especially during peak hours. This extra traffic causes congestion, an increased risk of accidents, increased air pollution from car exhausts, noise pollution, problems of car parking, and the loss of valuable land taken for urban road networks at the expense of housing and recreational purposes.

Figure 2 Population change in Northumberland villages

Village	1921	1931	1951	1961	1971	1981	1991
Alnham	270	254	174	155	109	104	101
Alwinton	223	220	155	154	119	105	104
Harbottle	410	294	224	200	183	207	187
Longframlington	531	552	514	575	593	700	762
Netherton	330	245	212	200	144	127	112
Rothbury	-	1603	1648	1784	1818	1733	1864

Figure 3 Northumberland villages

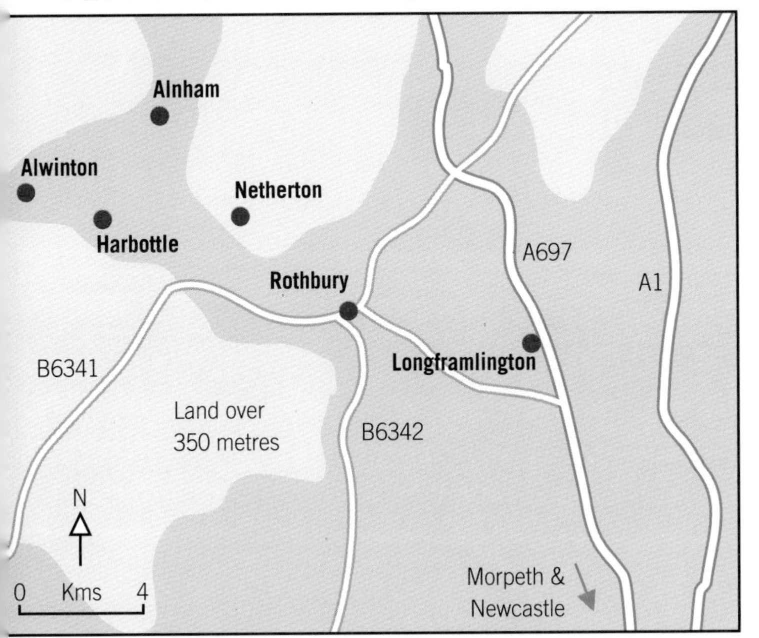

Figure 4 A population pyramid for Rothbury

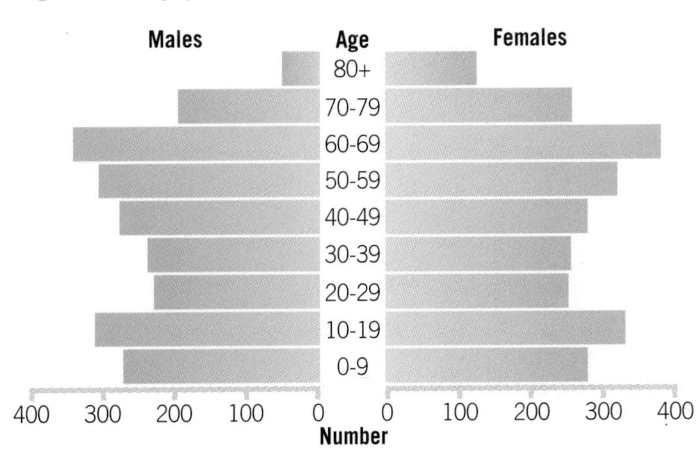

Figure 5 People can choose where to live

My husband is a bus driver for the Newcastle Bus Company. I work in one of the large department stores in the city centre. We've lived in Denton, in the north-west of the city, for the last ten years, and have no plans to move. We don't own a car, as we get a discount on bus services. This area is really convenient for the city and the local shops provide all our day-to-day needs. Of course, we'd like a garden, but there's a park nearby.

We moved out to Ponteland four years ago, because we wanted a better environment for our two children to grow up in. I work at the University, so I have to travel in to work each day. It takes about thirty minutes, but it's worth it once I'm home, away from the city noise and grime. As a family, we are very settled here. There's talk that the city Metro service is going to be extended to Ponteland, which would make my journey to work much easier and save me a lot of money in car park fees!

Activities

1 a) What is a commuter?
b) Why has the number of commuters increased?

2 a) Study the two maps in Figure 1. In what ways has the village changed?
b) Imagine that you have lived in this village all your life. What would you feel about the ways in which it has changed?

3 a) Look at the data in Figure 2.
b) Which of the villages have experienced an increase in population and which have experienced a decrease? Devise a technique for showing this on a sketch map of the area.
c) Why are some villages growing whilst others are declining? What effects are these changes having on the people and the economies of the villages? Annotate your answers onto your sketch map.

Dealing with traffic

Resource Bank

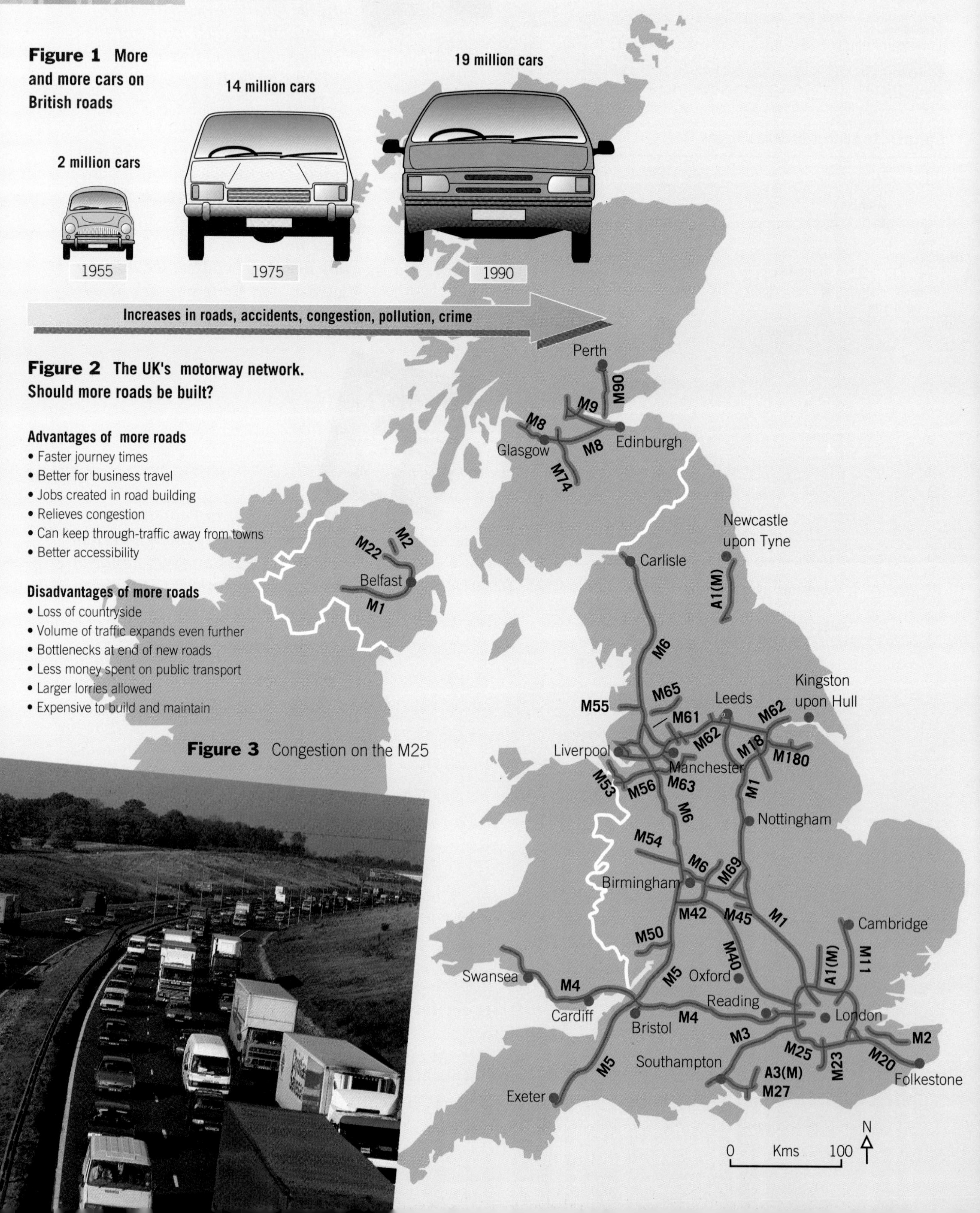

Figure 1 More and more cars on British roads

Figure 2 The UK's motorway network. Should more roads be built?

Advantages of more roads
- Faster journey times
- Better for business travel
- Jobs created in road building
- Relieves congestion
- Can keep through-traffic away from towns
- Better accessibility

Disadvantages of more roads
- Loss of countryside
- Volume of traffic expands even further
- Bottlenecks at end of new roads
- Less money spent on public transport
- Larger lorries allowed
- Expensive to build and maintain

Figure 3 Congestion on the M25

Figure 4 This cartoon shows a number of traffic control measures

Figure 5 Trams provide an alternative

Trams are electrically-powered vehicles that run on rails laid in a road. Tram systems were in use in a number of British cities in the first part of the twentieth century, but they then went into decline. Now, however, they are making a comeback.

Why trams died out

- The cost of electricity rose in the 1930s, just as the cost of petrol dropped.
- They were inflexible.
- The equipment became old and rundown.
- Tram networks were never extended to reach the new housing developments in the suburbs.
- They went 'out of fashion'.

Why trams are making a comeback

- They are seen as a solution to modern traffic problems.
- They are suited to city centres.
- They can be fast - up to 50 mph.
- Being electric, they are seen as 'green'.
- The rails indicate where the trains will turn up.
- There are no 'mugger's paradise' tunnels to travel through.
- Latest models allow for wheelchair access.

Manchester's new Metrolink tram system opened in June 1992. The city sees this efficient public mass transit system as essential to Manchester's development as Britain's second financial and professional centre after London. It is also designed to ease the congestion on the city's crowded roads.

Cleveland - Rust Belt city

Figure 1 Industry around the Great Lakes

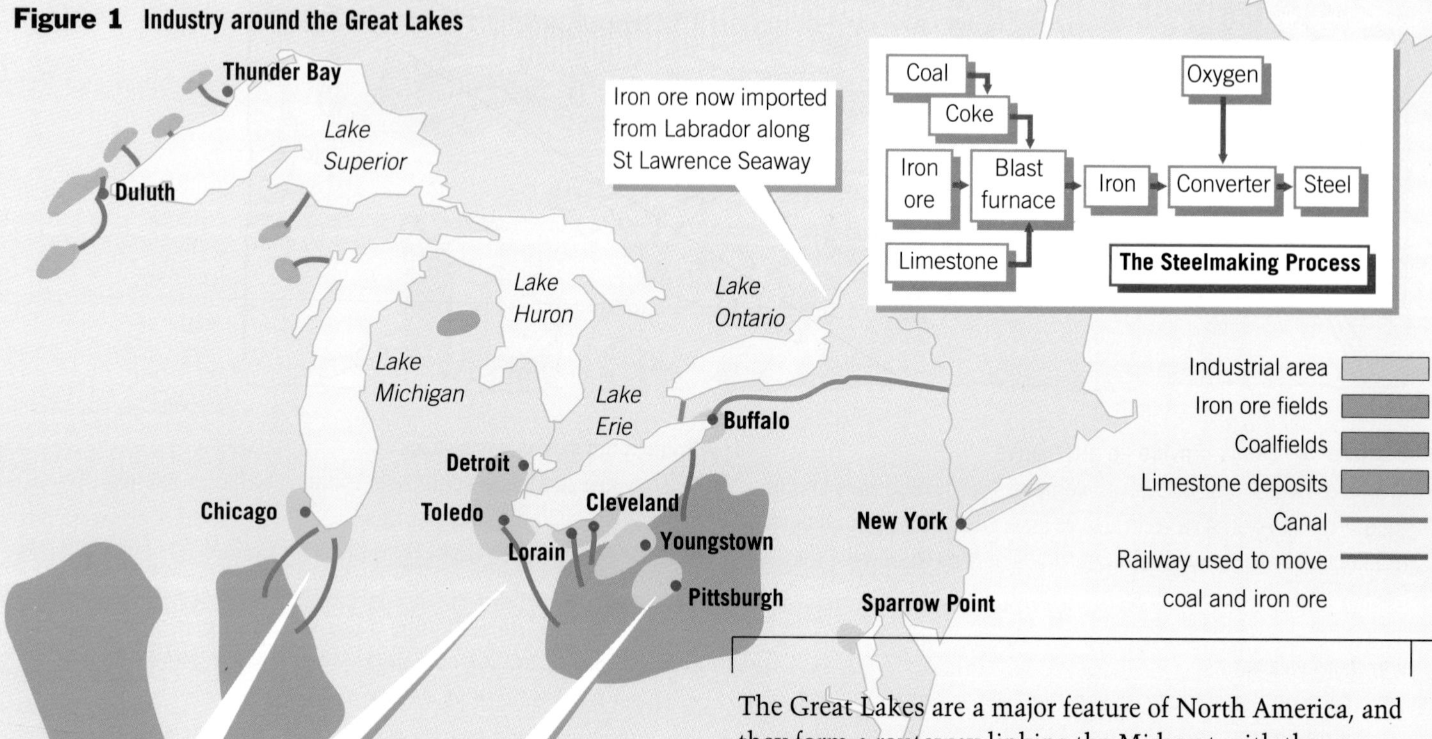

The Great Lakes are a major feature of North America, and they form a routeway linking the Midwest with the Atlantic Ocean. The lakes, and their associated rivers and canals, helped in the development of one of the most important industrial regions in the world. Steelmaking became the economic backbone of the region, making use of the raw materials found around the Great Lakes (Figure 1). The industry attracted manufacturers of vehicles, ships, and many other products. In the 1950s and 1960s, the Midwest was the source of a wide range of products that were sold throughout the world.

Figure 2
Cleveland. Derelict land and decaying buildings have become common sights as industries have closed and people have left. Huge job losses in steelmaking and related industries have placed a great burden on the welfare system

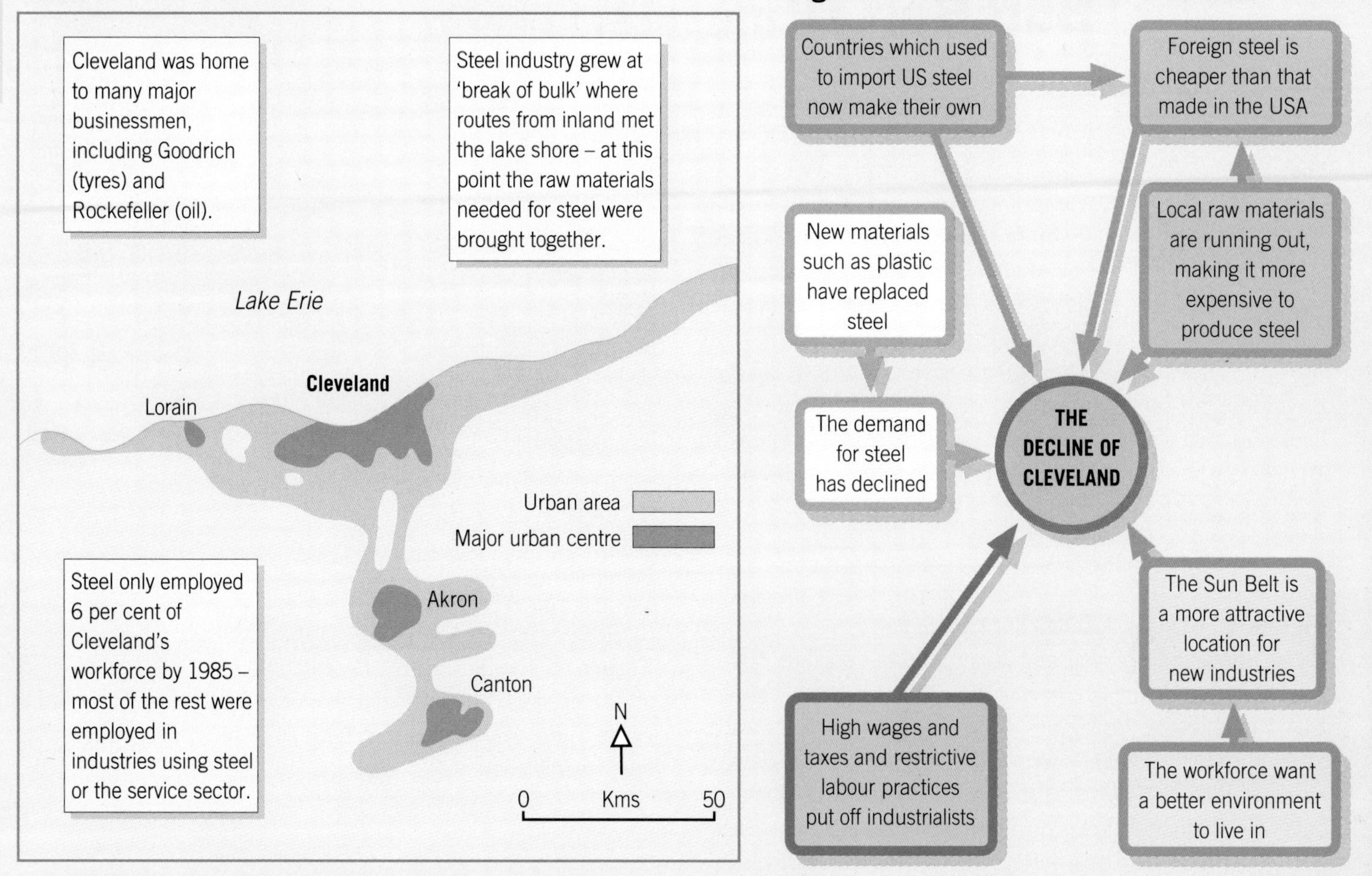
Figure 3 The Cleveland area
Cleveland was home to many major businessmen, including Goodrich (tyres) and Rockefeller (oil).
Steel industry grew at 'break of bulk' where routes from inland met the lake shore – at this point the raw materials needed for steel were brought together.
Lake Erie
Cleveland
Lorain
Urban area
Major urban centre
Akron
Canton
N
0
Kms
50
Steel only employed 6 per cent of Cleveland's workforce by 1985 – most of the rest were employed in industries using steel or the service sector.
Figure 4 Reasons for the decline of Cleveland
Countries which used to import US steel now make their own
Foreign steel is cheaper than that made in the USA
New materials such as plastic have replaced steel
Local raw materials are running out, making it more expensive to produce steel
The demand for steel has declined
THE DECLINE OF CLEVELAND
The Sun Belt is a more attractive location for new industries
High wages and taxes and restrictive labour practices put off industrialists
The workforce want a better environment to live in

Cleveland in Ohio on the southern shore of Lake Erie was just one of the manufacturing and steelmaking centres that grew up. At their peak, Cleveland and the towns of Akron, Canton, and Lorain had a population of over 3.3 million (Figure 3). But Cleveland now typifies the problems facing the Midwest industrial region. Industrial decline has been rapid (Figure 4). Unemployment has soared and Cleveland has the image of a dying city. Since the early 1980s, 60 per cent of the population has left in the search for a better life elsewhere. The Midwest has become known as the Rust Belt (or Frost Belt or Snow Belt) in contrast to the Sun Belt of South-Western USA. Cleveland has experienced some recent economic growth, with the help of government aid, but the industrial estates and shopping malls have tended to locate in the city suburbs; the centre of Cleveland continues to decline.

Activities

1 a) Study the map of the Great Lakes in Figure 1.
b) Using the inset diagram of the steelmaking process, explain why Cleveland was such a good location for the steel industry.
c) What other reasons were there for Cleveland's growth?

2 a) Look closely at the photograph. What impact of industrial decline does it show?
b) What other impacts can you think of?

3 Using the information in Figure 4, make two lists classifying the reasons for Cleveland's decline. One list should give local reasons, the other national and international reasons.

4 Imagine that you have just been made redundant after working in Cleveland for twenty years. Write a letter to your brother in California describing the pressures on you to move to the Sun Belt in search of a job. You should also describe the reasons why you would like to stay in Cleveland.

Sun Belt USA

The growth industries of the last thirty years have been high-tech industries such as electronics and computer technology. These industries often locate in areas where their highly skilled workforce can enjoy a pleasant environment and a high standard of living. The existence of good communications links is also a major consideration in their location. There are now several areas around the world that are famous for the high-tech nature of their industries. These include the 'Sunrise Strip' along the M4 motorway to the west of London, 'Silicon Valley' in California, and the 'Sun Belt' of the southern states of the USA.

Figure 2 The Biosphere 2 Research Centre, Arizona. High-tech industries are said to be 'footloose' in that they are relatively free to locate where they want as they have no restriction from access to their raw materials

Figure 1 USA: the Rust Belt and the Sun Belt
Urban decay and the decline of heavy industries such as iron and steel have led to high unemployment rates in north-western USA. Furthermore, the region's climate can be very harsh, with freezing, snowy winters. Consequently, people have drifted away from the 'Rust Belt' towards the 'Sun Belt' in the search for a better life. Although there is no official definition of the Sun Belt, it is generally taken to stretch from the Carolinas to California. It now contains more than half the US population. The Rust Belt is also known as the Frost Belt or Snow Belt

Figure 3 Population change in the USA, by state

	Net migration *thousands*		Percentage population change
	1960-1970	1975-85	1975-85
Alaska	16	44	17.1
Washington	249	64	3.6
Oregon	159	159	7.1
California	2113	623	12.4
Idaho	-42	64	16.3
Nevada	144	91	18.4
Montana	-58	25	9.9
Wyoming	-39	37	15.3
Utah	-11	35	18.4
Arizona	228	356	20.3
Colorado	215	237	18.3
New Mexico	-130	67	14.4
North Dakota	-94	-4	1.2
South Dakota	-94	-9	3.8
Nebraska	-73	11	4.9
Kansas	-130	-13	1.4
Oklahoma	13	107	13.4
Texas	146	543	14.7
Minnesota	-25	5	2.1
Iowa	-183	-3	1.0
Missouri	2	-32	3.7
Arkansas	-71	106	9.4
Louisiana	-130	-23	5.7
Wisconsin	4	27	4.1
Illinois	-43	-324	0.7
Michigan	27	-214	1.9
Indiana	-16	-138	0.3
Kentucky	-153	67	6.0
Tennessee	-45	119	7.7
Mississippi	-267	-1	6.3
Alabama	-233	50	8.6
Ohio	-126	-411	2.3
Maine	-69	42	7.1
Vermont	15	14	7.5
New Hampshire	69	56	6.8
Massachusetts	74	-7	4.1
Rhode Island	13	-45	3.9
Connecticut	214	-2	5.7
New York	-51	-640	-2.3
Pennsylvania	-378	-173	1.2
Washington DC	-100	-77	1.3
New Jersey	488	-38	3.4
Delaware	38	9	6.4
Maryland	385	65	5.2
West Virginia	-265	21	4.8
Virginia	141	162	5.1
North Carolina	-94	124	5.7
South Carolina	-149	97	7.9
Georgia	51	105	9.4
Florida	1326	1464	24.6

Figure 4 Why has the Sun Belt grown?

- The hot, dry climate and the beautiful scenery help the people of the Sun Belt to enjoy a wide variety of leisure activities. These include golf, tennis, and sailing as well as camping, hiking, and other ways of relaxing in the Great Outdoors.
- Many people retire to the sunshine of the Sun Belt, possibly after a lifetime of work and a fair amount of snow shovelling! Sun City and Sun City West on the outskirts of Phoenix are booming retirement developments offering a high level of service and leisure amenities. This does mean, of course, that a high proportion of Sun Belt residents are not employed, whilst requiring a good provision of medical and other facilities.
- Land in the Sun Belt is generally plentiful. As a result, land values are low and it is cheap to rent. These factors have helped to attract many new industries to the region.
- Cities like Phoenix are well linked to the US highway network, and they also have excellent rail and air links.
- Company taxes have been kept low in the Sun Belt, wage rates are generally lower, and trade union activity is restricted. These factors make the southern states of the USA a very attractive region for companies to invest in.

Activities

1 Read all the information on these pages. Make two lists, giving the reasons forcing people away from the northern parts of the USA and the factors attracting them to the Sun Belt.

2 Study the data in Figure 3 for 1975-85. Which five states have had the greatest in-migration? Which five states have had the greatest out-migration? Using an atlas to help you, name the two major cities in each of these states.

3 a) Use the data in Figure 3 to construct a choropleth map of the states of the USA showing their rate of population change between 1975 and 1985.

b) Is the pattern shown by your map what you would have expected, given the evidence in Figure 1?

Phoenix - city in the desert

Figure 1 Phoenix

A city in the desert may seem like a strange idea. But the city of Phoenix in Arizona, USA, is indeed found in a harsh semi-arid environment. In many ways it is a very attractive place in which to live and work and, as a result, it is one of the fastest growing cities in the USA.

But this growth has been accomplished at a price - economic, environmental, and social. Most residents of the city use huge amounts of electricity just to keep cool. As one person boasted 'I go from my air-conditioned house in my air-conditioned car to my air-conditioned office.' Water is also used in vast quantities, but supplies are running out and a series of problems lie in store for the future, as shown in Figure 3. In the past, the area has been best known for its farming produce, including cotton, fruit, alfalfa, and grains. Today, high-tech industries thrive. Many people have come to the city looking for work, although without the necessary skills they can find it very difficult to get employment.

Figure 2 Facts about Phoenix

- Name means 'few springs' in language of Papago Indians.
- State capital of Arizona (the Grand Canyon State) since 1889.
- First settled 1870.
- Population:

1910	11134
1940	65414
1950	106818
1960	439170
1970	581562
1980	789704
1990	950000 (approx)

- Area covered by the city:

1950	25.6 km sq
1960	476 km sq
1986	3674 km sq

- Climate. Dry and sunny. Average temperature 29 °C.
- Altitude 340m.
- Workforce in 1986: 544 966 employed, 31 561 unemployed
- Main industries: data processing, electronic research, computer components, aircraft, machinery.
- Employment structure:

Agriculture and mining	1.6%
Construction	8.4%
Manufacturing	18.0%
Transport /public utilities	7.2%
Wholesale trade	4.9%
Retail trade	17.7%
Finance/real estate	8.4%
Services	28.1%
Public administration	5.7%

- Tourism - popular winter and health resort

Figure 3 **Phoenix - a thirsty city**

Supply

- Dams on the Salt River and its tributaries store water from the summer and winter rains, thus ensuring a year-round supply.
- The Roosevelt Dam, completed in 1911, provides water for 141 000 ha of irrigated farmland.
- Four other dams on other rivers help to provide nearly half of the water needed to quench Phoenix's thirst.
- Boreholes now reach deep down to stores of groundwater and meet over half of the city's requirements.
- A new canal has had to be built to bring water from the Colorado River, over 300 km away. It has cost $3 billion.

Demand

- The Sun Belt lifestyle uses huge amounts of water. For example, lawns have to watered, swimming pools filled, golf courses greened, and lots of other leisure pursuits call for lots of water!

Problems

- Depletion and salinisation of groundwater.
- Drying up of rivers below dams.
- Excessive losses due to evaporation.
- Increased salinity of soil.
- Capacity of existing supplies has been reached.
- The future?

Figure 4 **Climate statistics for Phoenix**

	Jan	Feb	Mar	Apr	May	Jun	Jul	Aug	Sep	Oct	Nov	Dec
Rain *(mm)*	20	23	19	10	3	2	0	30	20	10	10	23
Temp *(°C)*	10	12	15	21	24	30	33	32	29	21	14	10

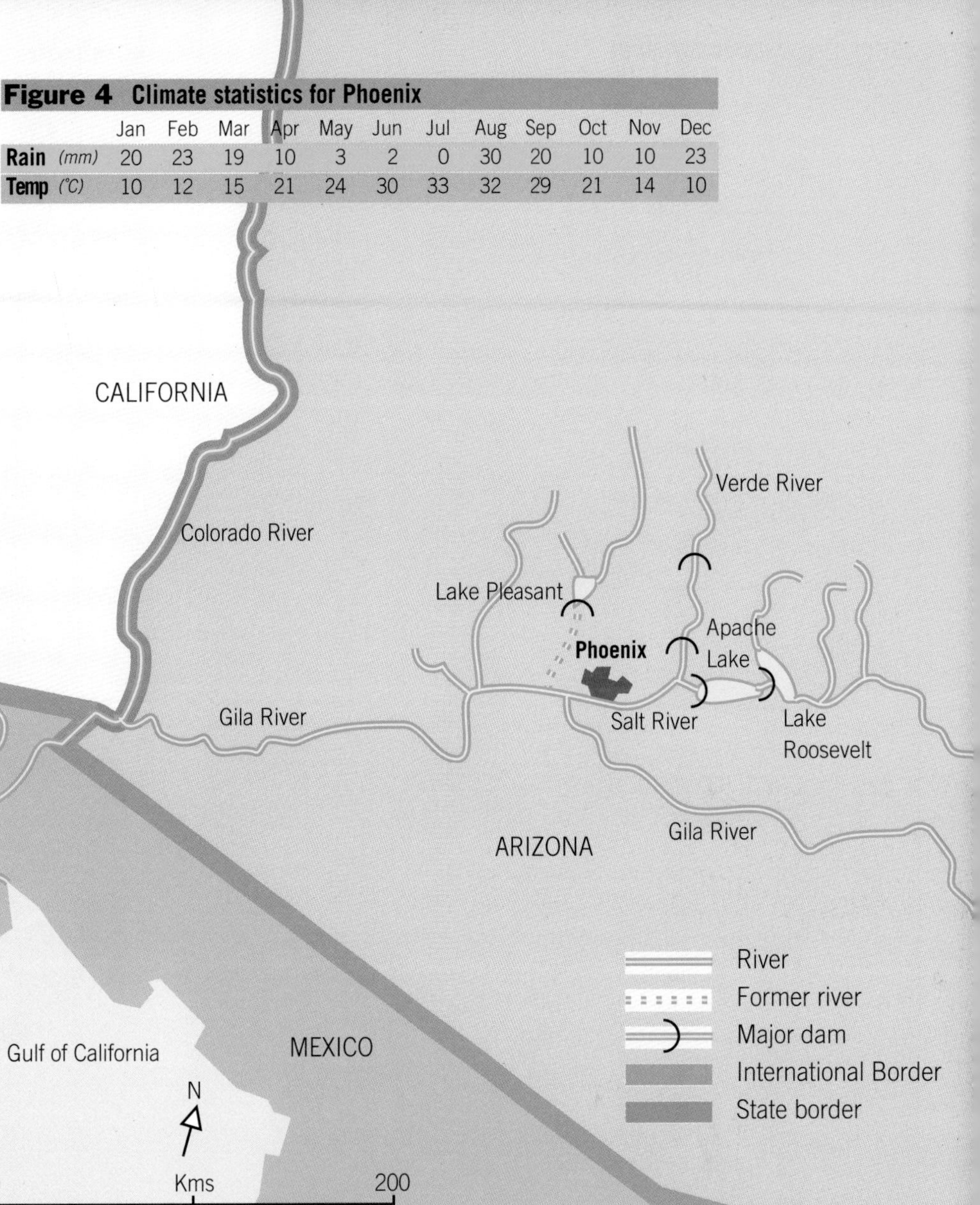

Activities

1 a) Study Figure 1. Draw a large sketch of the photograph.

b) Identify and label the major land use zones shown by the photograph.

c) Add further notes to your sketch, to say something about Phoenix and the Arizona environment.

2 a) Using the population figures in Figure 2, draw a line graph to show the population growth of Phoenix.

b) Can you explain the rapid growth rates in the 1950s and 1960s?

c) What factors continue to attract more people to Phoenix in the 1990s?

3 a) Using the climate data in Figure 4, draw a climate graph for Phoenix.

b) Has the climate influenced the development of the city? What sort of steps have been taken to overcome the climate?

4 Draw a pie chart of the employment structure in Phoenix.

5 Imagine that you work in the public relations department of the Phoenix Water Utilities Company. Your directors are very worried about obtaining extra water supplies to meet future increases in demand. They have asked you to design a poster to increase the public's awareness of the need to conserve precious water supplies.

— international boundary

• capital city

abbreviations:

AUST.	AUSTRIA
B	BOSNIA-HERZEGOVINA
BELG.	BELGIUM
C	CROATIA
CENT. AF. REP.	CENTRAL AFRICAN REPUBLIC
CZECH	CZECH REPUBLIC
L	LIECHTENSTEIN
LUX.	LUXEMBOURG
M	MACEDONIA F.Y.R.
NETH.	NETHERLANDS
S	SLOVENIA
SL.	SLOVAKIA
SWITZ.	SWITZERLAND
U.A.E.	UNITED ARAB EMIRATES
U.S.A.	UNITED STATES OF AMERICA

Modified Gall Projection

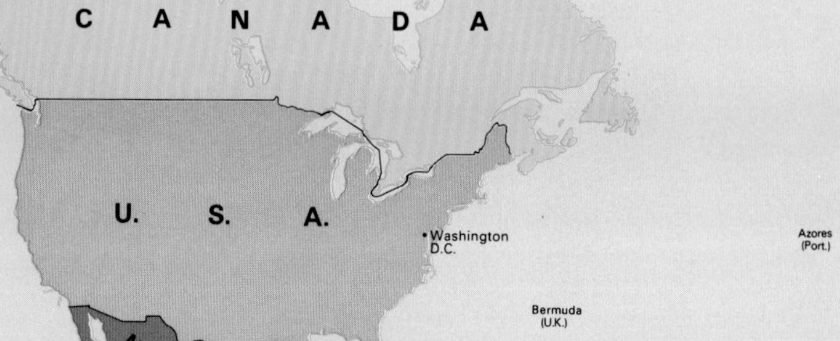

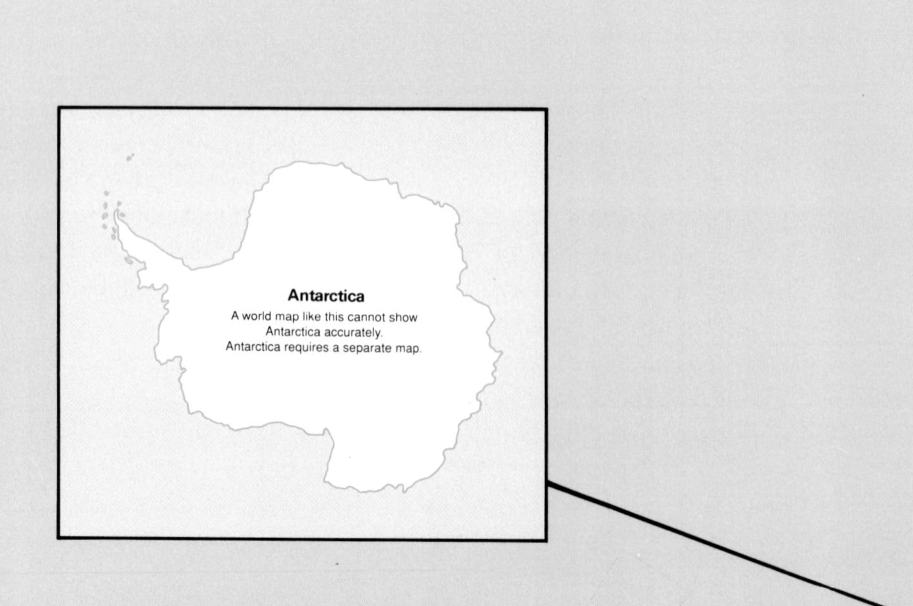

Jan Mayen (Den.)
Faeroes (Den.)
NORWAY
SWEDEN
FINLAND
Helsinki
Oslo
Stockholm
Tallinn
ESTONIA
LATVIA
Riga
DENMARK
Copenhagen
LITHUANIA
Vilnius
BELARUS
Minsk
Moscow
RUSSIA
UNITED KINGDOM
Dublin
London
Amsterdam
NETH
Berlin
Warsaw
POLAND
GERMANY
BELG
Brussels
LUX
CZECH
Prague
Kiev
UKRAINE
Paris
FRANCE
SWITZ
Bern
AUST
Vienna
Bratislava
HUNGARY
Budapest
MOLDOVA
Kishinev
Ljubljana
Zagreb
ROMANIA
Bucharest
Belgrade
YUGOSLAVIA
MONACO
ANDORRA
ITALY
Rome
BULGARIA
Sofiya
Skopje
Tirane
ALBANIA
GREECE
Athens
PORTUGAL
Madrid
SPAIN
Lisbon
GEORGIA
Tbilisi
Yerevan
AZERBAIJAN
Baku
ARMENIA
Ankara
TURKEY
KAZAKHSTAN
UZBEKISTAN
Tashkent
Alma Ata
Bishkek
KIRGYZSTAN
TURKMENISTAN
Ashkhabad
Dushanbe
TAJIKISTAN
MONGOLIA
Ulaanbaatar
NORTH KOREA
Pyongyang
Beijing (Peking)
SOUTH KOREA
Sŏul
JAPAN
Tōkyō
CHINA
Tunis
MALTA
Alger
TUNISIA
Tripoli
Rabat-Salé
MOROCCO
ALGERIA
LIBYA
Nicosia
CYPRUS
Beirut
LEBANON
SYRIA
Damascus
ISRAEL
Jerusalem
Amman
JORDAN
Baghdād
IRAQ
Tehrān
IRAN
AFGHANISTAN
Kābul
Islamabad
Cairo
EGYPT
KUWAIT
Al Kuwayt
BAHRAIN
QATAR
Doha
Abu Dhabi
U.A.E.
Masqat
OMAN
Ar Riyāḍ
SAUDI ARABIA
PAKISTAN
New Delhi
NEPAL
Kathmandu
BHUTAN
Thimpu
INDIA
Dhaka
BANGLADESH
T'ai-pei
TAIWAN
Hong Kong (U.K.)
MYANMAR (BURMA)
Rangoon
Hanoi
Vientiane
LAOS
VIETNAM
THAILAND
Bangkok
CAMBODIA
Phnom Penh
Manila
PHILIPPINES
MALI
NIGER
CHAD
Ndjamena
Khartoum
SUDAN
ERITREA
Asmara
San'a
YEMEN
Socotra (Yemen)
DJIBOUTI
Djibouti
Niamey
THE GAMBIA
BURKINA
Bamako
Ougadougou
NIGERIA
Abuja
Addis Ababa
ETHIOPIA
SOMALIA
CÔTE D'IVOIRE
Yamoussoukro
GHANA
TOGO
BENIN
Porto Novo
Lomé
Accra
LIBERIA
CENT. AF. REP.
Bangui
Yaounde
Malabo
CAMEROON
EQUATORIAL GUINEA
Libreville
GABON
CONGO
UGANDA
Kampala
KENYA
Nairobi
Mogadishu
SRI LANKA
Colombo
MALDIVES
MALAYSIA
Kuala Lumpur
BRUNEI
Bandar Seri Begawan
SINGAPORE
Kigali
RWANDA
BURUNDI
Bujumbura
ZAÏRE
Brazzaville
Kinshasa
Cabinda (Angola)
Dodoma
TANZANIA
SEYCHELLES
INDONESIA
Jakarta
PAPUA NEW GUINEA
Port Moresby
NAURU
SOLOMON IS.
Honiara
TUVALU
Luanda
ANGOLA
COMOROS
MALAWI
Lilongwe
ZAMBIA
Lusaka
Harare
ZIMBABWE
MOZAMBIQUE
MADAGASCAR
Antananarivo
MAURITIUS
Réunion (Fr.)
VANUATU
Vila
FIJI
Suva
New Caledonia (Fr.)
Nouméa
NAMIBIA
Windhoek
BOTSWANA
Gaborone
Pretoria
Maputo
Mbabane
SWAZILAND
Maseru
LESOTHO
REPUBLIC OF SOUTH AFRICA
AUSTRALIA
Canberra
NEW ZEALAND
Wellington
Kerguelen (Fr.)

Index